INSIGHT **CITYGUIDE**

PARIS

APA PUBLICATIONS

Part of the Langenscheidt Publishing Group

✳ INSIGHT GUIDE

PaRiS

Editor
Clare Griffiths
Art Director
Klaus Geisler
Picture Editor
Hilary Genin
Cartography Editor
Zoë Goodwin
Editorial Director
Brian Bell

Distribution

UK & Ireland
GeoCenter International Ltd
The Viables Centre, Harrow Way
Basingstoke, Hants RG22 4BJ
Fax: (44) 1256-817988

United States
Langenscheidt Publishers, Inc.
46–35 54th Road, Maspeth, NY 11378
Fax: (1) 718 784-0640

Canada
Thomas Allen & Son Ltd
390 Steelcase Road East
Markham, Ontario L3R 1G2
Fax: (1) 905 475 6747

Australia
Universal Publishers
1 Waterloo Road
Macquarie Park, NSW 2113
Fax: (61) 2 9888 9074

New Zealand
Hema Maps New Zealand Ltd (HNZ)
Unit D, 24 Ra ORA Drive
East Tamaki, Auckland
Fax: (64) 9 273 6479

Worldwide
**Apa Publications GmbH & Co.
Verlag KG (Singapore branch)**
38 Joo Koon Road, Singapore 628990
Tel: (65) 6865-1600. Fax: (65) 6861-6438

Printing

Insight Print Services (Pte) Ltd
38 Joo Koon Road, Singapore 628990
Tel: (65) 6865-1600. Fax: (65) 6861-6438

ABOUT THIS BOOK

This guidebook combines the interests and enthusiasms of two of the world's best-known information providers: Insight Guides, whose titles have set the standard for visual travel guides since 1970, and Discovery Channel, the world's premier source of nonfiction television programming.

The editors of Insight Guides give practical advice and general understanding about a destination's history, culture, institutions and people. Discovery Channel and its website www.discovery.com, help millions of viewers explore their world from the comfort of their own home and also encourage them to explore it first-hand.

How to use this book

Insight Guide: Paris is carefully structured both to convey an understanding of the city and its culture and to guide readers through its sights and activities:

◆ To understand Paris today, you need to know something of its past. The **History** and **Features** sections cover the city's culture in authoritative essays written by specialists.

◆ The main **Places** section provides a full run-down of all the sites. Principal placesand attractions of interest are co-ordinated by number with full-colour maps.

◆ The **Travel Tips** listings section provides practical information on travel, hotels, shops and activities.

Fountains in the
Place de la Concorde

tecture, and Canadian chef and food writer **Laura Calder**, resident in Paris, contributed a new chapter on food. The chapter on Shopping was drawn together from contributions made to Insight's specialist pocket guide *Shopping in Paris* by **Nicola Mitchell**, **Natasha Edwards**, **Joanna Hunter**, **Rosalind Sykes** and **Simon Cropper**.

The overview of the city's main art galleries and collections used work originally published in Insight's *Museum and Galleries of Paris* by **Natasha Edwards**, **Brent Gregston** and **Olivia Snaije**. The photo features were researched by Insight editor **Clare Griffiths**.

For this edition, American travel writer and long-term Paris resident **Brent Gregston** covered the new area of urban development at *Bercy and the New Left Bank* and contributed the insightful essay on the Parisians. He also updated all the chapters in the Places section, and worked on the *Travel Tips* section, originally compiled by Glaswegian writer and Paris resident **Hilary Macpherson**; Brent added his own selection of favourite restaurants and hotels.

Many of the photographs in the new edition are the work of regular Insight photographers **Jerry Dennis**, **Britta Jaschinski** and **Annabel Elston**.

The book was proofread by bi-lingual Insight editor **Carine Tracanelli** and indexed by **Isobel McLean**.

The contributors

This book builds on previous editions compiled by editors **Andrew Eames** and **Caroline Radula-Scott**, who gathered a team of writers with a firm knowledge of Paris.

In the original edition, bilingual writer **Jim Keeble**, who divides his time between England and France, did most of the leg-work for the *Places* section and **Marton Radkai** wrote the chapter outlining the city's turbulent history. Journalist **Susan Bell** was working in Paris for the London *Times* when she wrote the one-page features on different aspects of the capital.

French contributor **Philippe Artru** wrote the original chapter on archi-

CONTACTING THE EDITORS
We would appreciate it if readers would alert us to errors or outdated information by writing to:
Insight Guides, P.O. Box 7910, London SE1 1WE, England.
Fax: (44) 20 7403-0290.
insight@apaguide.co.uk

The Grand Palais from
Pont Alexandre III

Travel Tips

THE BEST OF PARIS

Unique attractions, festivals and events, top cafés and shops, family outings... here, at a glance, are our recommendations, plus some money-saving tips.

BEST CAFÉS

- **Au Petit Fer à Cheval**, 30 rue Vielle-du-Temple, 4th. With its tiny horseshoe-shaped bar, this Marais café is particularly atmospheric.

- **Café Beaubourg**, 43 rue St-Merri, 4th. Terraced café by the Centre Pompidou with a chic clientele.
- **Café Zéphyr**, 12 bd Montmartre, 9th. One of the few cafés with style on the Grands Boulevards.
- **Chez Prune**, 71 quai de Valmy, 10th. A cornerstone of the trendy Canal St-Martin area.
- **Ladurée**, 16 rue Royale, 8th. This elegant Salon de Thé is a Parisian institution.

Famous for its melt-in-the-mouth macaroons.
- **Le Café du Marché**, 38 rue Cler, 7th. Sit on the terrace with coffee or a glass of wine and enjoy the best view of the colourful market.
- **Le Rostand**, 6 place Edmond-Rostand, 6th. Spacious café opposite the Luxembourg gardens.
- **Le Sancerre**, 35 rue des Abbesses, 18th. This is one of the best cafés in Montmartre, drawing an eclectic, young, arty crowd.
- **Les Deux Magots** and **Café de Flore**, place St-Germain-des-Prés, 6th. These Left Bank literary cafés still retain something of the charm of their intellectual heyday.
- **Pause Café**, 41 rue de Charonne, 11th. A terraced café that sums up the tone of Bastille and the East.

BEST SHOPS

- **La Hune**, 170 bd Saint-Germain, 6th. A quintessential Left Bank bookstore, that keeps its doors open to bookworms until midnight.
- **E. Dehillerin**, 18 rue Coquillière, 1st. Packed to the rafters with traditional French cookware and kitchen utensils. Every cook's dream.
- **Le Bon Marché**, 24 rue de Sèvres, 7th. The slickest, most user-friendly department store in Paris.
- **Pierre Hermé**, 72 rue Bonaparte, 6th. Join the queue for the patisserie king's mouthwatering creations.
- **Galeries Lafayette**, 40 bd Haussmann, 9th. Slowly but surely, this revamped Art Nouveau department store is regaining its reputation for glamour and abundance.
- **Les Caves Taillevent**, 199 rue du Faubourg St-Honoré, 8th. A dazzling array of wines with the added bonus of a wine tasting room.

- **Colette**, 213 rue St-Honoré, 1st. Pioneering concept store that picks the best of what is stylish and innovative.
- **Barbara Bui**, 23 rue Etienne Marcel, 1st. Clean-cut super-smart clothes for the woman about town.
- **Charvet**, 28 place Vendôme, 1st. Venerable gentleman's outfitters.
- **Galerie Vivienne**, 6 rue Vivienne, 2nd. The best preserved of all the 19th-century shopping galleries, elegant precursors of the department store.

ONLY IN PARIS

- The city panorama from the top of the Eiffel Tower one hour before sunset and the light display it puts on after dark. *See page 165.*
- The fantastic view of the Champs Elysées from the top of the Arc de Triomphe. *See page 118.*

- The enigmatic smile of da Vinci's *Mona Lisa*, on display at the colossal Louvre. *See page 100.*
- Two of the finest Gothic churches in the Western world: Notre-Dame and Sainte-Chapelle, both on the Ile de la Cité. *See pages 71 and 74.*
- A Berthillon ice-cream on the Ile St-Louis. *See page 77.*
- The gilded dome of the Hôtel des Invalides, on a sunny blue-skied day. *See page 166.*
- The Impressionists at the Musée d'Orsay. *See page 169.*
- The picturesque 19th-century shopping arcades around the Palais Royal. *See page 106.*

- A coffee and a croissant in one of the literary cafés and a browse through the chic boutiques of St-Germain-des-Prés. *See page 141.*
- People-watching and market shopping on Rue Mouffetard. *See page 147.*
- The elegant mansions of the Marais and its glorious centrepiece, the Place des Vosges. *See page 80.*
- The offbeat boutiques and hip cafés of Bastille. *See page 134.*
- Rodin's beautiful sculpture garden. *See page 167.*
- Picasso's legacy to the French state. *See page 84.*
- A stroll down the newly fashionable Champs-Elysées. *See page 116.*
- The quiet, leafy backstreets and arty shops and bars of the Butte Montmartre. *See page 121.*
- The famous graves of the Père Lachaise cemetery. *See page 136.*
- Mint tea and a hammam in the Paris Mosque. *See page 149.*
- The lift to the top of the gigantic Grande Arche de la Défense. *See page 199.*
- The Hall of Mirrors and dancing fountains of Versailles. *See page 200.*

ABOVE: the Gothic splendour of Notre-Dame de Paris.
RIGHT: Napoleon's grand centrepiece, the Arc de Triomphe.
BELOW: the unmistakable Eiffel Tower.

FESTIVALS

- **April–May**: Foire du Trône. A huge funfair comes to town.
- **May–July**: Open-air jazz in the Parc de Vincennes.
- **June**: Fête de la Musique. Free street concerts and dancing.
- **26 June**: Gay Pride
- **13, 14 July**: Bastille Day. Street party on the night of 13 July at Place de la Bastille. On 14 July, a military parade and fireworks.
- **Sept**: Jazz à La Villette.
- **Sept**: Festival d'Automne. Modern theatre and dance.
- **Oct**: FIAC. International modern art fair.
- **Nov**: Fête du Beaujolais Nouveau.
- **31 Dec**: Parisians gather at the Champs-Elysées.
- **1 Jan**: La Grande Parade de Paris.

PARIS FOR FAMILIES

- **Disneyland Paris**. The most popular tourist attraction in Europe guarantees fun for all ages. *See page 18.*
- **Parc de la Villette**. Science museum, music and dance conservatory, a giant IMAX screen and children's museum, all set in futuristic gardens. *See page 179.*

- **Jardin du Luxembourg**. Puppet shows, tennis courts, model boats and honey bees in the quintessential Paris park. *See page 150.*
- **Grande Galerie de l'Evolution**. Revamped natural history museum with an impressive collection of stuffed animals and interactive displays for children of all ages. *See page 148.*
- **Bois de Vincennes**. Charming zoo, château, racecourse, boating lake, museum, floral park and adventure playground. *See page 181.*
- **Musée Grévin**. A fun wax-work museum, full of

cheerfully incompatible figures from Marie-Antoinette to Lara Croft. *See page 113.*
- **Canal St-Martin**. With its nine locks, the tranquil canal makes for an attractive boat trip, starting from Bastille. *See page 135.*
- **Bois de Boulogne**. Parisians' favourite Sunday afternoon playground, with woods and gardens, lakes and cycling tracks, a folk museum and an amusement park for children. *See page 176.*
- **Parc des Buttes-Chaumont**. Ice-skating, a boating lake, a fake mountain and waterfall, puppet shows and donkey rides. *See page 180.*
- **Jardins des Tuileries**. The well-manicured gardens adjacent to the Louvre are the perfect pleasure park: avenues of trees, statues, boules players, pony rides, toy boats, cafés and children's trampolines, and a giant Ferris wheel at Christmas and Easter-time. *See page 102.*

ABOVE: Place des Vosges, an enchanting 17th-century square, is a haven of relaxation in the heart of the bustling Marais.

AMAZING PARIS

- **The Eiffel Tower**. The tower weighs in at 10,100 tons, 60 tons of which is paint. It is repainted every seven years, and the work takes 15–16 months.
- **Métro madness**. The average commuter spends a year and four months of their life on the Métro.
- **Place des Vosges**. The first planned square in Paris and one of 338 squares, parks and gardens in the city.
- **Dense population**. Paris is more densely populated than Tokyo, London or New York.

- **Underground Paris**. There is a labyrinth of Métro lines, over 3,200km (2,000 miles) of sewers, which you can visit scores of garages and endless ancient quarries, which were converted into catacombs in the 18th century.
- **The Louvre fortress**. The foundations of the Louvre fortress and keep were only discovered in 1984.
- **Parklife**. There are 150,000 trees in Disneyland Paris, as many as in the whole of Paris.
- **Waterworld**. Beneath the auditorium of the Opéra lies an underground lake, draining water from the foundations.
- **Catacombs**. The bones of six million souls are neatly stacked in the underground galleries of an old quarry.

FREE PARIS

- **Free entry** to the permanent collections of 10 Paris museums. The list includes the Musée d'Art Moderne; Musée Zadkine; Musée Bourdelle; Musée Carnavalet; Musée Cognacq-Jay; Musée de la Vie Romantique and Musée Jean-Moulin. The former Parisian homes of writers Victor Hugo and Honoré de Balzac are also open to the public for free. All Réunion des Musées Nationaux (RMN) are free on the first Sunday of each month.

- **Open Studios**. During October, artists all over the Bastille and Ménilmontant area open their doors for Open Studios events.

- **Dancing in the streets** on 13 July, the eve of Bastille Day, when the firemen of Paris organise public balls across the city.

- **Visit the cemeteries of Paris**. Cimetière du Père-Lachaise, de Montmartre and du Montparnasse where countless notables from Balzac to Wilde have their memorials.

- **Basilique du Sacré-Cœur**. Visit one of the most spectacular religious buildings in Paris for free (paid entrance to the dome).

ABOVE: *An Argument in the Lobby of the Opera* (1889) by Jean Béraud, on show at the Musée Carnavalet, one of the major museums with no entrance fee.

ABOVE: a tomb statue in the Cimetière du Père-Lachaise.

- **Marché aux Puces de St-Ouen**. Go for a wander among the stalls one of the largest flea markets in the world or browse the *bouquinistes* (book stalls) on the banks of the Seine.

- **Jardins du Palais du Luxembourg** is the perfect Paris park for relaxing on a hot summer's day. It is one garden amid 338 squares, parks and gardens in the capital.

- **Exploring by foot** is the best (and cheapest way) to see Paris.

- **Free maps** of the Métro, bus and RER systems are available at airports and Métro stations.

MONEY-SAVING TIPS

- **Carte Musées et Monuments** (sold at museums, tourist offices, FNAC and Métro stations) gives you priority entrance at The Louvre and enables you to skip the queues while saving money.

- **Tickets to Ride**. A *carnet* of 10 tickets, (available from bus or Métro stations) gives reduced fares on public transport. The Paris Visit card is valid for one, two, three or five consecutive days on the Métro, bus and railway.

- **Two Kiosques Theatre** (15 place de la Madeleine and Montparnasse Square) sell half-price theatre tickets starting at 12.30pm for performances that day.

- **Comédie Française**. Reduced-priced tickets can be bought one hour before performances by under-27s.

- **Shop in the sales**. Traditionally the sales (*soldes*) are held in July and early January but many shops offer mid-season reductions.

- **For Disneyland Paris** discounts check the website www.affordabledisney.com

- **Food and drink**: don't eat breakfast in your hotel, pop into a local café for coffee and croissant; order the *plat du jour*; drink a *pichet* (jug) of wine and order tap water (*carafe d'eau*); stand at the bar rather than sit at a table to drink coffee or beer – outside tables at cafés cost more.

- **Marché d'Aligre** in Bastille is renowned for selling some of the best and cheapest vegetables in Paris.

- **Eat picnic-style** lunches with goodies bought from a supermarket or deli.

THE CITY OF LIGHT

Charles V, in the 14th century, described Paris as being not a city but a world. It still is, and it's a world that retains its ability to charm and captivate as well as, occasionally, to infuriate

Paris is a city of landscapes, set in a natural basin, cut through the middle by the slowly meandering River Seine and edged with gentle hills. The fascination of the French capital is eternal, a city in which "time is the architect, the people are the builder" – Victor Hugo's remark about Notre-Dame describes Paris itself. Throughout the centuries, each new generation has added its story to the stones, and each layer is full of history and intrigue. As a result, the "City of Light" has long been a magnet to artists, writers, philosophers and composers. According to writer Jean Giraudoux (1882–1944), the Parisian is more than a little proud to be part of a city where "the most thinking, talking and writing in the world have been accomplished".

Situated on longitude 2° 20'W and latitude 48° 50'N, roughly the same latitude as Stuttgart in Germany and Vancouver in Canada, all the French channels of communication lead to Paris. The city itself covers an area close to 100 sq km (40 sq miles), running 13 km (8 miles) east and west, and 9 km (6 miles) north and south. On the map, 20 *arrondissements* (administrative districts) spiral out like a snail's shell, a pattern reflecting the city's historical development and successive enlargements. The River Seine enters Paris close to the Bois de Vincennes in the southeast, and meanders gently north and south past three small islands – Ile St-Louis, Ile de la Cité and, on its way out, Ile des Cygnes. Chains of hillocks rise up to the north of the river, including Montmartre, the city's highest point at 130 metres (425 ft), Ménilmontant, Belleville and Buttes Chaumont; and to the south, Montsouris, the Mont Ste-Geneviève, Buttes aux Cailles and Maison Blanche. Mont Valérien is the highest point on the outskirts at 160 metres (525 ft), providing an immense panoramic view of Paris from the west. The lowest, at 25 metres (85 ft) above sea level, is at Grenelle.

The city is contained by the Boulevard Périphérique, a ring road stretching 35 km (22 miles) around it. Built in 1973 in an attempt to try and reduce traffic jams, the périphérique is invariably congested itself, particularly during the rush hours, when an estimated 150,000 cars storm its 35 exits. Forming two concentric rings wrapped tightly around Paris, the suburbs (*la*

PRECEDING PAGES: one of the old-style children's attractions of Paris; the Louvre Pyramid. **LEFT:** street cafés are part of the fabric of Paris.

banlieue) are divided up into *départements* or counties. The inner ring incorporates Hauts-de-Seine, Val-de-Marne and Seine-St-Denis, and the outer ring consists of Seine-et-Marne, Essonne, Yvelines and Val-d'Oise. These counties, together with Paris and the Greater Paris conurbation around it, constitute the Ile de France and are linked by eight major roads, five RER lines and an extensive rail network branching out in all directions from five stations in Paris.

At the beginning of the 19th century, Napoleon Bonaparte imposed a special status on the city of Paris, giving it the powers of a *département* in order to maintain a firm hold on the capital's politics and populace. Today, each *arrondissement* also has its own council and mayor to deal with local affairs. Nationally, Paris is represented by 21 delegates and 12 senators in the two houses of the French Parliament.

The role of the river

"She is buffeted by the waves but sinks not," reads the Latin inscription on the city's coat-of-arms, symbolising a Paris born on the flanks of the River Seine. Lutetia was indeed founded by the Romans, on the site of a Gallic Parisii settlement on the largest island in the river, but today it is the Seine that cuts a swathe through the middle of the city. The Seine is the capital's widest avenue; it is spanned by a total of 37 bridges, which provide some of the loveliest views of Paris.

The river is also the city's calmest artery, barely ruffled by the daily flow of tourist and commercial boat traffic. In the 19th century, the banks were encumbered with wash-houses and watermills, and its waters heaved with ships from every corner of France. Even more difficult to imagine now are the 700 brightly painted Viking warships, which used the river to invade Paris from the north in the 9th century, or the thousands of bodies that floated past in 1572, victims of the St Bartholomew's Day Massacre turning the Seine into a river of blood. Today, barges and pleasure boats on their way to Burgundy use the St-Martin and St-Denis canals to shorten their trip, cutting across the northeast of Paris.

Parisian ambience

One of the most persistent images of Paris is one of long avenues graciously lined with chestnut and plane trees. Flowers and plants abound in a patch-work of squares, parks and gardens, tended in the formal French tradition or following the English style so admired by Napoleon III. Divided up by two large series of streets, one forming a long line north to south (from Boulevard de Strasbourg to Boulevard St-Michel) and the other going east to west (from the Rue de Faubourg St-Antoine to as far as La Défense), Paris is a mosaic of *quartiers* (quarters) or villages, each one having a distinctive character. Chains of boulevards encircle the centre of the city, marking where the boundary was in medieval times. Many of the streets contain the word *faubourg*, which indicates that there was once a village or suburb in that area. Underground Paris is a labyrinth of Métro lines, over 3,200 km (2,000 miles) of sewers, which you can visit, and endless ancient quarries, which were converted into catacombs in the 18th century. ❑

RIGHT: taking in the splendour of Sacré-Cœur.

THE MAKING OF PARIS

The Parisii tribe discovered it, the Romans usurped it, the
Franks invaded it and Napoleon ruled it. The city's refined
culture and revolutionary politics changed the world

A s with many of the world's great cities,
the mysterious mists of antiquity veil the
origins of Paris. Around 300 BC, when
the Celts were chasing each other around
Europe, one tribe, the Parisii, settled on an
island in the Seine river (the Ile de la Cité).
They were good farmers and active traders,
hence the name Parisii, which is said to be
derived from a Celtic word for boat. A more
imaginative theory on the origins of the city's
name claims that the tribe's founder was Paris,
the emigré son of King Priam of Troy.

In 53 BC, a number of Gallic tribes failed to
appear at the annual council in Ambiani
(Amiens) summoned by the Romans, who
were in the process of colonising Gaul. Roman
Emperor Julius Caesar, sensing rebellion,
quickly transferred the council into the midst
of the restless Gauls, to the Parisii settlement
– just an agglomeration of huts – on the Seine.

The Romans soon realised the advantage of
the position, and developed the settlement for
themselves, naming it Lutetia. A wooden
bridge connected the island to the Left Bank,
and a town grew up with all the hallmarks of
Roman civilisation. Dominating the Right
Bank from its hilltop perch stood a temple to
Mercury where, more than three centuries
later, St Denis, a Christian agitator and the first
bishop of Paris, was beheaded, giving the hill
the name Mons Martyrium (Martyr's Mound)
– Montmartre in French. According to legend,
St Denis picked up his severed head and
walked 6,000 steps before being buried by one
of his apostles on the spot where the cathedral
of St-Denis now stands.

Lying as it did exposed on a plain, Lutetia
soon fell victim to frequent sackings by
marauding barbarian tribes. In AD 358,
Emperor Constantine sent his son-in-law,
Julian, to Gaul to deal with them. The young
man promptly fell in love with the town and
some say that it was he who renamed it Paris.
He became the Roman Emperor, abolishing
Christianity (officially tolerated since 313)
and, when not in battle, he sat in the palais,
organising the town's accounts.

Geneviève – patron saint of Paris

Just under a century later, around 451, Attila
the Hun appeared on the scene with his

hordes. The Parisians prepared to flee but were assured by the pious 19-year-old Geneviève, that the Huns would not harm the city, as long as they stayed with her and prayed. The marauders passed southwest of the town and ran straight into the swords of a hastily raised army of legionnaires. Thereafter, Geneviève became the patron saint of Paris.

She was still alive when Clovis I, king of the Salian Franks and founder of the Merovingian dynasty, invaded much of Gaul, seeing off the Romans, and sweeping into Paris. He promptly made it his capital (many believe it was he who gave Paris its name) and, installing himself in the palais, he converted

the town back to Christianity. Later a basilica was built where he and Ste Geneviève were buried, which eventually became the Panthéon, the last resting place for France's VIPs.

Merovingian law of succession was simple: the empire was divided among the previous ruler's offspring. As a result, for the next 250 years, instead of being used as an administrative centre, Paris frequently served as a battleground for the murderous family bickering of Clovis's descendants.

LEFT: Paris's coat of arms from the river worker's guild.
ABOVE: Roman stonework in the Musée National du Moyen Age – Thermes de Cluny.

Into the Middle Ages

The Carolingians, who ruled from 751 moved the political centre away from Paris, which was left in the charge of a count and his municipal guard. Charlemagne died in 814, leaving his son Louis – the first of many – in charge.

The Norman invasions of the mid-9th century brought Paris back into the limelight. After several sackings of the city, in 885, Eudes (Odo), Count of Paris, decided to resist by building fortifications around the Ile de la Cité. The first siege of Paris lasted a year and almost bore fruit: the Carolingian army came to the rescue. But King Charles the Fat, instead of attacking the siege-weary aggressors, let them sail up the Seine to pillage Burgundy. In defiance of the king, Eudes took the crown and Carolingian unity dissolved. A period of instability followed, as the French crown shifted from one dynasty to the next. The Saracens appeared in the south, Hungarians in the east, and the Vikings ran amok. All in all, it was not a happy time for France, until the ongoing power struggle led to Hugh Capet, son of Hugh the Great, a descendant of Eudes, becoming king of all France in 987. This marked the beginning of a new, long-lasting dynasty – the Capetians.

Paris prospered under the Capetians, new fountains were built to bring fresh drinking water to the citizens and *sergents de ville*, armed with clubs, walked a beat. With new cloisters and churches and a cosmopolitan population, Paris very soon grew into an intellectual centre. At the start of the 12th century, monks, scholars, philosophers, poets and musicians came to the city to learn, argue and teach.

Economic life in Paris rested in the hands of merchants and craftsmen, who organised themselves into guilds. The most powerful of these was the water merchants' guild, which included all river workers and gave its coat-of-arms to the city. Philippe-Auguste built Les Halles for the guilds and improved the Seine docks. The guilds took care of levying taxes, town-crying and other municipal duties. In 1190, six guild members, so-called Grands Bourgeois (city dwellers), were chosen to act as the king's officers. The number increased to 24, meeting in regular sessions to discuss municipal business.

Later, Louis IX (1226–70), who was made a saint, created three governing chambers. The

Bourgeois became an independent political force, often corrupt but, equally often, striving for democratic reforms, which had a long-lasting effect on political life. In 1200, the first student riot took place, which led to Philippe-Auguste (1180–1223) to found the University of Paris. Most European scholars visited its prestigious faculties on the Left Bank.

The first revolution

By the mid-14th century the Capetians had given way to the Valois and the devastating Hundred Years' War with the English began. The plague made its first deadly appearance. In 1356, the English captured King John the

alist. Three days later, John the Good's son, the Dauphin, entered the capital.

The new regent, who was to become Charles V (1364–80), hammered out a truce with the English, allowing France some time to put its house in order. Paris was relatively well treated, considering how fickle its loyalties had been: the Parliament still met but its powers were curtailed.

But Paris was seething with anger. In 1382, during the reign of Charles VI (1380–1422), a group of citizens calling themselves the Maillotins rebelled against high taxes and were brutally repressed. Then, in 1407, the Maillotins became enmeshed in the violent

Good at Poitiers. The citizens of Paris, tired of incompetent leadership, rebelled. Their leader, Etienne Marcel, a clothmaker and guild chairman, was the first in a long string of genial, but corrupt demagogues to emerge on Paris's political horizon. A motley crew of impoverished townspeople and peasants under Jacques Bonhomme chose the moment to begin a revolt, later known as the Jacquerie.

For support, Marcel unwisely chose the King of Navarre (Charles the Bad), an English ally. When the Parisians found out about the alliance, they turned on Marcel. In July 1358, as he was about to hand over Paris to the rival Navarre camp, he was assassinated by a loy-

struggle for power between the Burgundian John the Fearless and his cousin Louis d'Orléans, brother of the king, who was by now mentally deranged. John had Louis murdered and, in 1409, took control of Paris.

The advance of the English

While Louis's Armagnac son, Charles, raised a new army, Paris celebrated. Into the fray stepped a butcher, Caboche, demanding fiscal and administrative reforms. All hell broke loose as John's authority slipped into the hands of Caboche and his henchmen. The ensuing Reign of Terror gave Charles and his Armagnac army a chance to re-enter and "pacify" the city. Seeing France torn apart by civil war, the English resumed hostilities. Siding with the Burgundians, they defeated the Armagnacs at the Battle of Agincourt in 1415.

Four years later, John the Fearless was murdered, whereupon Henry V of England married Catherine, daughter of the mad King Charles, and occupied Paris in December 1420. The Dauphin, the legitimate French heir, had some support in the capital but he could not keep out the English invaders. Joan of Arc, a 17-year-old girl from Lorraine, came to his rescue in 1428 by defeating the English at Orléans and, a year later, Charles VII was crowned at Reims. However, Paris remained

goldsmiths, cabinet makers and masons, who set about the task of reshaping the city's lugubrious Gothic face. With the rebirth of the capital under François's graceful, iron hand, French culture also returned to life.

The advent of the printing press underpinned these activities; however, it also helped spread the new gospel of Protestantism through Catholic France. Paris, dominated by the conservative Sorbonne theologists, pushed for measures against the Protestants, known as Huguenots, often burning religious agitators.

Henri II's sons and heirs, François II (1559–60), Charles IX (1560–74) and Henri III (1574–89), proved inadequate in control-

in English hands until 1436, when Charles recaptured his tattered capital, driving the English back to Calais.

By the early 16th century, Louis XII (1498–1515) was ensconced in the Italian Wars. Then François I (1515–47) began the struggle against the mighty Habsburgs in Europe and, in 1525, he was captured at Pavia. The Parisians paid his ransom and he promptly moved into the Louvre. In his wake came an army of Italian architects, painters, sculptors,

ling France's religious factions. Nor were they helped by the intrigues of the Queen Mother, Catherine de Médicis. The country was plunged into a religious war.

War between the Henris

King Henri III's concessions to the Protestants infuriated the Catholics, who were led by the popular Henri de Guise and his Paris-based Holy League. In 1584, the Protestant Henri de Navarre, a Bourbon, became heir to the throne but he had to fight Henri de Guise for the right to accede to power. To this end, in 1589, Henri III had Henri de Guise assassinated. Paris threw up its barricades and the Holy League's

LEFT: boatmen in front of the Pont Notre-Dame.
ABOVE: Charles IX and Henri III, sons of the scheming Catherine de Médicis.

Council of Sixteen took power and deposed Henri III, who joined forces with Navarre. His army, however, joined the Catholics. That summer, Henri III was murdered by the friar Jacques Clément, and Henri de Navarre became Henri IV.

Civil war dragged on for another five years. Paris was the stage for the Council of Sixteen's gruesome repression of real and perceived plots. In 1593, Philip II of Spain, who had entered the war on the Catholic side, pressed to usurp the French throne. Henri IV, in a brilliant piece of opportunism, chose that moment to convert to Catholicism, whereupon Paris welcomed him and overnight the war-

Seine. Avenues cut through the dingy labyrinth. Architects built new houses, parks, palaces and schools and restored the old ones. Cardinal Richelieu, who largely governed on behalf of the young Louis XIII (1610–43) while the king was growing up, founded the Académie Française. Under the Sun King, Louis XIV (1643–1715), the spending spree reached its peak. His minister, Colbert, sanitised entire sections of the city and set up manufacturing plants to provide the French with luxury items. Louis XIV also had hospices constructed for the poor and Les Invalides was built to house war veterans.

The influx of money and the proximity of

weary nation fell in line. Henri IV patched up France spiritually and economically. In 1598, his Edict of Nantes set up guidelines for cohabitation between the religious groups. However, in 1610 the Catholic Henri IV, like Henri III before him, was murdered, bringing the young Louis XIII to the throne.

The glorious epoch

Despite massive deficits incurred by their violent foreign policy, the Bourbons lavished huge sums on Paris, while keeping it on a short political leash. Two deserted islets behind the Ile de la Cité became the residential Ile St-Louis. New bridges crossed the

the court attracted a huge crowd to the capital. Theatres echoed with the verse of Racine and Corneille and everyone laughed at the writings of Molière, Boileau and La Fontaine satirising the hustling and bustling society.

But storm clouds were gathering. In 1648, Paris revolted, demanding greater political representation. The 12 provincial parliaments joined a body promoting change, as did a conspiracy of nobles under Prince Condé. The Fronde, as it was called, eventually collapsed, but Louis XIV later had his lavish palace, Versailles, built outside the city limits to keep his distance from the unruly Parisian mob.

The beginning of the 18th century was a

period of great inequality in Paris. French high society was having a fine time in the court of the Sun King but the needs and wishes of the poor were ignored and they hit back dramatically as the century drew to a close.

The revolutionary years

French reputation no longer rested on royal glory in the latter part of the 18th century, but on the wisdom of its intellectuals – Voltaire, Rousseau, Diderot and Quesnay. Poverty increased, and when a bad harvest in 1788 caused the price of bread to soar and the people to become restless, Queen Marie-Antoinette is supposed to have made her famous pronouncement that the hungry should eat cake.

By 1789, France's debts had reached a critical stage. The king took the desperate step of summoning the Estates General, a legislative body made up of three estates: the Clergy, Nobility and the rest of the populace, commonly known as the Third Estate, to vote for reforms to the French Constitution. Craftily, the king only allowed one vote per estate, meaning that the massive Third Estate could be outvoted two to one by the smaller Clergy and Nobility.

Eventually forced out of the meeting, the Third Estate created a National Assembly in opposition to the king. On 14 July, the people of Paris stormed the Bastille prison for its weapons, proclaimed a Commune and formed a National Guard under the leadership of La Fayette, a French soldier.

The explosion of 1789 swept the past away. The First Republic was proclaimed and, in January 1793, King Louis XVI was decapitated in public on the Place de la Concorde, followed in October by his Queen, Marie-Antoinette. Paris was the centre of the French Revolution and its increasingly radical leaders. These included Mirabeau, Brissot, Danton and finally the fanatical Robespierre, egged on by Marat, whose assassination in July 1793 threw the Reign of Terror into top gear. Anyone suspected of stepping out of line was sent to the guillotine as a traitor.

In July 1794, it was Robespierre's turn for

LEFT: St Bartholomew's Day Massacre in 1572.
RIGHT: Madame de Maintenon, governess to the Sun King's children, who secretly became his wife.

the chop. The young General Napoleon Bonaparte finally drew the line under the Revolution, after quashing a royalist uprising in 1795. Four years later, he had seized power, crowning himself Emperor of a totalitarian and military state.

The Napoleonic Empire

The glorious Napoleonic empire ended once and for all with Paris occupied by three allied armies after the Battle of Waterloo in 1815. Bourbon Louis XVIII headed a constitutional monarchy, which placed an emphasis on law and order and laissez-faire economics. The Industrial Revolution might have turned Paris

into an opulent and mediocre business centre were it not for the apostles of Romanticism, led by Victor Hugo (1802–85). Inspired by the anti-establishment spirit of 1789, they waged a struggle against creaky academia and bourgeois respectability in garrets, cafés, journals and the "enemy's" own salons. The revolutionary spirit also remained in the Republican forces, who reached for the Parisian mob whenever despotism reared its head. In July 1830, Charles X revoked certain electoral laws, which led to three days of bloody rioting and his abdication. His cousin, Louis-Philippe, Duke of Orléans, held power until 1848, when another revolution forced him to abdicate.

The Second Empire

When Napoleon's nephew and president of the Second Republic, Louis Napoleon, crowned himself Emperor Napoleon III in 1852, he pre-emptively arrested more than 20,000 suspected political opponents to strengthen his position.

The Second Empire was a gaudy and grandiose period in the city's history. New railway tracks were built to connect the city with other European capitals. Twice, in 1855 and 1867, Paris hosted the World Fair. Basking in financial ease, the city abandoned itself to the pleasures of masked balls, Offenbach operettas and salon conversation. Aided by

eager speculators and fat taxes, the Prefect Baron Georges Haussmann gave Paris a new face, gutting and rebuilding the centre. New water mains and a sewage system were installed to service the two million Parisians. Elegant boulevards, avenues and squares appeared: the Champs-Elysées, St-Michel, St-Germain and Etoile, to name but a few. These served an aesthetic purpose, but they also facilitated swift troop deployment if trouble arose and were difficult for rioters to barricade. Families dispossessed by the construction were forced to move to eastern Paris. This influx only added to that area's already notoriously seditious spirit.

The Commune

In 1870, Napoleon III went to war with Prussia. Parisians lined the streets to cheer the ill-equipped, ill-led and ill-fated army as it marched east. Two months later, Napoleon was beaten, the Second Empire had become the Third Republic, and the Prussians were besieging Paris. In Bordeaux, the government of Adolphe Thiers waited for an uprising in heroic revolutionary style that never materialised.

On 28 January 1871, President Thiers, without consulting Paris, finally agreed to a ceasefire. A month later, the National Assembly ratified a peace treaty. The Prussians marched through Paris avoiding the eastern districts, home of the starving, belligerent and vengeful National Guard, which felt betrayed by the French government. Sensing trouble, Thiers moved his government to Versailles. He barely escaped the ensuing explosion.

On 28 March 1871, a Commune was proclaimed at the Hôtel de Ville after a municipal election was boycotted by the bourgeoisie. Civil war erupted and the Hôtel de Ville was burned. While the Communards hoisted red flags and argued over political and military strategies, Thiers was busy raising a new army. The government forces succeeded where the Prussians had failed and some 25,000 Communards were killed – most by summary execution – in the last weeks of May; the final 147 were shot in the Père-Lachaise Cemetery. With them went the revolutionary spark that had defied tyrants and kindled republics since 1789.

With the insurrectionist working class brutally tamed, Paris became the stage for the squabbles, plots, demonstrations, counter-demonstrations and oral and written polemics of the Third Republic. The Republicans split into pro-clerical and anti-clerical factions. In the 1890s, after recovering from the Commune, the left gathered around the socialist Jean Jaurès. On the right was an array of diehard monarchists and nationalists with a strong vein of anti-Semitism, as revealed by the Dreyfus Affair in the late 1890s. This scandal revolved around a Jewish army captain, Alfred Dreyfus, who was imprisoned on Devil's Island on trumped-up spying charges.

At the same time, the Métro was dug, the Eiffel Tower built for the 1889 World Fair and the first films were shown. Between 1880 and 1940, Paris housed more creative artists than any other metropolis. They chattered with philosophers, theorists, critics, anarchists and socialites in smoke-filled cafés.

Almost every artistic movement flourished in Paris – Realism, Impressionism, Cubism, Surrealism, Dadaism, and so on. In the pawnshops of Montmartre were paintings by Picasso, Utrillo and Modigliani. Debussy, Zola, Cocteau and his apostles were in town. In 1913, Diaghilev's Ballets Russes presented its superstar, Nijinsky, dancing to Stravinsky's latest composition, *The Rites of Spring*, scandalising the jam-packed auditoriums.

World War I dampened spirits and in Sep-

Between the wars

With one million dead, millions of others now crippled and the agricultural north destroyed by shelling, France's part in the victory over Germany in 1914 was tarnished. Conservative Republicans and left-wing coalitions, including the Communist Party (founded in 1920), tried to come to grips with the economic and social after-effects of the Great War. The extreme right, meanwhile, made some important gains.

Fascist-type organisations had started appearing in France in the late 19th century. In the 1920s and 1930s, such groups proliferated, fuelled by general discontent and fear of Bolshevism, and inspired by the successes of Mus-

tember 1914, the German army came within earshot. The military governor, Galliéni, rushed reinforcements, including the Paris taxi service, to the counter-offensive on the Marne. This rapid response ensured that the city was spared. Normal life began to return after the armistice was declared in 1918. From the east came Russian emigrés, and from the west came American writers and composers. In the 1930s, Paris became a temporary haven to the refugees of fascism in Europe.

LEFT: Louis XIV, the Sun King and a big spender.
ABOVE: Storming the Bastille, 14 July 1789.

solini and Hitler. They focused their efforts on Paris, parading in paramilitary garb and campaigning against the internationalists, the socialists and, above all, the Jews. On 6 February 1934, a coalition of fascist factions attempted a *coup d'état* in Paris. It failed, but the left was finally goaded into concerted action. In 1936, a front of radicals, socialists and communists, headed by the socialist Léon Blum, won the election. The so-called Front Populaire promised to fight fascism and improve the workers' lot. Initial euphoria was short-lived and the Front was split by its leader over Spain and then disappeared after a series of wildcat strikes.

World War II

When war broke out against Nazi Germany in September 1939, France shored up the utterly useless Maginot Line, mobilised an ill-equipped army, and waited. In Paris, statues were sandbagged and Louvre curators carefully prepared paintings for transport to safety. On 14 June 1940, the Nazis marched into the City of Light, having simply gone round the Maginot Line via Belgium. There was no siege, no National Guard, no *levée en masse*, no cabbies carrying reinforcements. The 84-year-old Marshal Philippe Pétain, the withered hero of Verdun, became the head of a puppet regime in Vichy in unoccupied France.

resumed without the extreme right. Tourists returned in droves. Bebop and rock 'n' roll arrived from across the Atlantic. But post-war thought was dominated by the dark existentialism of Jean-Paul Sartre and Albert Camus. In addition, France lost two major colonial wars, the first in Indochina (1946–54) and the second in Algeria (1954–62).

May 1968: the barricades are back

A bloody wave of bombings swept Paris in the early 1960s, when it became clear that President de Gaulle, who had come out of retirement to head the Fifth Republic in 1958, wanted to pull out of the Algerian quagmire.

While many Parisians collaborated with the Nazis, there were those who bravely resisted, joining the Free French Movement led from London by the Under Secretary for War, General Charles de Gaulle. Their defiance often cost them their lives. On 6 June 1944, Allied forces landed in Normandy and advanced on Paris. Dietrich von Choltitz, the German commander, received orders to blow up the city, but chose to surrender instead. On 24 August 1944, Paris was liberated and, two days later, General de Gaulle paraded with his forces down the Champs-Elysées. De Gaulle immediately formed a provisional government, which lasted until 1946. Political quarrelling

De Gaulle's manner in dealing with internal matters was patriarchal and authoritarian. The 1968 agitation began uneventfully enough in March with a sit-in by students to demand changes in the antiquated university system. But instead of initiating a civil discussion with the students, the *ancien régime* promptly called in the CRS, the riot police, to restore what they saw as a breakdown of order.

On the night of 10 May 1968, the police stormed 60 barricades in the Quartier Latin. Unrest spread to the factories and other cities. France was soon paralysed and Paris was left in a state of siege. Petrol was rationed and cautious housewives hoarded food. The state-run media broadcast heavily-monitored programming, while Parisians received the news from privateers on France's periphery or from the BBC in London. At the end of the month, de Gaulle announced new elections and warned against impending totalitarianism. The Parisian bourgeoisie awoke. An hour later, over 500,000 de Gaulle supporters were flowing down the Champs-Elysées. The Gaullists won the election, but were not in power for long. Disenchantment continued and the President resigned in 1969, leaving his Republic to his ardent follower Georges Pompidou.

Mitterrand and Chirac

The 1970s appeared tame but, when the Independent Republican President, Valéry Giscard d'Estaing, lost to socialist leader François Mitterrand in 1981, a huge crowd marched to the Bastille in celebration. However, in 1986, the exigent Parisian character revealed itself again, during the legislative elections. Voters on the left were dismayed by what they viewed as Mitterrand's sell-out, and conservative forces, led by Paris mayor Jacques Chirac, swept in with a rightist coalition.

Chirac was a mass of contradictions. In his student days, he had been a member of the Communist youth movement, then a gung-ho lieutenant fighting with French anti-independence forces in Algeria, and in the early 1970s, Prime Minister for two years under President Giscard d'Estaing. May 1968 had reaffirmed Paris's old rebellious spirit. Parisians still demonstrated at the drop of a hat – anti-racism, gay rights, against altering university entrance requirements, to name but a few. The zeitgeist of the 1990s found much to admire in the legacy of mai '68. The 1993 elections maintained the swing to the right, which was confirmed when Jacques Chirac succeeded François Mitterrand as president in 1995. Mitterrand died in January 1996. Despite the disquiet about his personal integrity, the French mourned him. Indeed, despite the decline in support for his policies, his grands projets – from the Louvre Pyramid to the Grande Arche at La Défense and the new Bibliothèque Nationale de France-François Mitterrand at

Tolbiac – made an indelible mark on Paris architecture. By 1997, Chirac's popularity had sunk to an all time low, which was borne out in the June elections when socialist Lionel Jospin was made prime minister, creating a second cohabitation with the right. By the end of 1999, the coalition was in a fairly stable position, with the economy booming and unemployment low. Then in the historic 2001 mayoral elections, disenchanted with the right-wing Jean Tibéri, Parisians voted for Bertrand Delanoë, the first leftist mayor of Paris for 130 years.

The French presidential elections of 2002 produced a shocking result: a runoff between centre-right incumbent Jacques Chirac and

far-right leader Jean-Marie Le Pen. Parisians took to the streets to express their rejection of Le Pen and his anti-immigration, anti-EU programme. They contributed massively to Chirac's second round victory on May 5, the most overwhelming in the history of France. President Chirac then led a determined opposition to the war in Iraq which saw his approval ratings at home soar, only to plummet after initiating reforms to the state pension and benefit system with his prime minister Jean-Pierre Raffarin. Then in August 2003 came the heatwave during which an estimated 15,000 old people died, leaving Chirac and Raffarin's popularity in tatters. ❏

LEFT: the liberation of Paris, August 1944.
RIGHT: quelling the student riots in May 1968.

Decisive Dates

The Gallo-Roman Era

c. 300 BC A Celtic tribe, the Parisii, settle on the Ile de la Cité and found the settlement of Lutétia.

58–52 BC Julius Caesar conquers Gaul and the Romans build Lutetia on the site left by the Parisii and on the Left Bank of the Seine.

c. AD 250 St Denis establishes the first Christian community and is eventually martyred on Mount Mercury in AD 287.

313 Christianity is tolerated until 350, when Roman Emperor Julian tries to abolish it.

360 Julian the Apostate is made Emperor of Rome while in charge of Lutetia and is believed to have changed the town's name to Paris.

451 Ste Geneviève saves Paris from Attila the Hun.

The Dark Ages

486 Frankish king Clovis pushes out the last Romans and, in 508, makes Paris the capital of his new kingdom.

496 King Clovis is baptised at Reims.

543 The monstery of St-Germain-des-Prés is founded.

635 Fair of St-Denis is established by King Dagobert.

751 The Carolingian dynasty begins, diverting power from Paris to Aix-la-Chapelle (Aachen) and the abandoned city goes into decline. Emperor Charlemagne rules from 768 to 814.

845-880 Paris sacked by the Vikings.

885 Count Eudes (Odo) defends Paris against the Normans and becomes king of the Western Franks in 888.

The Middle Ages

Paris develops into a city of learning and political power and spreads north of the river.

987 Start of the Capetian dynasty when Hugh Capet, Count of Paris, is made king.

1136 Abbot Suger begins the Basilica of St-Denis.

1108–54 Paris becomes an important trading centre.

1163 Building work starts on Notre-Dame.

1180–1223 Philippe-Auguste builds the Louvre fortress and a wall around Paris.

1215 The University of Paris is founded and given a papal charter.

1246–48 Louis IX builds the Sainte-Chapelle.

1226–70 Louis IX (St Louis) makes judicial reforms and the Sorbonne University opens in 1253.

1328 The House of Valois inherits the monarchy in preference to its English cousin Edward III, triggering the Hundred Years' War which begins in 1340.

1358 *Jacquerie* uprising of the peasants in Paris, led by clothmaker Etienne Marcel fighting for democracy.

1364 Charles V moves the royal court to the Louvre and builds Bastille and Vincennes fortresses.

1380 The Bastille prison is built.

1420 Paris surrenders to the English, who rule until 1436, despite Joan of Arc's efforts in 1429.

The Renaissance

At the end of the 15th century, wars with Italy expose the French to new ideas of art, wealth and luxury.

1463 The first printing press is introduced to Paris.

1469 First French printing works opens at the Sorbonne.

1516 François I brings Leonardo da Vinci with his masterpiece, the *Mona Lisa*, to France.

1528 François I starts to rebuild the Louvre.
1559 Henri II is killed in a jousting tournament. The new Louvre palace is completed and street lamps erected.
1572 23 August St Bartholomew's Day Massacre of Protestants on the orders of the Catholic monarchy.
1589 Henri III is assassinated.
1594 Bourbon Henri IV converts to Catholicism, ending the Wars of Religion.
1609 The Place Royale (now known as the Place des Vosges) and Pont-Neuf are built.
1610 Henri IV is assassinated.

Le Grand Siècle

In an age of extravagance, Louis XIV the Sun King moves to Versailles and starts an opulent building programme.
1629 Louis XIII's prime minister, Cardinal Richelieu, builds the Palais Royal.
1631 Paris's first newspaper, *La Gazette*, is launched.
1635 Louis XIII founds the Académie Française.
1648–53 Paris is occupied by the Fronde rebellion.
1661 Fall of Fronde.
1667 First street lighting in Paris.
1670 Hôtel des Invalides is built as a military hospital and retirement home for those wounded in battle.
1672 The Grand Boulevards, Portes St-Denis and St-Martin are built.
1680 Comédie Française is founded.
1682 Louis XIV moves his Royal Court to Versailles.
1686 Le Procope is the first café in Paris to open.

The Age of Enlightenment

The arts flourish, science develops and intellectuals, such as Voltaire and Rousseau, exchange ideas.
1700 The Spanish War of Succession begins.
1715 Louis XIV dies and Philippe d'Orléans becomes regent.
1751 First volume of Diderot's *Encyclopédie* published.

LEFT: Clovis I, king of the Franks, who saw off the Roman invaders.
RIGHT: Louis XIV (1643–1715), the extravagant Sun King, who built the palace at Versailles.

1753 Construction of Place Louis XIV (Place de la Concorde) is begun.
1760 Louis XV builds the Panthéon, Place de la Concorde and the Ecole Militaire.

The First Empire

The Revolution leads to the creation of a Republic, which is soon turned into an Empire by the warring, but reforming and popular, Napoleon Bonaparte.
1789 14 July after the storming of the Bastille, Louis XVI is forced to leave Versailles for Paris.
1791 21 June Louis XVI tries to leave Paris.
1792 22 September. A Republic is declared and the Royal statues removed.

1793 Louis XVI and Marie-Antoinette are executed.
1794 The ensuing Terror kills more than 60,000 people (more than 1,300 in six weeks alone). The Jacobins are overthrown and the Directoire takes over.
1799 Napoleon Bonaparte, the First Consul of France, seizes power and is crowned emperor in 1804.
1800 The Banque de France is established.
1806 Construction of the Arc de Triomphe begins.
1814 Napoleon is defeated and the Russian army occupies Paris.
1815 Napoleon regains power briefly before his

defeat at the Battle of Waterloo; the Bourbon monarchy is restored with Louis XVII ascending the throne.

The Restoration

Two more revolutions hit Paris, finally unseating the monarchy once more in 1848.

1830 Charles X is overtrhown and Louis-Philippe of Orléans becomes king.

1831 Victor Hugo's *Notre-Dame de Paris* is published.

1836 The Arc de Triomphe is completed.

1842 First French railway links Paris with St-Germain.

1848 Louis-Philippe, the Citizen King, is

construction of the Palais Garnier commences.

1863 Manet's painting *Le Déjeuner sur l'Herbe* scandalises the Académie.

1866 Founding of *Le Figaro* newspaper.

1870 Paris surrenders to Prussia and Napoleon III abdicates.

The Third and Fourth Republics

The Métro is dug and new inventions, such as the motor car, telephone and cinema, give rise to the term "*la belle époque*". The beginning of a new creative era.

1871 Uprising by Paris Commune with 25,000 people killed, the Tuileries palace destroyed and the Hôtel de Ville burnt down.

deposed. Louis-Napoleon Bonaparte is elected president.

The Second Empire

With Napoleon III at the helm, Paris is transformed into an efficient, modern city.

1852 Louis-Napoleon declares himself Emperor Napoleon III and the Second Empire begins.

1852–70 Baron Georges Haussmann undertakes a massive redesign of the city, laying sewers and creating parks. Bon Marché, the first department store opens.

1855 First World Fair. The second is 12 years later.

1862 Hugo's *Les Misérables* is published,

1888 Louis Pasteur sets up the Pasteur Institute as a hospital and research centre for infectious diseases.

1889 Eiffel Tower built for the World Fair. The Moulin Rouge opens.

1894–1906 The Dreyfus Affair.

1895 Lumiére brothers screen the world's first public film.

1909 The first Métro line opens, Pont Alexandre III, Grand Palais and Petit Palais are built.

1914–18 World War I: Paris is saved from German attack by the Battle of the Marne.

1919 Versailles Peace Conference.

1924 The poet and literary theorist André Breton publishes his *Surrealist Manifesto*.

1934 The Depression gives rise to riots and a series of strikes.
1937 Palais de Chaillot built. Léon Blum of the Popular Front is elected.
1940 World War II: Paris is bombed and occupied by the Germans.
1941-42 Mass deportation of Paris Jews.
1944 Paris is liberated by the Allies, and General Charles de Gaulle heads a Provisional Government until 1946, when a Fourth Republic is proclaimed.
1949 *The Second Sex* by Simone de Beauvoir is published.
1958 The Algerian crisis topples the Fourth Republic.

THE FIFTH REPUBLIC
General Charles de Gaulle returns as president of the Fifth Republic, launching Paris into the Space Age.
1958–63 The construction of La Défense begins.
1962 André Malraux, Minister of Culture, establishes a renovation and restoration programme. End of the Algerian war.
1968 Strikes and student riots against the university system and the Government forces de Gaulle to call an election. He wins but resigns a year later.
1969 Les Halles food market is moved to Rungis. De Gaulle resigns. Pompidou becomes president.
1973 The *périphérique* ring road is built in an attempt to reduce traffic jams. It is invariably congested itself, particulary during the rush hours, when an estimated 150,000 cars storm its 35 exits.
1977 The Centre Georges-Pompidou opens. Jacques Chirac is elected mayor of Paris.
1981 Socialist François Mitterrand is elected president and inaugurates the first of his *grands projets*, the renovation of the Louvre.
1986 Right-wing Chirac becomes prime minister in a unique *cohabitation* with a socialist president. The Musée d'Orsay opens. The Cité des Sciences at La Villette is completed.

1989 Bicentenary celebrations of the Revolution herald the opening of the Louvre Pyramid, Grande Arche and Opéra Bastille – more of François Mitterrand's *grands projets*.
1995 Jacques Chirac is elected president.
1997 Socialist Lionel Jospin becomes prime minister, creating a second *cohabitation*.
1998 France wins the World Cup. The Bibliothèque Nationale de France is relocated to new buildings at Tolbiac.
2000 Millennium celebrations focus around the Eiffel Tower.
2001 Bertrand Delanoë elected as the first leftist mayor to rule Paris in 130 years, and the first openly gay mayor of a major city.

2002 The euro replaces the franc. After the success of National Front leader Jean-Marie Le Pen in the first round of presidential elections, Chirac is re-elected president with 82 percent of the vote. Jean-Pierre Raffarin is prime minister.
2003 President Chirac opposes the US-led war in Iraq and his popularity ratings at home soar, only to plummet when a reform of the French state pensions and benefit systems is launched. In the summer, nearly 15,000 elderly French people die in an August heatwave. The government is seen as aloof and uncaring.
2004 Five people are killed when a new ultramodern terminal building at Charles de Gaulle airport collapses. ❏

LEFT: a section of Delacroix's *Liberty Leading the People* (1830, Musée du Louvre).
RIGHT: General Charles de Gaulle – war hero and a dominating president whose power was brought to an end by student unrest.

THE PARISIANS

Despite the stereotypes, there's no such thing as a typical Parisian. The people come from widely diverse ethnic and social backgrounds, but what almost all of them have in common is an obsessive enthusiasm for their city

F or many of the inner city's 3 million residents as well as the 25 million tourists who visit each year, Paris is a grand seductress, a love affair that often lasts a lifetime. While part of the allure is certainly the beauty of the city itself, Parisians, too, are an attraction, for their individualism, diversity, charm, and for all their quirks.

Today, Paris is more densely populated than Tokyo, London or New York, and the Parisians' high stress levels can be partly put down to the fact that they live literally on top of one another, squeezed into small apartments, packed into the city's 100 sq km (40 sq miles). A house and garden is an almost

unheard of luxury. There is intense competition for desirable living space, with an average of 150,000 people looking for a home at any one time. It is an oft-cited paradox that this battle for a place to live occurs in a city where 16 percent of apartments lie vacant. Furthermore, high rents contribute to the fact that many Parisians have neither the time nor the money to appreciate the city they live in, being trapped in a monotonous routine they describe as *métro-boulot-dodo* (commuting, working, sleeping).

Nonetheless, for anyone fortunate enough to live in the city centre the rewards far outweigh the demands. Human in scale, clean, safe, cosmopolitan, and lively, Paris lives up to its reputation as one of the best cities on earth for enjoying the good life.

Who are the Parisians?

Parisians, as a whole, form such a diverse collection of races and cultures that it is virtually impossible to stereotype them.

Still, there are ties that bind. Parisians are proud and impatient people, always complaining about their social systems, yet always defending them too. In general they are class conscious and fashion saavy, achingly traditional when it comes to their stomachs and polite behaviour, refreshingly open minded about art, politics and lifestyle. They're the most orderly people on the planet, and the most chaotic. They're forever in a hurry – and always late.

Appearances matter in a city where people-watching is one of the most popular sports.

Almost everyone pays attention to *le look* (pronounced *louk*): an English word used to describe not only your wardrobe but also your "style". Pulling yourself together is to *se looker*, and if you change your style people will notice and say you are *relooké(e)*.

A French sociologist once claimed that in his country, there were not three social classes but sixty-three. With their strong penchant for self-examination, Parisians are quick to create – and discard – stereotypes.

One entrenched classification is BCBG *(bon chic, bon genre)*: the French equivalent of the British Sloane Ranger or the American preppie. They can be spotted easily in their main

bourgeois as the BCBG crowd, only they play up their informality with more youthful clothes, trendy and *très chic*.

Breaking the rules

Paris probably has more rules and regulations than any other city on earth, but Parisians have a special talent for breaking them. Things like building codes, labour laws, pollution or taxation will probably not come to the visitor's immediate attention. What will hit home, however are things like dense clouds of cigarette smoke wafting through public spaces that are marked "smoking is strictly forbidden". Restaurants, by law, are supposed to have non-

stamping grounds of Neuilly, Auteuil and Passy (known collectively as NAP), the rich suburbs of the 16th and 17th *arrondissements*. If you are BCBG, your clothes are well cut, but never daring or flashy.

Another is *boho*, which stands for *bourgeois bohème*. These are the sort of bohemians who can afford the high rents and luxurious living of the Left Bank's St-Germain-des-Prés or the Marais. They're just as

PRECEDING PAGES: *vieille dame* of the Latin Quarter.
LEFT: taking a break in the Place des Vosges.
ABOVE: waiters are an important part of the atmosphere at any street-side café.

HOW SAFE IS THE CITY?

La sécurité was a key issue in the 2002 presidential elections. In the eyes of many, the ruling prime minister, Lionel Jospin, although regarded as an honest politician with a good record, was too "soft" on crime. According to statistics, the crime rate in France has shot up in recent years. In the Métro, a taped voice booms over the loudspeaker "take care of your wallets and personal affairs – there are pickpockets on the train". However, despite the latest trends, Paris remains one of the safest – and most heavily policed – cities in Europe. The Paris suburbs, however, are another story.

smoking sections, but it's rarely reinforced. Parisian drivers play chicken with pedestrians on crossings; they park in the middle of the street and will drive on the pavement if it represents a shortcut to where they are going; they stop paying parking tickets and run red lights during presidential elections (traditionally, the victor declares an amnesty). In theory, you can be fined for allowing your dog to leave its mess, yet the pavements are defiantly dotted with dog dirt.

La Politesse

This is not to suggest that Paris is one great free-for-all. For example, Parisian indiscipline

does not extend to bad manners; indeed, their reputation for rudeness (as long as they're not behind a wheel) is largely undeserved. Good manners are considered essential to everyday life. Indeed, *la politesse* can often become outright chivalry.

Visitors would be well advised to follow the same rules of courtesy. Whether you're buying a baguette, a bus ticket or a Hermès scarf, starting any transaction with a "*Bonjour Madame/Monsieur*," and finishing with those other magic words, "*Merci et au Revoir*" will make the world of difference to the service you receive. If you forget, you're likely to be reminded with a reprimand.

Taking to the streets

Somewhere in Paris someone is on strike almost every day of the year. The expression for going on strike – *faire la grève* – refers to the still existing practice of besieging Paris's Town Hall (located in the former Place de Grève) or marching from Nation and blocking all the streets all the way to Bastille. The strikes can involve many groups – transportation workers, teachers, sanitation workers, air traffic controllers, hospital staff, illegal immigrants, etc. These "social actions" might involve picketing school teachers, farmers dumping tomatoes on the Champs-Elysées or lorry drivers blockading the autoroute. Perhaps going on strike is compensation for the decline of the trade unions and the weakening of political parties. For example, nurses and doctors, bus drivers and firemen have taken to the streets with unsettled demands. But it can also seem rather more banal: a national sport in which Parisians are top of the league.

The protest march, with or without accompanying strikes, can be placed in the great Paris tradition of "the people" rising up. Parisians from all walks of life are willing to participate in street demonstrations for causes that matter to them. Several hundred thousand of them packed the streets in 2003 to protest against the war in Iraq. In fact, there were so many marches and strikes that year, there was even a major protest march against strikers.

Culture and multiculture

Paris considers itself to be the capital of everything French. Despite an official effort to promote regional development, there is still a lot of one-way traffic to Paris for the best and the brightest provincials in almost every field of human endeavour. The tendency of the capital has long been to look down on the provinces, despite the fact that areas such as Languedoc and Brittany have their own culture and language. In return, many French people who live outside Paris are disdainful of its inhabitants: "*Parigot, tête de veau*" (Parisian, calf's head). A national survey in the late 1990s put Parisians at the top of the list of most hated people in France (31 percent), easily topping traditional targets such as civil servants (21 percent), Corsicans (23 percent) and even policemen (18 percent).

However, as France moves gradually away from its rigidly centralising history, attitudes about the provinces are changing. The Paris press is full of stories about stressed-out Parisians who escape to a better life in the countryside. Regional development programmes are pumping a great deal of capital into cities like Bordeaux and Toulouse. And, the new high-speed trains, that zap south in a flash, are worshipped, not so much by provincials, but by Parisians who, much as they love their city, can't get out of it fast enough.

Aside from the provinces, the largest contributors to the Parisian cultural and racial pot au feu are the former colonies of West and North

current minister of the interior, Nicolas Sarkosy, has, amongst other initiatives, beefed up the country's security by expanding the police force and creating laws to make it more difficult for foreigners to enter and leave the country.

Village people

Paris is divided by the Seine into two lobes which look vaguely like the hemispheres of a brain, with the Ile de la Cité and Ile St-Louis in the middle. According to an old saying, the Left Bank was where you did your thinking – the Sorbonne university has been located there since the Middle Ages – and the Right

Africa. Other, earlier waves of immigration have brought an influx of Chinese, Vietnamese, Poles, Russians, Bosnians, Serbs, Armenians, Turks and Greeks. France has the largest Muslim population in Europe and Europe's largest Jewish minority outside of Russia.

If Paris on the whole displays genuine tolerance of other races and religions, "immigration" is still used as a code word – particularly by right-wing extremists like Le Pen – to express their fear of foreigners. The

LEFT: emulating the great at the Musée d'Orsay.
ABOVE: colourful but controversial, members of the extreme right National Front gather for a rally.

BALZAC'S PARISIAN

Throughout the ages, many writers have tried to define the Parisian character, Honoré de Balzac had this to say:

The Parisian is interested in everything and, in the end, interested in nothing… Intoxicated as he is with something new from one day to the next, the Parisian regardless of age, lives like a child. He complains of everything, tolerates everything, mocks everything, forgets everything, desires everything, tastes everything, feels everything passionately, drops everything casually – his kings, his conquests, his glory, his idol, whether made of bronze or glass…

Bank was the place to spend money. Over time, the city was organised into *arrondissements* (districts), running outwards in a snail-shaped pattern from the Ile de France (1st *arrondissement*) to the northeast (20th *arrondissement*), all of them contained within the *périphérique* (ring road). Today, when Parisians communicate about where they live, whether at the tax office or a party, they begin with the number of their *arrondissement*.

Within the various *arrondissements* there are recognised *quartiers*, or neighbourhoods, often worlds apart though linked by a short Métro ride. Each has its own shops, markets, cafés and local eccentrics. Parisians develop

the further left you will find yourself on the political spectrum. Rents are exorbitant in the western *arrondissements* while there is a substantial reservoir of affordable real estate in the east. City planners have been struggling for decades to improve the balance, culminating in massive urban renewal projects at Bercy and the "new" Left Bank in the southeast.

The East-West dichotomy is anchored in recent history. When Baron Haussmann began to demolish the city's medieval slums in 1860, the middle classes tended to relocate to the west while the working class moved east. The following decade was one of the most turbulent in the history of Paris and ended in the ter-

lifetime attachments to their own quartier. Although large supermarket chains are ubiquitous, residents still support local merchants and shop in specialised shops and local markets. Consequently, each quartier develops a village atmosphere in which residents are known by sight and often by name. All of these communities co-exist within Paris beneath the umbrella of a big city.

The east-west divide

The most important unofficial division in Paris is between the traditionally working-class eastern end of the city and the mostly bourgeois west. In general, the further east you go,

rible events of La Commune: hostage taking, class warfare and the summary execution of 20,000 Parisians, most of them inhabitants of today's 19th and 20th *arrondissements*.

Immigrants live on both sides of the Seine, east and west, from Chinatown in the 13th to the African Goutte d'Or in the 18th. However, the most diverse community of all is probably in the 19th *arrondissement*; in some schools half of the children have Arabic as a first language and there are nearly seventy other ethnic groups. The neighbourhood is dotted with mosques, churches of different denominations and synagogues.

Although the mythic *rive gauche* (Left

Bank) still pulls millions of tourists south of the Seine in search of the avant-garde, things have changed in the social geography of Paris since the days of Hemingway. The Left Bank's Latin Quarter is one the city's most expensive neighbourhoods, full of designer boutiques and fast-food outlets; it is not even close to being hip.

So, where do you go in Paris if you are young and adventurous? Starting in the 1980s and until recently, the simple answer was Bastille. The labyrinth of cobbled back streets and narrow passageways around Place Bastille still has a great bar scene – from the first *apéritif* through to the last tequila at 4am

housed in the *cités* (housing estates) of the *banlieue* (suburbs). Until recently, Paris seems to have turned a blind eye to the problems of its poorer suburbs, and most Parisians were rarely confronted with ghetto life unless they wanted to be.

The *cités* in the French suburbs were created in response to the housing shortage after World War II. Row upon row of ugly, grey rectangular high-rises were built to house French workers. Immigrants, encouraged to come to France during the economic boom of the 1960s, moved in later. With the oil crisis and recession of the 1970s, there was less and less employment. Crime and drug use soared.

– and trendy art galleries and cabaret theatre. However, nearby Rue Oberkampf and Rue Menilmontant are now much cooler, particularly for clubbing; Belleville is also on the map. If you are gay or lesbian, head straight for the Marais.

Beyond the périphérique

Paris proper has few ghettos to speak of. For the most part, they are beyond the *périphérique* where many of the poor are

The social problems of the French ghetto are gaining wider recognition and clearly made an impact on the last presidential election where law and order was the big political issue. The phenomenon of a French ghetto culture is also increasingly evident: French rappers like M.C. Solaar and N.T.M. have led the charts and in the past decade life in the ghetto has inspired a new genre of film. The best example is Mathieu Kassovitz's *La Haine*, which won a Palme d'Or at the Cannes Film Festival. It is a brutally realistic portrait of three kids from contrasting ethnic backgrounds in the *cité* – one Jewish, one black and one *Beur* (French-Arab). ❑

LEFT: a bookseller in a typical Left Bank book shop.
ABOVE: busking can be a means of artistic expression or a sign of economic hardship.

EATING IN PARIS

Traditionalists would regard any attempt to modify French cuisine as sacrilegious. But, without provoking riots, young chefs have allowed international influences to infiltrate

An enormous fuss has been made in recent years about the death of French food. Critics hail Spain as the "new France", or London, or Sydney, or New York; whereas Paris, they whine, is stuck in a rut, dead boring. It's not an entirely fair evaluation. It's important to remember when you eat in Paris, where the cooking of the whole country converges, that you're experiencing a long-established cuisine: a vast, yet coherent repertoire of dishes, ingredients and techniques that have stood the test of time. French cooking may be slow to evolve, but this is because France is a country that truly knows its food. A new ingredient or dish won't be welcomed into the cuisine until it proves itself worthy. The French are incredibly protective, disciplined and judicious in this regard.

For the traveller, if not for locals, this conservatism is appealing. You want real French onion soup? You've got it, and there won't be any star anise or fistfuls of coriander in there. The menu says *steak au poivre*? That means it's *steak au poivre*: flat, rare, with creamy peppercorn sauce spilling off the sides. No surprises. Everything is reassuringly real.

This is not to say that contemporary and international experiences are not to be found. In recent years, a wave of young chefs have been opening snazzy, yet relaxed restaurants – impervious to Michelin ratings – serving French food with a fresh, contemporary face, and integrating (ever so cautiously) more exotic flavours like ginger, peanut, coriander, curry and lime.

The international scene, although perhaps not as widespread as elsewhere, is also an integral part of the city's taste experience. Indeed, one thing that makes it exciting to eat in a country other than one's own is discovering the influences that immigrants from other places have brought to it, and these, naturally, change from place to place. San Francisco boasts great Chinese; London is famous for Indian; Melbourne and Sydney are pretty unbeatable for Italian, Greek and Southeast Asian. Paris, meanwhile, offers good North African, Vietnamese, Lebanese and Afro-island cooking. Seek it out and you'll be rewarded.

The full Parisian culinary experience offers a colourful array of options.

Street food and cafés

Street vendors with impromptu stands are a welcome sight, especially in winter, with chestnuts roasting over beds of coal, waffle irons and crêpe grills ever at the ready. Ice cream stands abound on the Ile St-Louis. Falafels are sold through the windows on the Rue des Rosiers. Your nose will lead you to middle-eastern kebabs and savoury turnovers throughout the city.

To fill a picnic basket with traditional French fare, your best bet is a *charcuterie*, where you'll find ready-cooked dishes such as quiches, salads, pâtés, sausages, cheeses and prepared dishes like *poulet basquaise*

a fried egg on top). Café salads are often hefty and filling, such as *Paysanne* (with potatoes, bacon and cheese) *Norvégienne* (with smoked salmon), *Landaise* (with duck breast), to name but a few.

Bistros and brasseries

No restaurants are more popular – or more Parisian – than the neighbourhood bistros and brasseries. Brasseries (breweries) were introduced to Paris in the 19th century, at about the time when modern methods of brewing were being perfected. Many brasseries serve Alsatian specialities, such as *choucroute* and *steins* of beer; others specialise in shellfish. Outside

(chicken with tomatoes and red peppers) or *brandade de morue* (salt cod purée). Next, head to the bakery (usually right next door) for a baguette or ready-made sandwiches.

If you're in a rush in the midst of shopping, traditional cafés will cater quickly while you give your feet a rest. Many will serve no more than simple baguette sandwiches. Others offer omelets, or the quintessential café favourite, *crôque-monsieur* (grilled ham and cheese on toast), or *crôque-madame* (the same, but with

the latter, you'll spot heaps of clams, mussels and langoustines on beds of ice, and burly men in overalls shucking oysters dawn 'til dusk. All brasseries serve a broad range of dishes, including standard bistro fare. They're a jolly experience: spacious, clamorous and festive, usually elaborately decorated in gracious Belle Epoque style.

For quieter, more intimate meals opt for the bistros. These are smaller, more humble nooks, offering more or less the same menus wherever you go: *hareng pommes à l'huile* (smoked herring marinated in oil with warm potatoes), *œufs en meurette* (poached eggs with red wine sauce), *blanquette de veau* (veal

LEFT: simple but elegant decor reflects the food served.
RIGHT: French café culture includes time to chat over coffee or read the newspaper.

in a white sauce), *coq au vin* (braised chicken in wine), *mousse au chocolat* (chocolate mousse), and *tarte Tatin* (caramelised upside down apple tart). A number of bistros have a regional bent, proudly boasting their provincial specialities. In Auvergnat bistros, think blue cheese, potatoes, walnuts and superb beef; with Southwestern bistros, it's *foie gras* and duck; Basque flavours include hot pepper, salt cod and ham; and Provençale bistros guarantee ratatouille, lamb and *bouillabaisse*. The origin of the name "bistro" supposedly lies in the days of the Allied occupation of Paris in 1814. The Russian military were forbidden to drink, so whenever they dived into a bar in Montmartre, they demanded their refreshments urgently – *bistrot* – to avoid being caught. Nowadays, really any restaurant with a relaxed atmosphere can call itself a bistro. They're not all necessarily as speedy, however, as they might once have been.

The star experience

For those who want to dress up and spend a bomb on dinner, there are countless prestigious restaurants in the city that will be pleased to see you arrive. A Michelin guide will point in the direction of restaurants that meet these starry standards. Be prepared to spend several hours at the table, to eat at least

A FEW BISTRO CLASSICS

La cuisine française is not one cuisine but a score, regional in origin, shading off into one another at their borders and all pulled together at Paris.
– American writer A.J. Liebling

Here is a selection of traditional dishes:
Andouillettes à la Lyonnaise: tripe sausages with onions
Bouillabaisse: Provençal fish stew
Coquilles Saint-Jacques: scallops in mushrooms and white wine, served in their shells
Escargots à la Bourguignonne: snails in a garlic and parsley butter, served in their shells

Gigot d'agneau rôti aux flageolets: roast lamb with dwarf kidney beans
Hareng pommes à l'huile: marinated herring with potatoes
Magret de canard: breast of duck Gascony style
Moules marinières: mussels in garlic and white wine
Petit salé aux lentilles: salt pork with lentils
Pot au feu: traditional meat stew
Poulet Basquaise: chicken with peppers Basque style
Crêpes Suzettes: pancakes with an orange, kirsch and curaçao sauce
Ile flottante: meringues floating in custard
Tarte tatin: upside-down caramelised apple tart

seven courses, and to have waiters buzzing around you like invisible winged butlers, whisking away empty bottles, replacing napkins, topping up your water glass… The food in starred establishments (whether one star or three) should blow you away, but this does vary. Some restaurants, unfortunately, rest on their laurels, while others produce meals you'll remember for a lifetime. To experience *haute cuisine*, these are the restaurants you're looking for.

Contemporary French cooking

There is no single name, really, for the recent sprouting of contemporary French restau-

that apart from what you find on the menus they don't feel particularly French.

The world

North African restaurants are probably the best represented in the French capital, offering emblematic dishes like *couscous* (steamed semolina with spicy meat or stewy vegetable toppings) and *tagine* (braised meat, often with preserved lemons and dried fruits). Japanese restaurants of the fast-food variety have all but taken over the 1st *arrondissement*, in and around the Rue des Petits Champs – not a bad option if you know you've got a starred meal coming up next. For cheap Vietnamese, head

rants: sleek, trendy, moderately priced, and with good, interesting food. Dinner usually consists simply of an entrée, plat and dessert. Dishes are lighter than in an average bistro, less complicated than in starred establishments. The wine list will probably include international options, the service is pleasant without being *de trop*, and the crowds are *très branché* (fashionable). All in all, a good way to get a taste of the future of French food. The only trouble with contemporary restaurants is

for the Porte d'Italie neighbourhood, not far from the student stomping grounds in the Quartier Latin. For Indian (not just restaurants, but also eclectic grocers) explore the 10th *arrondissement* around the Gare du Nord. African food is found in Belleville, northeast of the Place de la République. And, good Lebanese food is dotted somewhat all over. Whatever your craving, the trick is to pick out the gems within a sea of mediocrity. That is true anywhere.

Food for thought

Not all visitors to Paris are as enthusiastic about certain French classics as the French.

LEFT: *haute cuisine* establishments need to be booked weeks in advance, and you dress to impress.
ABOVE: ethnic food offers a vegetarian alternative.

Almost everyone knows that *escargots* are snails and *cuisses de grenouille* are frogs' legs, but many an innocent tourist has unwittingly ordered calf's head *(tête de veau)*, expecting simply veal; or *andouillette* in hopes of pork sausage only to discover tripe-filled concoctions. Remember, dishes such as these sound more frightening than they really are: after all, 50-million French (and many a foreign visitor) relish their taste. Besides, part of the thrill of dining in France is having the option of – if not the appetite for – pig's ears, beef muzzle and blood sausage.

Truly excellent fish is not especially easy to find in Paris, and where one does find it,

A VEGETARIAN DESERT

The vegetarian dishes of French cuisine are few and far between, which can be trying for herbivorous travellers. Even dishes that you're assured are meat-free often contain bacon or meat-based stocks. A solution is to order two meatless starters instead of a main course, or to stick to simple egg and potato dishes. This, however, will soon seem repetitive. In an upmarket restaurant, you can telephone ahead and request a vegetarian meal; this gives the cook time to concoct something just for you. Another option is to explore the ethnic restaurants of the city which serve meat-free snacks to three-course meals.

like anywhere in the world today, it comes at a price. Brasseries usually have a promising array, for example on their *plateaux de fruits de mer* (shellfish platters). Of course, it is generally in the more expensive restaurants that it will be cooked best. In France, meats tend to be served at one extreme or another: at the one end raw (for example, *tartare de bœuf* or *beef tartare*) or *saignant* (rare); and at the other *confit* (preserved) or stewed until falling from the bone. If you order steak in a French restaurant, it will come rare unless you specify "*à point*" (medium) or "*bien cuit*" (well done). Feel comfortable sending a dish back if the meat is not cooked to your liking. Fish is more difficult. At mid-range restaurants it tends to be overcooked, so if you like it just done, it's important to ask for your fish cooked "*rose à l'arrête*" (rare at the bone).

Cheese

Nowhere in the world is there a wealth of cheese to match that of France, where cheese is considered so important that an entire dinner course is devoted to it alone. Between the main course and dessert, out comes the trolley or platter, laden with a delectably smelly array. The most pungent are generally cheeses such as Epoisses, Mont d'Or, and Munster. If you're strictly a mild-cheddar personality, steer yourself, instead, towards fresh goat's cheeses, young comté or mimolette. Blue cheeses vary greatly in creaminess and strength, but usually aren't too overpowering. Brie and Camembert cheeses are well known, relatively mild and deliciously smooth. Try not to be overwhelmed by the amount of options. It can take years to become familiar with French cheeses. Just remember two rules: 1) In a cheese tasting, always start with the mildest cheese and work your way around to the strongest; and 2) Never steal "the nose" off a piece of cheese if you're serving yourself; always slice cheese in such a way as to preserve it's natural shape. This is considered proper behaviour because it means the last person served won't be left with just the rind.

Drinks

It is usual to be offered an *apéritif* before a meal in France. A glass of Champagne, white wine, or a *kir* (white wine with *cassis* – a blackcurrant liqueur) are most popular, but whisky and port are also enjoyed. Of course, it's not obligatory to order an *apéritif*; one can jump straight to the wine list.

In the minds of the French, wine is the *de rigueur* accompaniment not only to French food, but to eating in general. In starred restaurants, some to-do is generally made about what wine will go with what, but in most casual places, the rule is: drink whatever you want. Simple restaurants, in addition to bottles, sell wine by the glass or cheaply by the jug. *Un pichet de rouge* (a jug of red) will get you an inexpensive, potentially rough, but entirely drinkable red wine. Beer is usually only ordered with sandwiches, Alsatian meals or quick Asian lunches. Cider is similarly drunk, only in regional terms it accompanies Breton and Norman specialities such as *crêpes* or mussels. Numerous mineral waters will be on offer in all French restaurants. Request *pétillante* for sparkling; *plate* for still; or *en carafe*, if a jug from the tap suits you.

The French Meal

Entrée (Americans, take note) means starter, not main course. *Plat* is the main dish. *Dessert* is, not surprisingly, dessert or pudding. All three are often included in *prix fixe* (fixed price) menus, although increasingly a choice of *entrée + plat + dessert* is the norm.

In simple places, nobody minds if you order two *entrées* instead of a full meal. What is minded (disdained in upmarket establishments) is people ordering a few dishes and then flying them around the table like frisbees to share. Chefs take great pride in balancing the flavours on each plate to perfection and it is an insult to them if their exquisite scallops in saffron sauce are tasted only after a forkful of your neighbour's fiery curry. If you order a dish, eat it. If you want to try another, have it next time; or be tempted by a *menu dégustation* (tasting menu), which allows you to taste a greater number of dishes in smaller servings. In this event, it is best if everyone at the table orders the same, otherwise there's the

LEFT: cosy neighbourhood bistros offer simple food menus, often with a regional flavour.
RIGHT: the traditional red checked tablecloth is still a familiar and reassuringly old-fashioned sight.

> ### COSMOPOLITAN CUISINE
>
> Chinese/Vietnamese: between Avenue de Choisy and Avenue d'Ivry near Place d'Italie; Belleville.
> Indian: on the Rue du Faubourg St-Denis between the Gare du Nord and La Chapelle.
> Middle Eastern: around Strasbourg St-Denis and Goutte d'Or, near Montmartre.
> Jewish: Rue des Rosiers in the Marais.
> Japanese: Rue Ste-Anne near the Opéra.
> North African: Belleville and Goutte d'Or.

uncomfortable (potentially impossible) orchestration of serving some people three courses and others 10.

Coffee in France is served after, rather than with, dessert. *Café* means espresso, strong and black. If you like milk request a *café noisette*. *Café crème* (coffee with milk) is considered a breakfast food; ordering it after dinner will raise eyebrows. Finally, if caffeine will keep you up all night, ask for a *café décaféiné* (*déca* for short), or for *une tisane* (herbal tea).

Last but not least, the *digestif* (after-dinner drinks). These can range from Cognac to Armagnac to Calvados to other distilled fruit liqueurs. Experiment at leisure, but beware: too many and you'll pay for your pleasure in the morning. ❑

SHOPPING

Far from the shopping-mall mayhem of so many cities,
the boutiques of Paris make the French capital
one of the most relaxing places to shop

When shopping seems to be becoming more and more uniform, with the same international groups and luxury labels in every major city around the world, Paris can still put forward its claim to be the shopping capital of Europe. For one thing, there's an incredible variety of shops in what is a compact, beautiful and easily manageable city. For another, Paris retains its tradition of small specialist shops and personal attention.

Although there has been a notable tendancy for fashion labels to try and gain a citywide spread – with Left and Right Bank branches – there seem to be fewer chain stores here than in much of Europe. Thankfully, with the exception of the Forum des Halles and a couple of smaller shopping centres, Paris has remained largely free of the purpose-built *centres commerciaux* (shopping malls) and the rash of hypermarkets and discount stores that disfigure the Parisian suburbs and the outskirts of many provincial French cities. Instead, individual boutiques ensure that the historic heart of Paris remains a vibrant, living centre.

What to buy where

Paris's different *quartiers* each have their own mood and atmosphere, and their shops often reflect their history and the type of people who live there. Expect conventional, classic BCBG ("bon chic, bon genre", the Parisian equivalent of a Sloane or Preppy) wear with a fair dose of St-Tropez gilt in Passy; boho designers on the

LEFT: Au Printemps, *grand magasin* rival to Galeries Lafayette. RIGHT: Galerie Vivienne is the best preserved of all 19th-century shopping galleries.

hilly streets of Montmartre; designer couture and an international clientele along Avenue Montaigne and Faubourg St-Honoré; and street-wise streetwear congregated around Les Halles and Rue Etienne-Marcel, minutes from the busy Châtelet-Les Halles public transport interchange through which suburban youth flock into the city.

Other areas take a bit more delving: the exclusive residential western sector of the 7th *arrondissement* is particularly good for city-slicker menswear and equipment for the golfing brigade, along with upmarket interior design boutiques and furnishing fabrics. Although Place Vendôme is the place to find sparkly diamond-encrusted baubles, you'll find more original jewellery designs amid the fine 17th- and 18th-century architecture of St-Germain or the Marais. Similarly, if opulent 18th-century antiques are on offer around the Quai Voltaire in the 7th and Faubourg St-Honoré in the 8th, you're more likely to spot 1950s and 1960s retro furnishing and ceramics near the more alternative Bastille or Montmartre.

However, the geographical shopping map of Paris is far from static, reflecting an ebb and flow that goes with the rise and fall of different *quartiers*. The Champs-Elysées, which zig-zagged from the epitome of glamour in the early 20th century to that of fast-food tourist

dross in the 1980s, returned to favour with a vengeance at the end of the 1990s. The staid Rue St-Honoré has now become the focus for a more avant-garde fashion set, chasing the latest trends at Colette or Maria Luisa. Equally, in the past few years, designer fashion has migrated to St-Germain, which was always best known as a literary quarter – to the chagrin of those who bemoan the disappearance of favourite, long-standing bookshops and foodstores, although some arrivals such as Karl Lagerfeld's Lagerfeld Gallery have a distinctly Left Bank edge.

If the Marais was first *à la mode* in the early 17th century, when many of its finest aristo-cratic mansions were built, it subsequently fell

PARISIAN MARKETS

Paris's numerous markets *(see page 50)*, whether upmarket, tatty, daily or weekly, pull in bargain hunters, gourmets and collectors alike.

Fleamarkets: The fleamarkets of Paris developed in the 19th century, today they range from the huge and classy Marché de St-Ouen to the tatty Marché de Montreuil and the venerable Marché d'Aligre.

Roving markets: It's at the "roving" street markets that pop up two or three mornings a week (7am–2.30pm) all over town that you'll often find the most authentic produce and a true local flavour that varies from quartier to quartier.

Street markets: There are over 50 street markets in Paris; some consist of just a handful of stalls, others, such as Marché Bastille or Avenue Daumesnil, stretch for hundreds of metres and have outstanding ranges of produce. Market streets, like Rue Mouffetard (5th) in the Latin Quarter, have food shops with stalls that spill out onto the pavement and are open Tuesday to Saturday all day, with a very long break for lunch, and on Sunday morning.

Covered markets: Covered markets are usually open at the same time as street markets. The best-preserved and most authentic cast-iron covered market is the Marché St-Quentin, built in the 1880s.

into decline with the departure of Louis XIV to Versailles and only began its slow recovery in the 1960s. By the 1990s it was back on top of the desirable areas list. Restoration of its beautiful golden stone *hôtels particuliers* and the installation of important museums such as the Musée Picasso and Musée Cognacq-Jay have turned the Marais into an international district and a focus for youthful fashion and quirky gift shops.

A parallel specialist enclave, is the Marais' gay area, the hub of which is around Rue Vieille du Temple. The past few years have seen the arrival of not just bars but gay-oriented bookshops and men's clothing stores, often replacing Jewish bookshops and bakeries in what had been the main Jewish district.

Other districts reflect the changing population of Paris. In the 13th *arrondissement* "Chinatown", with a large South-East Asian population, you'll find Chinese supermarkets and *pâtisseries*. Other previously uncharted territories have arrived on the map, notably, the Canal St-Martin, where the colourful, kitsch Antoine & Lili set up its flagship store.

Other *quartiers* have not fared so well: Les Halles seems to be in perpetual decline with its flagging array of chain stores and dodgy reputation, and the aristocratic past of the Boulevards Bonne-Nouvelle and Montmartre is a distant memory blurred by the ranks of discount stores and fastfood chains.

Made in France

The fashion industry is still a tangible presence in Paris, from the mass-market sweatshops concentrated around the Sentier to the haute-couture houses on Avenue Montaigne. However, French designers no longer dominate the world fashion stage. But between the couture tags and the high-street chains, you can discover small local boutiques with their own take on French style, street-wise retailers picking out exciting young talents, and the one-off boutiques of individual fashion designers. At a number of atelier-boutiques, especially those around the Bastille and Montmartre, you can buy directly from

designers and may well see the clothes being made in the back of the shop.

Other aspects of French design other than clothing are also worth exploring. Paris has an enviable art and craft tradition, from the classic hallmarks of quality such as Lalique glass, Limoges porcelain and Pierre Frey fabrics to contemporary design gurus such as Philippe Starck, and the rising generation of French designers, including Tsé & Tsé Associés and the Bouroullec brothers, who can be found at outlets such as Edifice or Sentou Galerie.

Then there's food, of course, Paris is a remarkably lived-in city and every *quartier* has its *chocolatiers*, superb *pâtisseries* and *boulan-*

geries, delicatessens, ripe-smelling cheese shops and bustling street markets.

Shopping is the perfect excuse for getting to know the city, its layout, people and food. What better way to appreciate its beauty and character than to window-shop in elegant Place Vendôme, meander along the Boulevard St-Germain, rummage through the book stalls on the banks of the Seine, peer into the eccentric dens of the covered passages, choose fruit at the foot of the Eiffel Tower or stop off for a bite to eat at a neigbourhood bistro?   ❏

LEFT: kitsch colours at Antoine & Lili.
RIGHT: self-indulgence at beauty-product emporium Sephora.

● *For a full listing of shops in Paris see Insight Guide: Shopping in Paris.*

BEST BUYS IN THE MARKETS

The markets of Paris define the character of the different *quartiers* of the city and are an integral part of everyday life for most residents

Visitors who tire of the cool chic of haute couture Paris or the impersonality of the Grands Boulevards should plunge into the nearest market. The flavour of Paris is rarely further than a couple of Métro stops or streets away. Foodies will be beguiled by the tantalising smells of the roving street food markets; photographers intrigued by the predominantly North African Marché d'Aligre. Browsers may prefer the *bouquinistes*, the book stalls that line the banks of the Seine. Specialist buyers head to the markets dedicated to flowers, birds, postcards and stamps. There are funky Left Bank markets selling secondhand designer clothes, rural markets laden with fresh farm produce and bargains or genuine antiques to be had at one of the city's regular fleamarkets.

LEFT: The fleamarkets of Paris developed in the 19th century, as scrap-metal merchants and rag-and-bone men camped in the unbuilt zone outside the Thiers fortifications, thus avoiding the duties within the city walls.

ABOVE AND BELOW: food markets say a lot about the way Parisians live. The key to most is that they sell fresh, quality ingredients. Prices are not cheap but the emphasis is on the best that is in season and most residents prefer them. There are two main types of food markets: the roving street markets and market streets that appear a couple of mornings a week and reflect the character of various quartiers; and the historic covered markets. **RIGHT:** not all flea markets sell antiques, the Marché Malik for example has its fair share of discount clothing and shoes. Vides-Greniers are local affairs where residents of a street or district empty out their attics and cupboards. Expect clothes, household china, children's toys and books.

THE BEST MARKETS

Paris is known for it many flea *(puces)* and food markets. Here are some of the best:

Marché de St-Ouen: in the north of Paris (Métro Porte de Clignancourt). Reputedly the largest flea market in Europe, with over 2,500 dealers spread over a dozen markets and arcades. A huge range of specialists, with prices to match. Be prepared to bargain.

Marché de Montreuil: tattier and more anarchic than St-Ouen, Montreuil (Métro Porte de Montreuil) sells car parts, tools and unwashed clothes. Open Sat, Sun and Mon.

Marché de Vanves: smaller than St-Ouen and Montreuil, Vanves (Métro Porte de Vanves) is a relaxed, easy-going flea market within the *périphérique* ringroad. Mostly bric-à-brac. Open weekends.

Marché d'Aligre: the oldest fleamarket in Paris on the square next to the Rue d'Aligre (Métro Ledru-Rollin) food market. Handful of stalls selling overpriced antiques and junk. Open Tues–Sun mornings.

Marché Bastille on boulevard Richard Lenoir (Thurs and Sun am) and **Avenue Daumesnil** (Tues and Fri am)**:** street markets that stretch for hundreds of metres, with outstanding ranges of seasonal produce.

Rue Mouffetard: characterful food market street in the Latin Quarter open Tues–Sat (closed for lunch) and Sun morning.

Marché St-Quentin: 85 boulevard Magenta, 10th, is the best-preserved and most authentic cast-iron covered market. Stalls sell fresh produce and exotic snacks. Open Tues–Sat and Sun morning.

ARCHITECTURE

**It didn't happen by accident. Paris is one of the world's most
centrally planned cities, moulding a variety of styles, from
Gothic to Modern, into an impressively harmonious whole**

Two thousand years of history and seven centuries of artistic brilliance have made Paris a city rich in architecture. Although invasions, sieges and insurrections destroyed a number of the capital's early masterpieces, fine examples remain, spanning many ages, and making modern-day Paris one of the most beautiful, fascinating – and intact – cities in the world.

More fortunate than many of its European counterparts, Paris escaped catastrophe (by a hair) in 1944. As Allied troops approached the city, Hitler gave General Dietrich von Choltitz, the occupying governor of Paris, the order to blast every single historical edifice to pieces, so that the Allies' triumphant entry would be greeted by a field of smoking ruins. Charges of dynamite were laid under Les Invalides, Notre Dame, the Madeleine, the Opéra, the Arc de Triomphe and even at the foot of the Eiffel Tower. But, at the last minute, loathe to perpetrate such sacrilege, von Choltitz couldn't bring himself to give the order. Instead, he surrendered the city, undamaged, to General Jacques-Philippe Leclerc, liberator of Paris.

Today's Paris boasts examples of all France's architectural styles, especially from the 12th century and the beginnings of the Gothic era onwards, creating a textbook of architectural history. It requires little imagination to conjure up a sense of the past. Over the centuries, the best architects, sculptors, masons and painters have preserved this sense, while at the same time looking forward and making room for the new. This explains the extraordinary juxtaposition of different styles of architecture, from the Sainte Chapelle to the Eiffel Tower to the Centre Pompidou at the heart of the city.

Roman remains

Nothing is left of the wooden huts occupied by the Gallic Parisii on the Ile de la Cité. However, thanks to the Romans' development of an extremely durable concrete made from stone quarried out of Mont Ste-Geneviève, their ruins – the site of their settlement, Lutetia – can still be found in the Quartier Latin. Several streets, such as the Rue St-Jacques and the Boulevard St-Michel are built on ancient Roman roads. Lutetia was not an important city, but it was equipped with the buildings necessary to Roman civic life – a palace, forum, theatre, arena, baths and temples. The vestiges of one of these baths can be seen in the garden at the Musée National du Moyen Age – Thermes de Cluny and the ruins of the arena (Arènes de Lutèce) have also survived.

Unfortunately, nothing is left of the Merovingian and Carolingian eras (6th–9th centuries); the Vikings burnt and pillaged Paris on several occasions during this period.

Romanesque and Gothic

The Romanesque era, with its propensity for ponderous, gloomy structures, left hardly a

is distinguished by pointed arches and the combined use of ribbed vaults with flying buttresses, a technique which allowed windows to replace walls and walls to soar towards the heavens.

The most famous sacred building in Paris, the cathedral of Notre-Dame, epitomises the perfection of Gothic style. The construction of Notre-Dame began in 1163 on the site of a Romanesque church, which had been built on the foundations of a Carolingian basilica, which in turn had been built on the site of a Roman temple. It took 200 years and several generations of architects and craftsmen to finish it. Like all medieval churches, Notre-

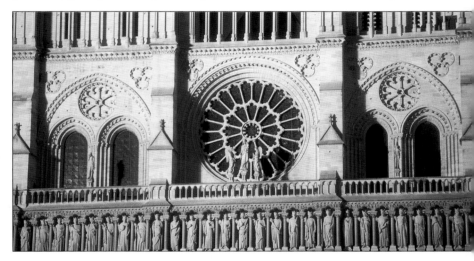

trace, either. The steeple of St-Germain-des-Prés church is one of the few remnants of this artistic and religious movement that spread throughout France at the turn of the first millennium. In the 12th century, Paris and the Ile de France turned to the newest rage in religious architecture: Gothic. Lighter, more slender and luminous than previous architecture, Gothic coincided with the strengthening of the French crown and a fresh religious fervour inflamed by the Crusades. Gothic architecture

Dame was once completely painted on the inside. The paintings were, of course, how illiterate medieval citizens learned the Bible stories, and the use of colour was felt to glorify God and breathe life into the sculptures. The building began to decay during the 17th century, but restoration by 19th-century Gothic revivalist Eugène Viollet-le-Duc (1814–79) eventually started in 1841, as a result of Victor Hugo's novel, *Notre-Dame de Paris (The Hunchback of Notre-Dame)* and prodding by the Romantic movement. The restoration took almost 23 years.

Close by stands Sainte-Chapelle, a fragile-looking church in the High Gothic style,

LEFT: vestiges of a Roman bath can be seen in the garden of the Musée National du Moyen Age.
RIGHT: Notre-Dame, a Gothic masterpiece.

which differs from Notre-Dame in that the vast stained-glass windows (the oldest in Paris) are supported by only a thin framework of stone. Nestled within the walls of the Palais de Justice, the church was built by King Louis IX in 33 months to shelter the Crown of Thorns, which he bought from Emperor Baudouin II of Constantinople, and other relics he acquired later from Byzantium.

Renaissance

War in Italy, in 1495, brought the French into contact with Renaissance grandeur, and the style, characterised by contempt for all Gothic forms and a rediscovery of antiquity, was imported to France. In architecture, the ribbed vault disappeared in favour of flat ceilings with wooden beams. Medieval fortresses gave way to genteel palaces and Greek-style colonnades were re-established.

Among Paris's main exponents of the Renaissance were architect Pierre Lescot (1510–78), whose finest work is the west wing of the Louvre, and Jean Goujon (1510–68), who sculpted the magnificent reliefs on Lescot's facade at the Louvre and worked on the Hôtel Carnavalet (1544) in the Marais. Goujon's work can also be seen on Lescot's Fontaine des Innocents near Les Halles, an example of Renaissance sensuality.

THROUGH THE AGES

Architecture in Paris embraces a wide spectrum of styles. Here are a few examples:
Gothic: Notre-Dame (1160–1345), Sainte-Chapelle (1245), Tour St-Jacques (1523)
Renaissance: Cour Carrée facade of the Louvre (1549–56), St-Eustache (1532–1637)
Classical: Versailles (1668), Les Invalides (1671–76), Place Vendôme (1698)
Neo-Classical: Panthéon (1764–90)
19th-century: Opéra Garnier (1862–75)
Modern: La Défense, Louvre Pyramid, Opéra Bastille (all 1989); Bibliothèque Nationale de France (1998)

The Classical influence

At the end of the 16th century, while the Renaissance had succumbed to the Baroque movement in the rest of Europe, French architects were looking towards sobriety and Classicism. A desire for strength and clarity, born of rationalism, dominated architecture. The Classical style is based on symmetry, simplicity of line and great, wide-open perspectives. The Pont-Neuf, the first bridge to be built without houses on it in 1606, and now the oldest in Paris, was one of the first examples of such architecture. During this period, large squares were created, surrounded by uniform buildings and with a statue of the king in the middle of the large central garden. The Place des Vosges, commissioned by Henri IV in 1609, was the first and most elegant of the Classical-style royal squares. Edged with graceful arcades, the square started out as the Place Royale, until it was changed in the Revolution.

In grand style

The Sun King left his mark on Paris and the Ile de France, but imposed his personality in the grandest style on the palace of Versailles. Started in 1668, the château symbolised the absolute power of the monarch and employed the top designers of the time – architects Louis

NOTHING BUT THE BEST

For centuries, Paris has traditionally attracted the best architects, sculptors, masons and painters.

built Place de la Concorde and the Ecole Militaire, and Jacques-Germain Soufflot designed the Panthéon, originally a church and today a necropolis for the great and the good of France.

With the coronation of a triumphant Napoléon and the installation of a new Empire at the beginning of the 19th century came the triumphal arch (Arc de Triomphe du Carrousel and Arc de Triomphe) and the triumphal neoclassical Rue de Rivoli.

Le Vau and Hardouin-Mansart, painter Charles Lebrun and landscape gardener André Le Nôtre. Other fine examples of the Classical style are the Palais du Luxembourg (1631) and the Hôtel des Invalides (1670).

After Louis XIV's death, building was kept to a minimum until the 1750s, when the neoclassical movement turned to forms lifted directly from antiquity, taking the utmost care to reproduce what recent progress in archaeology had brought to light. Jacques-Ange Gabriel

Baron Haussmann's legacy

Except for a few elite neighbourhoods, post-Revolution Paris was a squalid city. Poverty-stricken communities, with their filthy, narrow alleyways and miserable, overpopulated shacks, were constantly on the brink of revolt. For obvious reasons of sanitation, but also to circumvent riots, Napoléon III and the Prefect Baron Georges Haussmann began a sweeping urbanisation programme in the 1850s. Medieval Paris all but disappeared. Whole quarters were razed and wide, tree-lined avenues, harder to barricade than narrow alleys, took the place of grimy backstreets.

The city of Paris is still strongly stamped

LEFT: Sacré-Cœur, built much later than its architectural style implies in 1876.
ABOVE: the imposing dome of the Hôtel des Invalides.

with Haussmann's ideas. After clearing out slums and opening up the area around the Louvre, he concentrated on expanding the system of boulevards through the city centre, started by Louis XIV. A small hill then known as the Butte St-Roch, occupied by windmills, a gallows and a pig market, was intended to be their centre. It is hard to picture that today as you stand on the busy Place de l'Opéra, looking at Garnier's opera house, the Second Empire's most sumptuous construction.

Monsieur Eiffel's tower

The second half of the 19th century was very rich in creativity. Wrought-iron architecture

higher and higher, bets were placed on when it would topple over. When the engineer himself climbed up to plant the French flag atop his iron latticework fantasy, crowds of ordinary Parisians who admired his vision cheered; the snobbish aesthetes stayed away.

This was an eclectic period. After being burnt down during the Commune of 1871, the Hôtel de Ville (town hall) on the Right Bank was rebuilt Renaissance-style, while the Sacré-Cœur fused neo-Byzantine and Romanesque styles. Numerous churches toed the neo-Gothic line. Reacting against these academic approaches and inspired by Japanese art, the Belgian Hector Guimard estab-

made its debut with the Grand Palais, the Pont Alexandre III and, of course, the Eiffel Tower. Panned by the architectural critics during its construction in 1889 for the World Fair, the tower is now the universal symbol of Paris. It was originally designed to be a temporary exhibit, along with "a grotesque city of plaster, staff and pasteboard... buildings from an Asian temple to a Swiss chalet, from Kanaka hut to medieval Paris, Chinese pagoda to Montmartre cabaret", as one contemporary visitor remarked on a trip to the city. The tower symbolised the uneasy relationship between science, industry and art in Paris. As Gustave Eiffel's controversial creation rose

lished the Art Nouveau movement. The sinuous organic forms and curving lines, natural and Baroque at the same time, were decried by some as "noodle style". Guimard designed several buildings in the 16th *arrondissement*, including the Castel Béranger (14 rue de la Fontaine), and also the city's Métro entrances, many of which, such as Porte Dauphine and Abbesses, still remain.

The modern age

Both the modern movements of the 1920s and 1930s and Art Deco were born in the 16th *arrondissement*. Mallet-Stevens and Le Corbusier were the main artisans of the Cubic style of architecture, all pure lines and concrete. The Palais de Chaillot is a typical example of this grandiose, neo-classical architectural style.

From the 1960s, Paris underwent a transformation. Facades were cleaned, the Métro was modernised and old parts of the city, such as Les Halles market place, were demolished. New architectural projects were developed, keeping up with technical advances by building upwards (La Défense and Tour Montparnasse), expanding indoor space (Centre Georges-Pompidou, Cité de la Villette, Bercy) and experimenting with new materials that capture, reflect and admit light.

vel) achieves a kind of harmony by reflecting the neighbouring buildings and the ever-changing Parisian sky. Gothic architecture, in its time, held a mirror to society in much the same way.

Innovation continues apace. The imposing Bibliothèque Nationale de France, also known as the Très Grande Bibliothèque, which opened in 1997, is at the heart of the "new" Rive Gauche (Left Bank), a vast urban renewal project between the Gare d'Austerlitz and the Boulevard Masséna. In 2003, La Cité de l'Image et du Son MK2, the largest cinema complex in the city, opened near by. The city's newest footbridge, the Passerelle de Bercy-Tolbiac, will open before the end of 2005, on

In the 1980s, Sino-American architect I.M. Peï designed a new entrance and orientation centre for the Louvre: an illusionistic "landscape" of pyramids in stainless steel and specially created polished glass. Lauded for its beauty and efficiency, the central pyramid has undoubtedly earned its place on the architectural stage of Paris.

Like Peï's pyramid, the bankside Institut du Monde Arabe (designed in 1987 by Jean Nou-

the heels of the 1999 opening of the Passerelle de Solférino linking the Tuileries with the Musée d'Orsay.

Building is currently underway on Chirac's new Musée des Arts Premiers, another Nouvel design, due to open in 2006 at Quai Branly, which will house the former Museum of Mankind collection *(see page 162)*

If you want to get a complete overview of the history of architecture in Paris, you could pay a visit to the permanent exhibition in Le Pavillon de l'Arsenal (21 boulevard Morland, 4th), which is itself a remarkable piece of 19th-century design, with natural light pouring through a superb glass roof. ❏

LEFT: the Ecole Militaire seen through an arch of the unmistakable Eiffel Tower.
ABOVE: the facade of the Biblothèque Nationale de France, one of President Mitterrand's *grands projets*.

ART GALLERIES

The museums and galleries of Paris are among the most splendid and most visited in the world. The Louvre alone contains enough treasures for a lifetime's worth of visits

There is an overwhelming choice of museums and art galleries to visit in Paris. What follows is a brief outline of the city's major collections.

The **Musée Carnavalet** (*see page 83*) recounts the history of Paris from its origins as the Gallo-Roman settlement of Lutetia to a modern-day metropolis, as seen through the eyes of contemporary artists. It is spread across a network of intimate rooms in two adjoining city mansions: the Hôtel Carnavalet (16th and 17th centuries), home of Madame de Sévigné from 1677 to 1696, and the Hôtel Le Peletier de St-Fargeau (17th century). There are over one hundred rooms and galleries to explore. Those with plenty of time can follow the floor plan supplied at the entrance and tour the museum chronologically. If you have only an hour or so to spare it may be more beneficial to target a particular theme, such as the French Revolution or Parisian Life under Louis XIV. Like Paris itself, the Carnavalet can also be a rewarding place for a purposely aimless walk through centuries of Parisian art and decor, misery and grandeur.

France may have been at the forefront of artistic experimentation at the start of the 20th century, but it took a curiously long time to establish a national museum of modern art. When it finally arrived in 1945, the **Musée National d'Art Moderne** (*see page 90*) was born out of the fusion of the collections of living French art (then housed in the Musée du Luxembourg) and foreign art (then at the Jeu de Paume). The museum amalgamated in 1967 with the CNAC (Centre National d'Art Con-

temporain) and the launch in 1969 by President Georges Pompidou of an international architectural competition for a cultural centre that was to be both museum and centre of creation.

Chosen from 681 entries, the winning project, inaugurated in 1977, put the young Italo-British duo Renzo Piano and Richard Rogers on the international map with their revolutionary high-tech design. At the time highly controversial, the steel and glass structure had a radical inside-out solution. The Musée National d'Art Moderne and temporary exhibition galleries are just one aspect of a multi-disciplinary institution which also contains a large public library, performance space, auditorium and cinema, as well as neighbouring avant-garde music institute IRCAM.

Only a small proportion of the Pompidou Centre's 50,000-strong collection can be seen at any one time. Nonetheless, you can appreciate substantial displays of Cubism and Surrealism, an unrivalled holding of Matisse and whole rooms or sections devoted to such artists as Braque, the Delaunays, Kandinsky and Klein. Entered on level 4, the collection now begins with the contemporary before going up to the historical on level 5. The period covered shows an incredible diversity, underlining the dramatic change in what is now considered art.

ways or chunks of the medieval fortress: a portrait of Louis XIII by Philippe de Champaigne adorns a wall amid Egyptian pharaohs. There are countless stairways and courtyards, areas of crisp new walls, glazed atria and modern escalators, and other parts where you find yourself amid a Rococo riot of putti, gilding and allegorical ceiling paintings. The most visible feature of the Grand Louvre project is the glass pyramid designed by Sino-American architect I.M. Pei. Opened in 1989, this serves as a new entrance and focus of the underground Carrousel, where the museum has been enriched by an auditorium, shops, restaurants and exhibition spaces. After initial controversy,

The **Musée National du Louvre** (*see pages 97 and 108*) first opened to the public as a museum in 1793 but it was François Mitterrand's Grand Louvre project that doubled the gallery space and made the Louvre one of the most modern and enterprising museums in Paris. The Louvre is not simply a palace housing a museum of art. Many of the works are also intimately linked to the palace, with their origins in the royal collections; and here and there you'll find painted ceilings, carved stair-

the Pyramid has become an admired part of the landscape, providing a striking contrast with the carved golden facades of the palace.

The sheer extent of the collections can be mind boggling. There are not merely Rembrandts but followers of Rembrandt, portrait busts, kilometres of maiolica plates, countless Aphrodites, innumerable ancient Greek terracottas and legions of Egyptian mummies. While the different collections are colourcoded, and there are numerous signs and orientation maps, it's still easy to get lost at times.

The Decorative Arts Museum complements the Louvre's Objets d'Art department, but is different in that its collections go right up to

LEFT: Centre Pompidou, containing the Musée National d'Art Moderne.
ABOVE: the Sculpture Court at the Louvre.

the present. Upstairs, the Advertising Museum's collection includes some 50,000 posters dating from the end of the 13th century to World War II, and another 50,000 produced since 1950, along with promotional memorabilia, advertising clips and packaging. The Fashion Museum changes its display annually to reflect different aspects of the collection, which ranges from rare 17th-century dresses to the very latest designer wear.

The national museum of 19th-century art, the **Musée d'Orsay** *(see pages 169 and 172)*, found its ideal home in the former Gare d'Orsay, an ornate Beaux-Arts railway station designed by Victor Laloux. Opened in 1900 to

serve passengers to the Exposition Universelle, it was built around a metal frame with a long, glass-roofed nave hidden behind an imposing stone facade. In 1977 President Giscard d'Estaing saved the building from demolition and declared that it would be converted into a new national museum. Italian architect Gae Aulenti came up with the design for a skylit, central sculpture aisle along the line of the old tracks, inserting large internal partitions to create a series of rooms on either side. The Musée d'Orsay was finally opened to the public by Mitterrand in 1986.

The museum's collection, which covers the period from 1848 to 1914, is best known for the Impressionists collection, but encompasses all the key movements in later 19th-century French art, beginning with the late Romantics and official salon painters, and going via Realism, Impressionism and Symbolism to Post-Impressionism and the Nabis. Seen in the context of these movements, the Impressionists are better understood.

Although overwhelmingly dominated by French painting, the Musée d'Orsay has also acquired works by European and American artists from the same period. The collection also covers the art of photography, presented in temporary exhibitions of the work of pioneers like Fox Talbot, Daguerre and Niepce, portraits by Nadar, Muybridge's experiments with movement and photos by artistic amateurs such as Zola and Lewis Carroll.

Housed in the 17th-century Hôtel Salé, the **Musée National Picasso** *(see page 84)* displays a large proportion of Picasso's personal

NOTABLE MUSEUM ARCHITECTURE

Musée du Louvre: Royal palace and art collection, with sculpted Renaissance and Baroque facades, monumental staircases, medieval fragments and the 20th-century intervention of I.M. Peï's glass pyramid.

Musée du Moyen Age: Housed in Roman baths and the Gothic mansion of the abbots of Cluny.

Musée Picasso: Well-restored 17th-century mansion built for one of Louis XIV's tax collectors.

Musée de l'Histoire de France – Archives Nationales: Grandiose early 18th-century Marais mansion with fine Rococo interiors in Paris.

Musée de l'Armée: Grand classical architecture designed

on a geometrical plan by Libéral-Bruand in the 1670s as a military hospital for the Sun King.

Musée Jacquemart-André: Opulent, eclectic style of a 19th-century *haute-bourgeoisie* mansion.

Musée d'Orsay: Pompous Belle Epoque railway architecture, given an inspired conversion in the 1980s.

Musée des Arts d'Afrique et d'Océanie: Modernist classical revival of 1931, with striking Art Deco rooms.

Centre Pompidou: High-tech icon by Renzo Piano and Richard Rogers with exposed services and flexible floors.

Institut du Monde Arabe: Jean Nouvel's design marries high-tech glass and steel with Arabic references.

collection, donated to the state by his family in lieu of inheritance tax. His paintings, drawings, ceramics, sculptures, collages and manuscripts are laid out in chronological order, covering every stage of his life and work. All Picasso's works, but particularly his paintings, ooze life, humour and sex in a career that can never be separated from his personal life, his children and his various wives and lovers.

With its gracious, curved, entrance courtyard, watched over by sphinxes, and grandiose cherub-adorned stairhall, the Hôtel Salé is one of the finest mansions in the Marais. It was built in 1656–59 by Jean Boulier for the wealthy tax collector, Pierre Aubert de Fontenay. He was responsible for collecting the *gabelle* or salt tax, hence the hotel's nickname "salty". However, not long after he had moved in, Fontenay was forced to leave due to his involvement in the trumped-up scandal surrounding Louis XIV's minister Fouquet.

After the Revolution, it went through various incarnations, first as a school, then a wrought-iron workshop and technical college, until it was finally renovated and reopened as the Picasso museum in 1985 (a small display in the old chapel shows archive prints and photos, including ones of the chemistry labs that once stood in the courtyard).

The **Musée National Rodin** *(see page 167)* displays work that is considered a bridge between Classical 19th-century sculpture influenced by antiquity and the Renaissance, and the sculpture of the 20th century. Rodin was born in 1840 into a modest family in the Latin Quarter. He studied drawing and maths at the "Petite Ecole" but failed to get into the Ecole des Beaux-Arts. Instead, he was forced to earn his living as an ornamentalist. During a visit to Italy in 1876, he discovered Michelangelo and it transformed his career. The resulting sculpture, *The Age of Bronze*, scandalised the 1877 Salon, where critics found it so naturalistic that they believed Rodin had cast it directly from a live model. By 1900, Rodin was a successful artist, honoured with a pavilion by Pont de l'Alma for the Exposition Universelle, where he exhibited hundreds of his small groups. He was an

artist of his time, allied to Symbolism and, in his search for naturalism, to his Impressionist contemporaries. But he was also an innovator, as he pared back his compositions and cut out extraneous detail, or combined and fragmented figures to maximise expression.

Built in 1728–32 by Jean Aubert for the Peyrenc family, the Hôtel Biron was variously used for public balls, as a cardinal's residence, by the Russian ambassador and by a religious community before becoming home to numerous artists and writers at the start of the 20th century. Rodin himself moved here in 1908 and campaigned to save the house when it was threatened with demolition. The French gov-

ernment bought the mansion and in return Rodin agreed to leave all his collections to the state. These included hundreds of sculptures and drawings, and his collections of furniture, antiquities and Impressionist paintings, all of which formed the basis of the Rodin museum, which opened in 1919. The carved Rococo panelling in the two circular drawing rooms has recently been restored and two of François Lemoyne's overdoor paintings of mythological scenes have been returned to the house, giving some idea of its original decoration. ❑

LEFT: the Main Hall, Musée d'Orsay.
RIGHT: the *Burghers of Calais*, Musée Rodin

● *For full coverage of all the city's museums see Insight Guide: Museums & Galleries of Paris.*

PLACES

A detailed guide to the city, with all the principal sites clearly cross-referenced by number to accompanying maps

"**P**aris is the city of cities," as Victor Hugo put it. Where matters of French administration, politics and cultural life are concerned, Paris plays an absolutely dominant role in determining France's character and values. Yet it is so unlike much of the rest of the country that it has been described as virtually a city-state in its own right. On the global stage, its political influence has waned since the days of empire, but it remains indisputably the world capital of chic.

Largely undamaged by two world wars, Paris has been created by centuries of grandiose urban planning. Its monuments and museums provoke a sense of déjà vu to people from all over the world. Yet, for all its glorious past, the City of Light seems bent on change. I.M. Peï's pyramid in front of the Louvre and the Bibliothèque Nationale are evidence of that. But there are regrets in this process of evolution.

What doesn't change is the fascination of Paris: from Gothic Notre-Dame to 19th-century boulevards and 21st-century designer window shopping. The city is always a spectacle and a fête. There's endless entertainment here for the observant, who will learn as much about Paris from walking the streets as from visiting the great museums.

The chapters that follow cover the key destinations on both banks of the Seine, as well as venturing further afield to outlying parks and markets and to destinations that can easily be visited in a day – the palace at Versailles, Monet's house at Giverny and the cathedral at Chartres.

This is a city that is best discovered on foot. But one of the beauties of Paris is its superb public transport system – and it is thanks to the RER and SNCF that the region surrounding the capital is so easily accessible. ❏

PRECEEDING PAGES: the view from Pont Alexandre III; Hôtel de Ville.
LEFT: the Eiffel Tower at night.

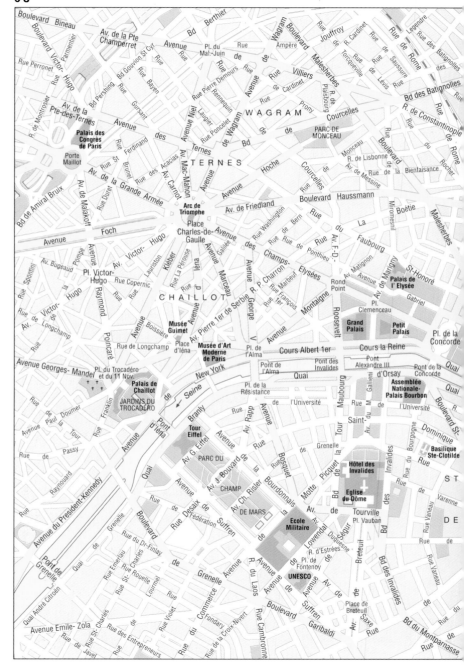

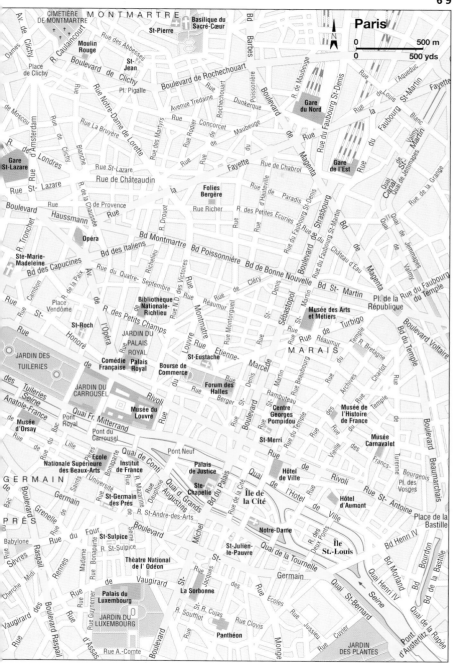

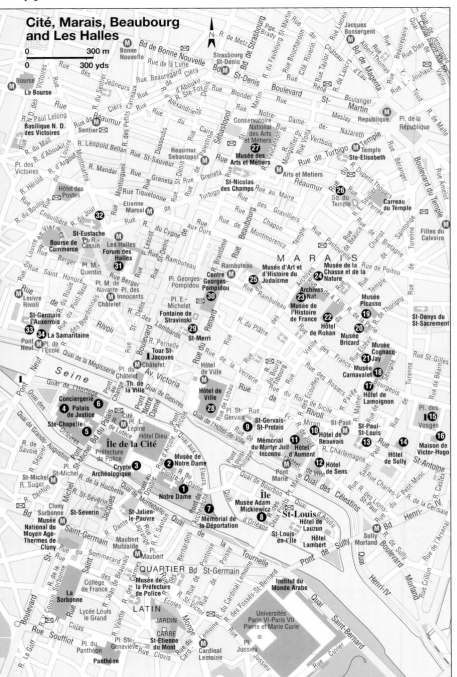

ILE DE LA CITÉ AND ILE ST-LOUIS

The soaring Gothic edifices of Notre-Dame and Sainte-Chapelle rub shoulders with the dour Conciergerie on Ile de la Cité across from the genteel mansions on Ile St-Louis

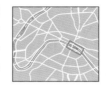

The Ile de la Cité in the middle of the Seine is the birthplace and topographical centre of Paris and has been its spiritual and legislative heart for more than 2,000 years. Invading the Parisii settlement already established there in 53 BC, the Romans built a prefect's palace, law court and temple to Jupiter on the island. Across the river on the Right Bank, the Hôtel de Ville has been the cauldron of political debate since the Middle Ages, while just to the north, the area of Les Halles fed the city's stomachs from AD 1110 until 1969. This is the core of the capital, an area which, in many ways, embraces the essence of Paris.

Notre-Dame

The Ile de la Cité is dominated by the soaring cathedral, **Notre-Dame de Paris** ❶ (tel: 01 42 34 56 10; www.cathedraledeparis.com; open daily 7.45am– 6.45pm; free), that occupies the eastern end of the island. Gazing up at the cathedral's finely sculptured facade, it is hard to imagine the building's poor condition when Victor Hugo *(see page 23)* wrote his novel *The Hunchback of Notre-Dame* in 1831. He and his Romantic followers were appalled at the state of the building and, in 1841, succeeded in triggering a massive restoration programme, headed by Viollet-le-Duc *(see page 53)*. For the next 23 years, the meticulous architect repaired the cathedral's structure literally from the foundations to the roof tiles, recreated stained-glass windows by copying remaining ones and replaced sculptures destroyed in the Revolution, such as the Gallery of Kings, by studying those of other Gothic cathedrals.

He also added a sacristy to the south side, now the Trésor de Notre-Dame (Mon–Sat 9.30am–6pm, Sun

Map on page 70

BELOW: the soaring Gothic towers of Notre Dame.

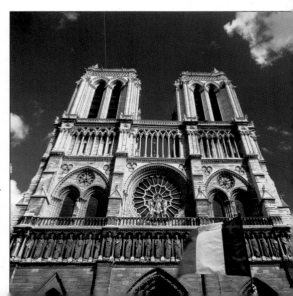

1.30–5.30pm; entrance fee) housing the alleged Crown of Thorns, among other relics and manuscripts.

The church of "Our Lady" was built on the site of earlier pagan fertility worship by Celts and Romans. In the 6th century, Clovis, the conquering Frankish king, erected an impressive Christian basilica, which was replaced by a Romanesque church. By 1159, a young bishop, Maurice de Sully, decided that Paris deserved bigger and better. Work on the cathedral began in 1163 and took just under 200 years to complete, following plans by Pierre de Montreuil, who was also the architect of Sainte-Chapelle.

Even before it was finished, Notre-Dame had become the venue for national ceremonies, state funerals, and thanksgivings; in 1239, Louis IX deposited in the cathedral the Crown of Thorns, and other relics acquired on a Crusade, while Sainte-Chapelle was being built. Since then, Notre-Dame has been witness to a string of historical events: in 1572, the cathedral's strangest wedding took place. The bride, Marguerite de Valois (a Catholic), stood at the altar, while the bridegroom Henri de Navarre (a Protestant), called in his vows from the doorstep. Later, in 1589, Henri was crowned in the cathedral, having decided to convert to Catholicism saying, "Paris is well worth a Mass".

Come the Revolution, Notre-Dame was ravaged by enthusiastic citizens, who melted down and destroyed anything that hinted of royalty, lopping off the heads of the kings of Judah along the top of the main portals.

The cathedral was then turned into a Temple of Reason and by the end of the Revolution was being used for wine storage.

By the time Napoleon decided to crown himself Emperor in 1804, the cathedral was in such a shabby state that bright tapestries were hung up to cover the crumbling decor. Pope Pius VII attended with reluctant obedience and, when he hesitated at the altar, Napoleon snatched the crown and to the crowd's cheers of "Vive l'Empereur!" placed it on his head himself. In August 1944, at the thanksgiving ceremony for the

BELOW: riverside view of the floodlit cathedral.

Liberation of Paris, the Resistance hero and leader of the new government, General Charles de Gaulle, was shot at during the Te Deum.

Gothic architecture

Notre-Dame is magnificent from any angle, but its Gothic facade is particularly impressive. Viewed from the front on the Place du Parvis, the twin towers soar to the heavens with dramatic grace. The cathedral's three doors each have a distinct design – an asymmetry typical of medieval architecture. Originally, the stone figures were finely painted against a gilt background and were designed to illustrate the Bible to an illiterate populace.

On the left, the Portal of the Virgin depicts the ark of the covenant and the coronation of the Virgin. The Portal of the Last Judgement, in the middle, shows the Resurrection, the weighing of souls and their procession to heaven or hell. The Portal of Ste Anne portrays the Virgin and Maurice de Sully. Above the doorways, the Rose Window, depicting the Virgin and Child in deep blues and rich reds, is a miracle of engineering. Picture the rickety scaffolding and the armies of stonemasons, who with simple measuring techniques constructed an intricate masterpiece that has lasted for 750 years. The glass, however, has been restored.

The ascent of the **Tours de Notre-Dame** (open daily 9.30am–7.30pm in summer, 10am–5.30pm in winter; closed some public holidays; entrance fee) is a religious experience for those who love heights and a taste of hell for claustrophobes with vertigo. From the top of 387 steps Paris stretches to the horizon. "Emmanuel", the 13-tonne bell of Notre Dame, is rung only on state occasions. Dating from the 17th century, legend has it that the purity of the bell's tone is due to the gold and silver jewellery cast into its heated bronze by the most beautiful women of Paris.

Cathedral interior

Inside, the cathedral is edged with 37 side chapels. Supported by flying buttresses, the vault of the chancel

Map on page 70

The devilish gargoyles scowling down from the upper gallery are not medieval nightmares but the playful creations of the 19th-century Gothic revivalist architect Viollet-le-Duc.

BELOW: the intricately sculpted facade.

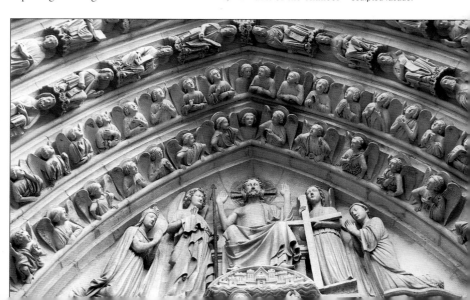

Vedettes du Pont-Neuf (tel: 01 46 33 98 38) run cruises along the Seine lasting about an hour. Boats leave from the Square du Vert-Galant (Métro: Pont-Neuf) every half hour in the high season (see page 229).

BELOW:
the lower chapel of Sainte-Chapelle.

seems almost weightless, with stained-glass windows distributing rays of coloured light into the solemn shadows. The exquisite 13th-century north and south rose windows are the transept's two star attractions. The most spectacular north window still has most of its 13th-century glass but the south rose had to be reconstructed completely by Viollet-le-Duc.

The 18th-century carved choir stalls, depicting the life of the Virgin Mary, were commissioned by Louis XIV, who was fulfilling the vow his father made 60 years earlier that he would build a high altar and devote the east chancel to the Virgin, if he were to have an heir. Louis XIII's statue stands behind the high altar, along with Guillaume Coustou's *Pietà*.

Outside on Rue du Cloître-Notre-Dame is the **Musée de Notre-Dame de Paris** ❷ (open Wed, Sat, Sun 2.30–6pm; entrance fee), which charts the history of the cathedral and has exhibits of ancient pottery found beneath the parvis, Gallo-Roman artefacts, works of religious art and a

cup, dating from the 4th century. In the **Crypte Archéologique** ❸ (tel: 01 43 29 83 51; open Tues–Sun 10am–6pm; entrance fee), underneath the parvis in front of the cathedral, are excavations of buildings dating back to the 3rd century, including parts of a Lutetian house inhabited by the Gallic Parisii.

Sainte-Chapelle

Across from Notre-Dame rise the imposing walls of the Palais de Justice and the Conciergerie. At one time, the **Palais de Justice** ❹ (tel: 01 44 32 50 00; open Mon–Sat 8am–6pm; free) was a royal palace and Louis IX had his bedroom in what is now the First Civil Court. In the 14th century, Charles V moved out, installing his parliament there with full judiciary rights. A wander around the hushed corridors, past fleeting black-robed figures, is a reminder of the tense days of the Revolution when a new judicial system was imposed and the public prosecutor, Fouquier-Tinville, sent thousands of people to the guillotine. The present legal system has been passed down from Napoleon Bonaparte.

Within the walls of the Palais de Justice, **Sainte-Chapelle** ❺ (tel: 01 53 73 78 51; open daily summer 9.30am–6.30pm, winter 10am–5pm; closed some public holidays; entrance fee) stands like a skeletal finger pointing heavenwards – an ethereal counterpoint to the stones of the establishment.

This miracle of High Gothic ingenuity is an obligatory pause on any visit to Paris. Completed in just 33 months by Pierre de Montreuil and consecrated in 1248, the chapel was built to house the Crown of Thorns, bartered from the Venetians by Louis IX. Seemingly constructed without walls, the chapel's vaulted roof is supported by a thin web of stone, from which descend veils of richly coloured stained glass. A

replica Crown of Thorns decorates the top of one of the pinnacles.

Built in two tiers, the lower chapel was designed for the palace staff and is consequently smaller and gloomier. From the shadows, climb the spiral staircase into the crystalline cavern of the upper chapel. The soaring windows catch the faintest of lights, creating kaleidoscopes of colour which are still vivid, despite being nearly 800 years old. Depicted are 1,134 scenes from the Bible, which begin by the staircase with Genesis and proceed round the church to the 15th-century rose window. Regular orchestral concerts are held in the chapel.

The Conciergerie

In the northeast wing of the Palais de Justice, the **Conciergerie** ❻ (tel: 01 53 40 60 97; open Mar–Oct daily 9.30am–6pm, Nov–Feb 9am–5pm; closed public holidays; entrance fee) looks like an intimidating castle, its four towers rising insolently above impenetrable walls. It isn't hard to imagine this fortress as a merciless medieval prison – which it was

(although much of the facade is 19th-century). It was originally built as a palace, but when Charles V moved his residence to the Hôtel Saint-Pol, the palace was used to house Comte des Cierges – hence the name, Conciergerie.

The Comte was in charge of the king's lodgings and taxes until the Conciergerie became a prison in the 14th century, when his job changed to that of chief gaoler. The Capetian palace came into its own during the Revolution, when it housed nearly 2,600 prisoners awaiting the guillotine, including Marie-Antoinette. Ironically, her prosecutor, Danton, resided in the next cell before his trip to the guillotine, as, in turn, did his nemesis Robespierre. In the merry-go-round of retribution, 1,306 heads rolled in one month at Place de la Nation. To the west is the Cour des Femmes, a rough courtyard where the women were allowed during the day.

The tower at the back is called Bonbec (the squealer), for it was here, from the 11th century, that torture victims told all. At the front

Map on page 70

Stained-glass perfection at Sainte-Chapelle.

BELOW: replica of Marie-Antoinette's prison cell.

Notable Inmates

A prison for four centuries, the medieval Conciergerie hosted, among others, Captain Montgomery, a Scot, who fatally wounded Henri II during a tournament in 1559, and Ravaillac, who assassinated Henri IV in 1610. During the Revolution, celebrity inmates included Madame du Barry, Louis XV's favourite mistress; Marie-Antoinette, Louis XVI's wife; the Revolutionary leader Danton; Charlotte Corday, who murdered Marat, another Revolutionary leader; the poet André Chenier; and even Robespierre himself. During the massacres of September 1792 that marked the beginning of the Revolutionary Terror, more than 300 prisoners were killed here.

is the 14th-century Clock Tower containing the first public clock in Paris, still ticking today.

Inside, the original kitchens are still intact. They were built to feed up to 3,000 people using four huge fireplaces and have a Gothic canopied ceiling supported by buttresses. The adjacent Salles des Gens d'Armes is a magnificent four-aisled Gothic hall where the royal guards, or men-at-arms, used to live.

The Mémorial de la Déportation, commemorating the thousands of Jews transported to Nazi death camps during World War II.

BELOW: Ile St-Louis.

Exploring the island

Escape the shadows of the Revolution on Quai des Orfèvres, along the south bank of the island, now home to the Police Judiciaire (CID), where goldsmiths *(orfèvres)* once fashioned Marie-Antoinette's jewellery. Beyond the Square du Vert-Galant and the statue of Henri IV, the river slides silently past the tip of the island, caressing wistful willows. Pont-Neuf, bisected by the island, is the oldest surviving bridge in Paris.

It was made of stone, rather than wood, and was the first bridge to be built without houses on it. In 1985, the American artist Christo famously wrapped the whole Pont-Neuf in golden fabric.

You can return to the east end of the island via the colourful Marché aux Fleurs in Place L. Lépine, opposite the Préfecture de Police and Haussmann's Hôtel Dieu. Built on the site of a medieval hospital, which was the recipient of generous donations from Louis IX, the Hôtel Dieu, now a city hospital, was the scene of intense battles when the police resisted the Germans in 1944.

In contrast to these forbidding structures, the market is an array of small glasshouses selling flowers and plants underneath classical, black street lamps. On Sunday, the stalls become a market for caged birds and the jabbering of parakeets fills the air.

On the north side of Notre-Dame is the Quartier des Anciens Cloîtres (Ancient Cloister Quarter), home and study area for 12th-century monks and scholars who belonged to the cathedral chapter, including the theologian Pierre Abélard, famous for his love letters to the

beautiful Héloïse. The area was once a warren of medieval churches and houses until Haussmann razed them to the ground, moving 25,000 inhabitants to the suburbs, to provide the present vista. As you pass along Rue de la Colombe, note the remains of the Gallo-Roman wall in the pavement.

On the eastern tip of the island lies the **Mémorial de la Déportation** ❼ (open daily; closed noon–2pm; free; tel: 01 46 33 87 56), a bleak but moving monument commemorating the tens of thousands of French Jews sent to their deaths in Nazi concentration camps. The chambers of this prison-like structure are etched with the names of the deported victims.

Ile St-Louis

Away from the tourists and camcorders, across the pedestrian Pont St-Louis, Ile St-Louis is a privileged haven of peace and wealth. The island's elegance is 17th-century and its mansions are home to Paris's elite.

Turning right along the south bank, you will come to the small **Musée Adam Mickiewicz** ❽ (closed for restoration until 2005; tel: 01 55 42 83 83). Adam Mickiewicz (1798–1855) was a Polish poet, living in Paris from 1832–40, who devoted his work to helping oppressed Poles. The 17th-century building includes the Polish Library and memorabilia of the Polish composer Frédéric Chopin.

Continuing eastwards round the island to the north bank, you will pass Hôtel Lambert. Built in 1640 by Louis Le Vau, an advisor to Louis XVIII, it is now owned by the Rothschilds. Further on is the Hôtel de Lauzun where the poets Théophile Gautier and Charles Baudelaire lived in 1845 and where Baudelaire wrote part of *Les Fleurs du Mal*. The house now belongs to the City of Paris, and is reserved for official guests. Behind, the Rue St-Louis-en-l'Ile is full of gift shops, bars, restaurants and quaint tearooms. Also on this street is the church of the same name. Built between 1664 and 1765, **Eglise St-Louis-en-l'Ile** has a classical Baroque interior and holds popular classical concerts. ❏

TIP

Ile St-Louis's favourite attraction is edible: Berthillon, opposite the Pont St-Louis, purveys 100 flavours of the city's most delicious ice cream.

Restaurants

Brasserie de l'Isle St-Louis
55 quai de Bourbon, 4th. Tel: 01 43 54 02 59; fax: 01 46 33 18 47. Open: L Fri–Tues, D Mon–Sun. €€ (set menu) €€€ (à la carte) The tables outside look up to Notre-Dame's soaring buttresses. The heavy Alsatian menu offers succulent pork knuckle and lentils or *choucroute* as a main. Wines are reasonable; skip the overpriced coffee and ice cream and head for Berthillon instead.

Isami
4 quai d'Orléans, 4th. Tel: 01 40 46 06 97. Open: L Tues–Sat, D Tues–Sun. €€ (set menu) €€€ (à la carte) The sushi and sashimi, arguably the best in Paris, is a work of art and the Seine-side dining room is cosy. This small Japanese restaurant has a minimalist menu to match the stripped-back decor. Two tables give out over the Pont Marie. Prices reflect the quality. Book ahead.

Le Réminet
3 rue des Grands Degrés, 5th. Tel: 01 44 07 04 24; fax:

01 44 07 17 37. Open: L & D Wed–Sun. € (set menu) €€ (à la carte) Norman chef Hugues Gournay has a deft hand with classical and regional fare. The weekday menus are a remarkable bargain. Wines are fairly priced.

Le Sarrasin et le Froment
84/86 rue St-Louis-en-l'Ile, 4th. Tel. 01 56 24 32 06. Open: L & D daily. €€ Only a short walk from the buttresses of Notre-Dame. If you like cheese, order your crêpe with Roquefort and

walnuts, or melted Camembert. There are salads and delicious omelettes, too.

Le Vieux Bistro
14 rue du Cloître-Notre-Dame, 4th. Tel: 01 43 54 18 95; fax 01 44 07 35 63. Open: L & D daily. €€ Right in the shade of Notre-Dame. Just the right place to tuck into a classic boeuf bourguignon. The atmosphere and portions are medieval.

● *Price categories:*
€ = under €25 ; €€ = €25–40; €€€ = €40–60; €€€€ = over €60.

THE MARAIS

Steeped in political history, this lively quarter
offers medieval streets, trendy bars and boutiques,
museum-filled mansions and the city's oldest
and most beautiful square

There's nowhere quite like the Marais, an elegant district that oozes charm and character with everything to recommend it: mansions and museums, chic boutiques and kosher grocers, gay bars and cosy cafés, all bundled together in a labyrinth of narrow streets and alleyways. Stretching west to east from Beaubourg to Bastille, straddling the 3rd and 4th *arrondissements*,with the rue des Francs-Bourgeois pulsing across it like a central artery, the Marais offers arguably the most fun you can have on the Right Bank.

It's hard to believe that for centuries the area was a mosquito-infested swamp ("marais" means marsh), cut through the middle by Rue St-Antoine, the old Roman road. The marshes were drained in Philippe-Auguste's reign and when, in 1358, Charles V moved his royal court from the Ile de la Cité to the area around the Tuileries, a royal influx to the Right Bank began. In 1609, Henri IV built a sumptuous nest for his court around the Place des Vosges, shifting the political and financial focus from the Louvre. As a result, the finest architects and stonemasons in Europe descended on the Marais, building countless grand residences, or *hôtels*, for the nobility, each more spectacular than the last. The Place des Vosges itself, initially known as the Place Royale, was the first planned square in Paris and, with its red brick-and-stone façades tapering into arched walkways, it remains as beautiful as ever.

The fall and rise

The pendulum of fashion swung away from the Marais after Louis XIV moved his court to Versailles in the 1680s and the nobility moved to the Ile St-Louis, then westwards to the Faubourg St-Honoré and the Boulevard St-Germain. During the

**Map
on page
70**

LEFT:
the impressive facade
of the Hôtel de Ville.
BELOW:
a café in the arcades of
Place des Vosges.

An eye-catching mural in the Jewish Quarter of the Marais.

BELOW: the *Horses of Apollo* sculpture in the Hôtel de Rohan court-yard.

Revolution, the area was abandoned to the people and the Marais's graceful hôtels fell into disrepair.

In the 19th and 20th centuries, the quarter became a centre for small industries and craftwork, and successive developers dug up and widened its picturesque streets. In 1962, André Malraux, President de Gaulle's Arts Minister, set wide-scale renovation work in motion to preserve what had by now become a very rundown area. By the 1990s, the Marais had regained its status as one of the most fashionable – and costly – places to live in Paris.

The Jewish and working class communities that once occupied the area have been marginalised by the relentless gentrification process. The character of the Marais is now defined by its designer boutiques, trendy bars and cafés, and a thriving gay community.

A tour of the old hôtels

Most of the *hôtels particuliers* have been converted into luxury apartments or offices, but a number of them have been left intact and now house museums. A good place to begin a tour of the Marais is at the Hôtel de Ville (City Hall), on the Seine-side of the Rue de Rivoli *(see page 89)*, that marks its western boundary. Just behind it stands the 17th-century church of **St-Gervais-St-Protais ❾** (open Tues–Sun; free) with a triple-tiered facade, a flight of Italianate steps and some monstrous-looking gargoyles. The church is renowned for its 18th-century organ and concerts are frequently held here. As a parting shot at the end of World War I, the church was shelled by the German army, killing more than 100 worshippers.

Rue François-Miron leads away from Place St-Gervais into the heart of the Marais. By the end of World War II the houses along here were practically derelict, but they have since been carefully restored. At the corner of Rue Cloche-Perce is a half-timbered medieval house, and at No. 68 stands the **Hôtel de Beauvais ❿**, built by Catherine Beauvais in 1654 with money and land from Louis XIV, who had greatly enjoyed her favours. Catherine is also rumoured

to have entertained archbishops here. A more innocent young Mozart stayed here during his first visit to Paris at the tender age of seven.

Neighbouring Rue de Jouy contains **Hôtel d'Aumont** ⓫, designed by the Versailles architect Louis Le Vau *(see page 55)*, renovated and enlarged by the French Classical architect François Mansart (1598–1666) and decorated by Versailles painter Charles Le Brun (1619–90). With a formal garden designed by Le Nôtre *(see page 55)*, the mansion now functions as the city's administrative court.

Further on down Rue Figuier stand the château-like turrets of one of Paris's few medieval residences, the **Hôtel de Sens** ⓬ (open Tues–Fri 1.30pm, Sat 10am–8.30pm; entrance fee; tel: 01 42 78 14 60), which now houses the city's historical and fine arts library, the Bibliothèque Forney. Built at the end of the 15th century for the Archbishop of Sens, the mansion is military in style, with simple but immaculate gardens. Henri IV lodged his first wife, Marguerite de Valois (Reine Margot), in the hôtel when he could no longer put up with her promiscuity. Here she continued to leave a trail of broken hearts. When a jealous ex-lover murdered her current beau, Marguerite had him beheaded outside the house.

The Village St-Paul

Opposite the Hôtel de Sens, the Rue de l'Avé-Maria intersects with the Rue des Jardins St-Paul a block away. This leads into the Village St-Paul past two towers and ramparts, the remnants of Philippe-Auguste's city wall, shadowing the antics of local schoolchildren. The restored "village" consists of a series of small courtyards and fountains, sheltering bustling antique shops and various secondhand stalls. At night, it is tranquil beneath the halo of old streetlamps.

On Rue Charlemagne, wooden walkways running between the buildings have been restored to the way they were the Middle Ages. Left along Rue St-Paul is an ancient passageway leading to the church of

Map on page 70

The modern Cité Internationale des Arts (behind the Hôtel de Sens) stands out in its mostly 17th-century neighbourhood; the building provides studios and a year's lodging for artists from around the world.

BELOW: inside a neighbourhood café.

For a true Parisian meal, Le Temps des Cerises in Rue de la Cerisaie, where 1,000 cherry trees used to grow, is a bistro that hasn't changed with the times, providing fresh market produce served by jocular waiters.

BELOW: in the gardens of Place des Vosges.

St-Paul-St-Louis , an amalgamation of two parishes, constructed by Jesuits in 1627, copying the Gesù church in Rome. Here, the hearts of Louis XIII and Louis XIV were embalmed and kept as relics until the Revolution, when they were removed and sold to an artist who crushed them to mix with oil for a varnish for one of his pictures. Later he gave what was left of Louis XIII's heart to the newly installed King Louis XVIII, in return for a golden snuffbox.

Place des Vosges

Rue St-Antoine is the ancient Roman road that led east out of the city. Built wide and straight in typical Roman fashion, it became a site for jousting tournaments until, in 1574, Henri II was knocked off his horse by his Scottish Captain of the Guard, Montgomery, with a blow to his eye. In a drastic bid to save his life, Henri's physician, Ambroise Paré, ordered the immediate decapitation of every prisoner on death row and had their heads rushed to the surgery so that he could experiment on them in a bid to rescue his king. Needless to say he didn't succeed and Henri died 10 days later. The unfortunate Captain Montgomery lost his head too.

At No. 62 Rue St-Antoine, roughly halfway between Métro St-Paul and Place de la Bastille, is **Hôtel de Sully** (courtyards open daily 10am–6.30pm), one of the finest mansions in the Marais. Under the courtyard's grumpy statues, Voltaire was beaten with clubs by followers of the Count of Rohan, following a slanging match between the two at the Comédie Française *(see page 104)*. Through the courtyard, the **Mission du Patrimoine Photographique** (open Tues–Sun 10am–6.30pm, closed Mon; tel: 01 42 74 47 75 or visit www.patrimoine-photo.org; entrance fee) hosts exhibitions of historical photography.

The intimate garden with clipped privet hedges *à l'anglaise* is an unexpected surprise. A door in the back right corner leads to the **Place des Vosges** . Initially called the Place Royale, this enchanting 17th-century square, with a garden surrounded by 36 arcaded residences, was constructed by Henri IV as a showcase for his court. Here courtiers paraded, preened and pranced. After the Revolution, when the melted-down statue of Louis XIII had been reforged and replaced, the square was named after Vosges, the first *département* to have paid its taxes promptly.

Today, this is the most beautiful square in Paris and one of the capital's most sought-after addresses. The arcades house chic cafés and boutiques and in summer play host to classical concerts – the same place Mozart gave his first recital in 1763.

In the southeast corner is the **Maison de Victor Hugo** (open Tues–Sun 10am–5.40pm, closed public holidays; free; tel: 01 42 72 10 16). The Romantic writer's Paris home for 15 years is a museum to the great man, containing portraits of his family, manuscripts, pen-and-ink drawings and pieces of furniture knocked together by Hugo in his spare time.

The Jewish Quarter

Between the northwestern corner of Place des Vosges and Rue Vieille du Temple runs the Rue des Francs-Bourgeois, a shopper's paradise crammed with boutiques and curiosity shops, many of which have retained the shop signs from their previous incarnations as butcher's or baker's. A left-hand turning just past the Musée Carnavalet leads to Rue Pavée and the **Hôtel de Lamoignon ⓱**, built in 1584 for the Duchesse d'Angoulême. Sixty people were murdered here during the massacres of 2 September 1792. The hôtel now houses the city's historical library.

Rue des Rosiers, a little further on, is the hub of what remains of the Jewish quarter. As the area has become increasingly popular with bar and boutique owners, the Jewish community has retreated to a small pocket centred on this narrow street lined with kosher delis, falafel stands and tiny shops packed with religious artefacts. Originally an Ashkenazy community, with its origins in eastern Europe, the community was depleted during the Holocaust. Numbers swelled again with the influx of Sephardic Jews from north Africa following the independence of Algeria in the 1960s, giving the area a Middle Eastern feel. Among the restaurants and bookshops that surround the synagogue, look out for Chez Marianne, the perpetually busy restaurant for Jewish specialities such as rollmops and falafels. For an overview of the area and the people who have lived there, visit the nearby Jewish Museum *(see page 85)*.

Rue des Rosiers leads on to the **Rue Vieille du Temple**, one of the best and liveliest stretches for cafés and bars in Paris.

Carnavalet and Picasso

One of the most fascinating of the many Marais museums is the **Musée Carnavalet ⓲** (tel: 01 44 59 58 58;

Map on page 70

The Mémorial du Martyr Juif Inconnu (Memorial to the Unknown Jew) stands on Rue Geoffroy l'Asnier, south of the Jewish Quarter. Its eternal flame in an underground crypt is a poignant reminder of the Holocaust.

LEFT: the formal garden of the Musée Carnavalet.

Victor Hugo – Man of Words

Poet, dramatist, novelist, politician and leader of the Romantic movement, Victor Hugo (1802–85) lived at 6 Place des Vosges from 1832 to 1848. This was a highly creative period of his life. His Parisian salon – now a museum *(see page 82)* – drew many great luminaries of the day, including Balzac, Lamartine and Dumas. "…the king of modern poetry reigned for 15 years, surrounded by his devoted courtiers, who were full of admiration for the master," wrote Eugène de Mirecourt, one of the many literary regulars. The rooms on the second floor of the house trace the story of Hugo's life, which he himself divided into three stages: "before exile, during exile and after exile". In 1841, after two attempts, Hugo was elected a member of the Académie Française and, in 1845, he accepted a political post under King Louis-Philippe. The 1848 Revolution threw Hugo into the thick of political struggle and he became a chief in the Democratic party against Louis-Napoleon. In 1851, he went into exile to the Channel Islands, where he wrote a large part of *Les Misérables* (1862). At the fall of the Empire in 1870, Hugo returned to Paris and continued writing there until his death.

A reminder of the German occupation during World War II.

www.paris.fr/ musees; open Tues–Sun 10am–6pm; closed public holidays; free). Occupying two mansions, the main 16th-century Hôtel Carnavalet and the neighbouring 17th-century Hôtel le Peletier, the museum covers the history of Paris chronologically from its beginnings as a Gallo-Roman settlement to its transformation into a modern-day metropolis. The evolution of the capital is traced through paintings, objets d'art, sculpture and costume. Madame de Sévigné, whose celebrated letters provide an insight into 17th century Parisian high society, lived in the Hôtel Carnavalet between 1677 and 1696 and there is a gallery devoted to her life.

Opposite, Rue de Thorigny leads to one of the finest buildings in the Marais district, the mansion that houses the **Musée Picasso** (5 Rue de Thorigny; tel: 01 42 71 25 21; open Wed–Mon 9.30am–6pm in summer, 9.30am– 5.30pm in winter; closed some public holidays; entrance fee). The Hôtel Salé was constructed with the booty of a 17th-century tax collector. Three centuries later, the French tax authorities scored another coup. Following his death in 1973, Pablo Picasso's family was faced with an enormous inheritance tax bill and so, in lieu of payment, they donated to the French nation a large collection of his works: 200 paintings, more than 3,000 drawings and 88 ceramics, along with sculptures, collages and manuscripts, as well as Picasso's own private collection of works from contemporaries like Cézanne, Matisse and Modigliani.

The museum shows all Picasso's different periods, in chronological order, including the Blue, Pink, Cubist, Classical and Post-Cubist phases. The famous beach pictures of the 1920s and 1930s are here, as well as remarkable portraits of his model-mistresses, Marie-Thérèse and Dora Maar. There is also a huge amount of sculpture made of driftwood, scrap iron and bicycle parts which serve as a reminder of Picasso's motto: "I do not seek, I find".

A cluster of museums

The Rue du Parc Royal is lined with magnificently restored 17th-century

A Spanish Genius

Born in Málaga in Spain, Pablo Picasso (1881–1973) finally settled in Paris at the age of 23, having studied art in Barcelona and Madrid. However, he never lost his Spanish touch as his work so often revealed. His works ooze life, humour and sex in a career that could never be separated from his personal life. A leading figure in modern 20th-century art, his work developed through many phases, including a Blue Period, when he painted his *Self Portrait* (1901), and Cubism, a primitive and monumental form of art, which he also explored in sculpture. In the 1920s and 1930s, Picasso produced his most abstract work and, in 1937, he painted *Guernica*, a harrowing representation of the Spanish Civil War. He remained in Paris, in the Rue des Grands-Augustins, during World War II, moving to the South of France afterwards. His last paintings were long considered a splashy and crude decline, but they have been rehabilitated as proof of the painter's continuing energy and inventiveness right up to his death in 1973 in Mougins. He left behind him a massive collection of paintings, sculptures, drawings and ceramics.

mansions, one of which houses the **Musée Bricard de la Serrure** ❷⓿ (Place de Thorigny; tel: 01 42 77 79 62; open Mon–Fri 10am–noon, 2–5pm, closed Aug and public holidays; entrance fee). The elegant hôtel was built by Libéral Bruand, the architect of Les Invalides (*see page 165*). This unusual museum exhibits a fascinating array of locks, keys, knobs and knockers, some of which date back to Roman times.

A few minutes' walk away, down Rue Elzévir, the exquisite Hôtel Donon houses the **Musée Cognacq-Jay** ❷❶ (tel: 01 40 27 07 21; www.paris.fr/musees; open Tues– Sun 10am–5.40pm; closed public holidays; free), the art and antiques collection of Ernest Cognacq and his wife Louise Jay, founders of La Samaritaine department store (*see page 151*). The collection, which includes works by Rembrandt and Canaletto, is displayed over a succession of salons and small rooms, which are furnished to give the feel of a private house.

A little further west, at the end of Rue Barbette, is the stunningly restored **Hôtel de Rohan** ❷❷, temporary home to the collection of the Musée de l'Histoire de France (*see below*). Even if you don't go inside, take a look in the courtyard at the magnificent sculpture of the *Horses of Apollo* over the stables (*see page 80*). On the Rue des Francs-Bourgeois a few minutes' walk southwards, behind an austere facade, lies the Crédit Municipal, the state pawnbroker. Nicknamed *Ma Tante* (My Aunt), the lending facility was opened in 1777 and you can still obtain cash on the value of objects surrendered to its charge.

Opposite this house of the poor stands a house of the rich, namely the **Hôtel de Soubise**, home to the **Musée de l'Histoire de France** ❷❸ (closed for renovation until 2005).

This early 18th-century mansion has rooms handsomely decorated in the Rococo style. Here, too, are the National Archives in which over 6 million official documents, on 290 km (180 miles) of shelving, demonstrate the French nation's love affair with the rubber stamp.

Rue des Archives leads up to a fine collection of stuffed animals and objets d'art related to hunting, in the **Musée de la Chasse et de la Nature** ❷❹ (tel: 01 53 01 92 40; open Tues–Sun 11am– 6pm, closed Mon and public holidays; entrance fee). A little further west at 71 rue du Temple, the grand Hôtel de St-Aignan now houses the **Musée d'Art et d'Histoire du Judaïsme** ❷❺ (tel: 01 53 01 86 60; www.mahj.org; open Mon–Fri 11am–6pm, Sun 10am– 6pm; entrance fee), a fascinating museum of Jewish art, culture and heritage.

Quartier du Temple

To the north of the Marais, about a 10-minute walk up Rue des Archives, the Quartier du Temple was once the headquarters of the

Map on page 70

BELOW: the Marais streets are a showcase for urban style.

Map
on page
70

TIP

The Marais is one of
the few places in the
city where you can
shop on a Sunday, its
busiest and most
crowded day of the
week.

Knights Templar. A 13th-century
secret society of soldiers, originally
formed to protect pilgrims in the
Holy Land, the Knights Templar
owned much of France and were in
charge of the royal treasury until
1307, when Philippe the Fair burnt
their leaders at the stake on an island
in the Seine and the society was
forced to go underground.

With the Revolution, the Temple
Tower became the most famous
prison in France and was where the
Royal Family was imprisoned. It
was from here, in 1793, that Louis
XVI went to the guillotine. The
Temple Tower was eventually razed
by a superstitious Napoleon, and
Haussmann replaced it with a
wrought iron, covered market, the
Carreau du Temple, which still sells
inexpensive and secondhand clothes
and cloth by the metre.

Along the tree-lined Rue Perrée
lies all that remains of the Temple
fortress, the **Square du Temple** ㉖,
a tree-lined garden which echoes
with the gentle sound of table tennis
balls on its two outdoor tables. Not

far from the Temple district, about
another 10 minutes along Rue Réaumur, is France's most prestigious
technical college, the Conservatoire
National des Arts et Métiers, and the
Musée des Arts et Métiers ㉗ (tel:
01 53 01 82 00 or visit www.cnam.fr;
open Tues–Sun 10am–6pm, Thur
until 9.30pm; entrance fee), the oldest museum of science and technical
innovation in Europe. The best part
of this fascinating museum of technology is the converted 11th-century
chapel that houses, among other
innovations, Foucault's pendulum (a
copy of which hangs in the Pantheon,
see page 147), immortalised in
Umberto Eco's novel *Foucault's
Pendulum*, and Blériot's aeroplane.

To end a visit to the Marais head
down Rue du Temple past the jewellery boutiques (about a 10-minute
walk) to No. 41 and its courtyard.
Once the headquarters of the Aigle
d'Or, the last stagecoach company
in Paris, it is now a bustling corner,
where the Café de la Gare puts on
alternative theatrical and musical
performances. ❏

Restaurants

Au Bascou
38 rue Réaumur, 3rd. Tel: 01
42 72 69 25. Open: L & D
Mon–Fri. €€
Generous meals from *la
terre basque*: squid,
roast lamb, sweet
stuffed peppers,
pipérade and smoked
tuna are on the menu in
this small, friendly place.
An exceptional and
unusual wine list too.

Au Petit Fer à Cheval
30 rue Vieille-du-Temple, 4th.
Tel: 01 42 72 47 47. Open: L
& D daily (until 2am). €
Fin de siècle café/wine

bar where an eclectic
mix of locals and foreigners gather around the
original marble-topped
horseshoe bar. An excel-
lent place to people
watch and very atmos-
pheric. Try the excellent
warm goat cheese salad.

Chez Omar
47 rue de Bretagne, 3rd.
Tel: 01 42 72 36 26. Open: L
Mon–Sat & D daily. €
Couscous is king here in
an old brasserie setting.
Popular with artists and
the chattering classes.
No reservations, so
arrive early to avoid
queuing. No credit cards.

Le Dôme du Marais
53 bis, rue des Francs-Bourgeois, 4th. Tel: 01 42 74 54
17. Open: L & D Tues–Sat. €€
(set menu) €€€ (à la carte)
This quiet, airy 18th-cen-
tury dining room, topped
with a glass dome, is
unique. It is hard to
believe that such a
romantic place was once
a state-owned pawnbro-
ker's shop.

Mi-Va-Mi
23 rue des Rosiers, 4th.
Tel: 01 42 71 53 72. Open: L
Sun–Fri & D Sun–Thur. €
A candidate for best
falafel in Paris. The
falafel special comes

with hummous and fried
aubergine. Excellent
choice for lunch or light
supper.

Sacha Finkelsztajn
27 rue des Rosiers, 4th.
Tel: 01 42 72 78 91. €
A bakery with central
European specialities,
including a sumptuous
array of kosher cakes
with a strong emphasis
on apple and cream
cheese. *Vatrouchka*
(cheesecake) is
recommended.

● *Price categories:*
€ = under €25 ; €€ =
€25–40; €€€ = €40–60;
€€€€ = over €60.

Café Life

The neighbourhood café is the Parisian's decompression chamber, easing the transition between *Métro-boulot-dodo* – commuting, working and sleeping. It provides a welcome pause in which to savour a *p'tit noir* (espresso) or an *apéritif*, to empty the mind of troublesome thoughts and to watch the people go by. The café is also the place to meet friends, have a romantic tryst or even to do business in a relaxed atmosphere.

The first café ever to open in France was Le Procope in 1686 and the literati soon started to congregate there, keen to discuss ideas with each other. More establishments quickly sprang up all over the country and it wasn't long before there was at least one café in every village and hamlet where people kept each other company. During the 18th century, the neighbourhood "zinc", named after its metal counter, became part of the fabric of French life.

In Paris, each café developed its own character, attracting different types of clientele, and with the widening of the boulevards in the 19th century, the tables spilled out onto the pavements. By 1910, there were 510,000 zincs in France, but now café life is waning.

While the invasion of fast-food restaurants is partly to blame (a nearby McDonald's, "McDo", can slash a café's profits by 30 percent), changes in the French way of life are also culpable. When customers move out to spacious homes in the suburbs, they tend to "cocoon", staying in to watch television and the local café eventually has to close. Then there are the ageing proprietors to consider. The café is traditionally a family business but, today, fewer sons and daughters are prepared to take on gruelling 16-hour days with sparse holidays and little reward or profit.

Sadly, even the atmosphere of remaining cafés is not what it was. Now there is formica where once there was marble. Piped muzak and the electronic beep of video games have replaced the song of the accordionist and the furious volleys of players on the *Baby-foot* machines. Only the Gauloise-induced haze (attitudes to the 1992 smoking ban are casual) and the hazards of the lavatories (some are still holes in the ground) remain the same.

Yet all is not lost. Authentic "zincs" are still to be found in Paris and many are thriving. Try the stylish Café de l'Industrie on Rue St-Sabin, La Palette on Rue de Seine or the tiny but lovingly restored Le Cochon à l'Oreille on Rue Montorgueil. For literary atmosphere order *un verre* (glass of wine) at Les Deux Magots, which has been home to almost every Paris intellectual from Rimbaud to André Breton. At the nearby Café de Flore, Sartre and Simone de Beauvoir wrote by the stove. "My worst customer, Sartre," recalled the patron. "He spent the entire day scribbling away over one drink." Clearly not a writer who needed alcohol to inspire him.

But go soon, before things change too much. For if you have never nipped into a French café to make a quick phone call, met your lover for an *apéritif* on a terrasse or negotiated the crouch of the *toilettes*, you cannot claim truly to know Paris. ❑

BEAUBOURG AND LES HALLES

The Pompidou Centre, with its "inside-out" design, is one of the most visited sites in the world. Les Halles, for centuries the capital's main produce market, is now blighted by a charmless shopping complex, but vestiges of the historic quarter remain in the warren of streets around it.

Sandwiched between the Louvre and Palais Royal to the west and the Marais to the east, this central chunk of the Right Bank is one of the city's most hyperactive commercial and cultural centres. The area is dominated by the Forum des Halles, a vast shopping and leisure complex. Next to the monumental grandeur of the neighbouring Louvre, Les Halles is a scruffy poor relation, an unsightly multistorey blot on the landscape. The other landmark building here is the Pompidou Centre, Paris's modern art museum. Unlike the 1970s monstrosity of Les Halles, this hulking mass of pipes, ducts and scaffolds painted in primary colours is strangely alluring, and is one of the world's most visited sites.

Hôtel de Ville

Place du Châtelet is a good starting point for exploring the area. Flanked by two theatres (Théâtre de la Ville and Théâtre du Châtelet for opera and modern dance), the square lies above one of Paris's biggest Métro and RER stations. To the northeast, rises the Gothic **Tour St-Jacques** (open Tues–Sun afternoons), a lone belfry once attached to a church that was destroyed during the Revolution. Look out for the statue of scientist and philosopher Blaise Pascal

(1623–62) who carried out pioneering experiments on atmospheric pressure from the top.

Opening out at the eastern end of Avenue Victoria is the wide esplanade of the **Hôtel de Ville (Mairie de Paris)** ㉘ (tel: 01 42 76 54 04; www.paris.fr; open Mon–Fri; free), ornate home of the city council. In medieval times, the square was the site of hangings and macabre executions. No traces of its horrific past remain. Today, the pedestrianised Place de l'Hôtel de

Map on page 70

LEFT: Henri de Miller's giant sculpture in the Jardin des Halles, St-Eustache.
BELOW: Pompidou Centre, Beaubourg.

Ville, which overlooks the Seine, is a pleasant place to stroll through, especially in the evening, when the fountains and town hall are floodlit.

The elaborate 19th-century building, with its splendid Mansard roofs, carved facade and army of statues, was rebuilt after the original 17th-century town hall was destroyed by fire in the 1871 Commune. The most notable features inside are the majestic Salle des Fêtes (ballroom), a magnificent staircase and lots of chandeliers. Such grandeur and opulence are a fitting backdrop for the city's governing powers and the grand halls are often used for banquets and ceremonial receptions.

Heading north up Rue St-Martin, towards the Pompidou Centre, you pass the richly adorned 16th-century church of **St-Merri** ㉙, built in Flamboyant-Gothic style. Its bell, dating from 1331, is the oldest in Paris, and the organ used to be played by Camille Saint-Saëns (1835–1921). Between the church and the Pompidou Centre, the playful waterworks of the Fontaine de Stravinski were inspired by the

French composer's ballet, the *Firebird*. Created by artists Niki de Saint-Phalle and Jean Tinguely, the forms and figures in the fountain represent the story – a heart, a snake, a bare-breasted torso, pursed red lips and the firebird in the middle spin and spit water in all directions. In fine weather, this square is a favourite sightseers' picnic spot.

Beaubourg

Known locally as Beaubourg, the **Centre National d'Art et de Culture, Centre Georges-Pompidou** ㉚ (tel: 01 44 78 12 33, www.centrepompidou.fr; closed Tues; open Mon and Wed–Sun 11am–10pm; entrance fee to galleries) welcomes 8 million visitors a year. Its architects, Richard Rogers and Renzo Piano, placed all the infrastructure – escalators, lifts, ducts, etc – on the outside. The high-tech design caused an uproar when the building opened in 1977, but its popular appeal soon silenced the critics. As well as housing one of the world's most important modern art collections, the cavernous interior

The Pompidou's primary-coloured pipes are not just for show: the blue convey air, the green transport water, the yellow contain electricity and the red conduct heating.

BELOW: Fontaine de Stravinski by Niki de Saint-Phalle and Jean Tinguely.

accommodates a large public library, an educational area, a performance space, auditorium and cinema, and the neighbouring avant-garde music institute IRCAM.

The **Musée National d'Art Moderne** is on the fourth and fifth floors. Incredibly, the works on display represent only a small proportion of the 50,000-strong collection, which is why the museum has regular rehangs, so as to rotate the works of art and allow the public access to as many as possible.

The fifth floor covers the period from 1905 up to the 1960s, with works by Picasso, Matisse, Kandinsky, Klee, Klein and Pollock, and sections on Dadaism and Surrealism. The fourth floor is devoted to the wonderful comtemporary collection, from the 1960s up to the present day, and includes work by Andy Warhol, Xavier Veilhan, Claude Viallat, Verner Panton, Joseph Beuys, Gerhard Richter and Jean Dubuffet. Displays of 20th-century design and architecture, as well as installations, are now interspersed among the paintings.

Also on show is a reconstruction of Brancusi's studio, l'Atelier Brancusi. The outdoor terrace looks over towards Les Halles, displaying sculptures by Tinguely.

Les Halles

The Les Halles quarter gets its name from the city's historic food market which stood between 1183 and 1969 on the spot now occupied by the biggest shopping complex in Paris. Large scale construction has been a feature of the area since 1851, when Napoleon III ordered architect Victor Baltard to design ten colossal cast-iron hangars to go over the market. Stallholders, restaurant owners, pickpockets, artists, prostitutes and police inhabited this vast market that novelist Emile Zola called "the belly of Paris". By the 1960s the site had become impractical. The market decamped to the suburbs of Rungis and the hangars were tragically pulled down, leaving a gaping hole that became a national joke. It was filled in the 1980s by the **Forum des Halles ❸**, an underground shopping mall with

Map on page 70

Shoppers with a passion for fashion should avoid the soulless Forum des Halles and head instead for the trendy Rue Etienne Marcel, home of Yohji Yamamoto, Diesel, Barbara Bui, Joseph and other hip high-street labels.

BELOW: Bourse du Commerce.

Fontaine des Innocents

The Fontaine des Innocents, a Renaissance fountain decorated with water nymphs by Pierre Lescot and Jean Goujon, stands on the site of the infamous Cimetière des Innocents, southeast of Les Halles. In use since the 12th century, the graveyard, encircled by a high wall, had become a putrid necropolis by the 18th century, as the dead – mostly paupers – were carried there among produce bound for the market at Les Halles. Gruesome tales are told about how people ground up bones for bread when Paris was under siege in 1590, and used the skeletons for firewood. By 1780, corpses were overflowing above street level and the area was teeming with rats, which started to gnaw their way into people's homes. It was recognised that something had to be done so the cemetery was finally closed and its contents moved to the Catacombs, where remains can still be seen (see page 155).

Today, the square is a meeting place for the city's youth, and the pedestrianised Rue des Lombards is a centre for nightlife with bars, restaurants and the Duc des Lombards jazz club.

Map on page 70

The area around Les Halles makes frequent appearances in 19th-century French literature (Zola set his novel Le Ventre de Paris – The Belly of Paris – *here), and the Baltard halls and workforce were later photographed by such distinguished snappers as Doisneau and Cartier-Bresson.*

BELOW: the Gothic gaze of St-Eustache.

shops, two multiplex cinemas, an Olympic swimming pool and a film centre – practical but devoid of charm. The immediate surroundings have been blighted by notoriously bad landscaping. However, surrounding the market area are remnants of a bygone age with brasseries staying open around the clock (the clientele no longer formed by hard-working market porters in the early hours, but exhausted partygoers) and sleazy Rue St-Denis, the age-old domain of prostitutes. The best place for a glimpse of the old Les Halles is **Rue Montorgueil**, a narrow, pedestrianised street packed with romantic cafés, wine and cheese merchants, friendly butchers and colourful fruit and vegetable stalls. This short, attractive strip is one of the few places in Les Halles where it is easy to linger – even if you end up buying nothing more than a coffee.

Around St-Eustache

North of the Forum, the beautiful **St-Eustache ㉜** is a rose among thorns. The colossal church, modelled on Notre-Dame (note the flying buttresses) took over a hundred years to build (1532–1637). The interior is a Renaissance feast of majestic columns, arches and stained glass windows. During the French Revolution it was converted into a "Temple of Agriculture". Berlioz and Liszt played here in the 19th century and concerts are held regularly using the church's 8,000-pipe organ. A memorial in one of the chapels portrays the fruit and vegetable sellers leaving the city like refugees.

Outside the church, a sculpture of a giant head and cupped hand by Henri de Miller attracts children and pigeons to its benign seat. The stretch of gardens lying between Les Halles and St-Eustache is peopled by dog-walkers, loitering teenagers and down-and-outs. The green space features glass pyramids which contain a hothouse full of palms, papayas and banana trees. Metal walkways pass through them to the **Bourse du Commerce** (tel: 01 55 65 55 65; open Mon–Fri 9am–6pm; free), a circular building erected in the 18th century as a corn exchange and now a busy commodities market for coffee and sugar.

Head back towards the Rue St-Honoré, south of Les Halles, an elegant street with a rich history and upmarket shops. A little further on is the church of **St Germain-l'Auxerrois ㉝**. At midnight on 24 August 1572, the church bells rang as the signal to start the St Bartholomew's Day Massacre *(see page 23)*, when thousands of Protestants were butchered on the orders of Catholic Catherine de Médicis. Behind the church on the banks of the Seine, **La Samaritaine ㉞** is a historic department store with lovely Art Nouveau decor, spread over five buildings joined by overhead walkways *(see page 216)*. The roof terrace restaurant offers one of the finest views of Paris – at a reasonable price. ❑

RESTAURANTS & CAFÉS

Restaurants

Barlotti
35 place du Marché-Saint-Honoré, 1st. Tel: 01 44 86 97 97. Open: L & D daily. €€
Fashionable Italian restaurant where a young and vibrant crowd enjoys top-class carpaccio and a long list of adventurous pasta dishes.

Café Beaubourg
25 rue Quincampoix, 4th. Tel: 01 42 77 48 02. Open: L & D daily (until 2am). €€
Designer café opposite the Centre Pompidou. Ideal for a light bite to eat and a spot of people-watching. Either gaze out from the terrace onto the Pompidou forecourt or turn your gaze inwards, to the café's habitués.

La Fresque
100 rue Rambuteau, 1st. Tel: 01 42 33 17 56. Open: L & D daily (until midnight). €
Sitting elbow to elbow at one of the big wooden tables is part of the charm here, as is the decor (white faience tiles, frescoes). Bistro fare like beef stew and duck are excellent and the staff is friendly if sometimes harrassed. There is always one vegetarian main course.

Georges
6th floor, Centre Georges-Pompidou, place Beaubourg, 4th. Tel: 01 44 78 16 80.
Open: L & D Wed–Mon (until 1am). €€€
The chic clientele don't go to Georges' restaurant for the food but to see and be seen in a unique setting at the top of the Pompidou Centre.

Le Hangar
12 impasse Berthaud, 4th. Tel: 01 42 74 55 44. Open: L & D Tues–Sat. €€ (set menu) €€€ (à la carte)
Minimalist and cosy, this modern bistro is just steps from the Pompidou Centre, hidden in an alley. Pan-fried foie gras with puréed potatoes is always on the menu as well as a towering chocolate soufflé.

Le Petit Marcel
65 rue Rambuteau, 4th. Tel: 01 48 87 10 20. Open: L & D daily (until midnight). €
In a great location, a stone's throw from the Centre Pompidou, this café/bar is a real find. Art Nouveau tiles decorate the interior. Good drinks selection, food and friendly service.

Le Père Fouettard
9 rue Pierre-Lescot. Tel: 01 42 33 74 17. Open: L & D daily (until midnight). €
Totally relaxing, the café terrace is leafy in summer, heated in winter. Brochettes of beef from the Aubrac region are on the menu as well as vegetarian options.

Au Pied de Cochon
6 rue Coquillière, 1st. Tel: 01 40 13 77 00. Open: daily, 24 hours. € (set menu) €€ (à la carte)
In its heyday, the legendary all-night brasserie catered for the market workers; now it's rather more upmarket. But the house speciality remains the same: grilled pig's foot with béarnaise sauce. If that isn't your thing, there are oysters and seafood. And the onion soup is good for hangovers.

Chez Clovis
33 rue Berger, 1st. Tel: 01 42 33 97 07. Open Mon–Sat L & D.
Good hearty cuisine in the heart of Les Halles in a simple terraced café. Generous helpings and good-humoured waiters provide an uncomplicated eating experience and set you back on the tourist trail.

Au Chien qui Fume
33 rue du Pont-Neuf, 1st. Tel: 01 42 36 07 42. Open non-stop daily noon–2am. €
The "smoking dog" has an extensive brasserie menu and is not a bad place to lap up the late night atmosphere in Les Halles.

PRICE CATEGORIES

Prices for three-course dinner per person with a half-bottle of house wine:
€ = under €25
€€ = €25–40
€€€ = €40–60
€€€€ = over €60.

RIGHT: Barlotti offers slick service, thoughtful presentation and a cosmopolitan crowd.

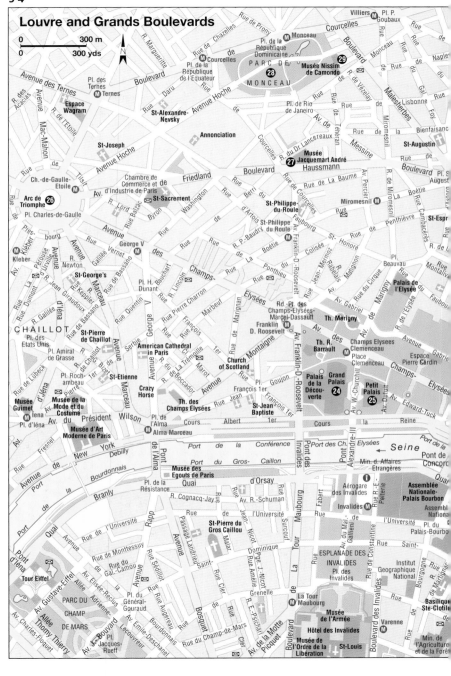

Louvre and Grands Boulevards

0   300 m
0   300 yds

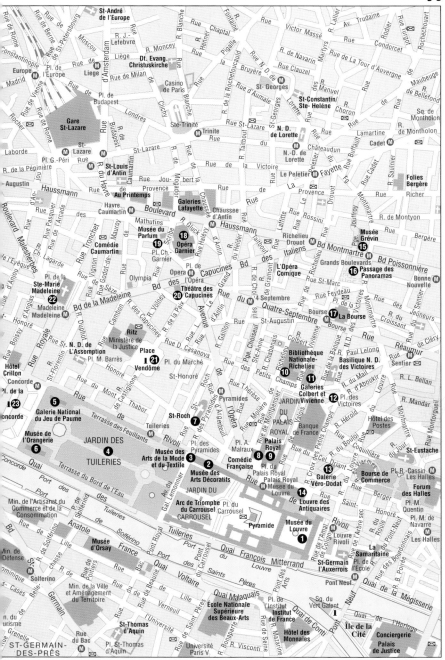

THE LOUVRE AND QUARTIER DES TUILERIES

The royal heart of Paris embraces the ornamental Tuileries gardens, the tranquil Palais Royal, and the world's largest museum of art

Map on pages 94–95

O n the Seine's Right Bank expanses of beautifully laid out gardens stretch into ostentatious squares, and wide tree-lined boulevards overflow with upmarket restaurants and designer boutiques, interspersed with royal palaces, an opulent opera house and the world's most famous museum. Meticulously planned by Prefect Baron Haussmann, the elegant buildings, boulevards and open spaces engulf the visitor in 19th-century grandeur.

This chapter covers the royal heart of Paris, from the Louvre and Palais Royal westwards to the Jeu de Paume gallery and the Musée de l'Orangerie at the far end of the Tuileries Garden. The grandiose squares – place de la Concorde and place Vendôme and place de la Madeleine – with the Champs-Elysées, the Grands Boulevards and the Opéra are covered in the next chapter.

The Louvre

Once the seat of royalty, the **Musée du Louvre ❶** (tel: 01 40 20 51 50; www.louvre.fr; open Mon, Thur–Sun 9am–6pm, Wed until 9.45pm, closed Tues and some public holidays; reduced entry fee Sun; first Sun of month entrance free) has been the home of fine art since a colony of painters and sculptors moved into the empty halls after

Louis XIV decamped to Versailles in 1682. The Louvre's art collection goes back even further, to 1516, when François I invited Leonardo da Vinci to be the Royal Court painter and he brought with him his masterpieces of the *Mona Lisa* and *Virgin of the Rocks*.

Originally built as a fortress in 1190 by King Philippe-Auguste to protect a weak link in his city wall, the Louvre was transformed into a royal château in the 1360s by Charles V, who established his

LEFT: statue in the Jardin des Tuileries.
BELOW: the Louvre and the Triumphal Way from the air.

Foundations of the Louvre fortress and keep, discovered in 1984.

BELOW: Coustou figures in the Sculpture Hall at the Louvre.

extensive library in one of the towers. Successive monarchs demolished, rebuilt and extended various sections until Louis XIV moved out. The squatters who consequently took up residence in the palace included Guillaume Coustou, sculptor of the Marly Horses, now one of the Louvre's most prized exhibits. A fine artistic reputation grew out of the decaying passageways and galleries and, in the 18th century, the fine arts academy, which had joined the Académie Française and other academic bodies in the royal apartments, set up salons for artists to exhibit their work, a tradition which lasted for more than 120 years.

During the Revolution, in a moment of creative fervour, the rebels decided to inaugurate the palace as a museum, ironically fulfilling the plans of Louis XVI, the king they had just beheaded. Opened in August 1793, the museum benefited from the growing collection of royal treasures, augmented by Napoleon's subsequent efforts to relocate much of Europe's artistic wealth, following his victorious military campaigns in Italy, Austria and Germany. After Napoleon was defeated at Waterloo in 1815, many of the stolen masterpieces were reclaimed by their rightful owners. But many more remained.

In 1981, President Mitterrand commissioned a massive renovation of the Louvre, one of his "Grands Projets", transferring in the process the Finance Ministry from the Richelieu Wing to Bercy, in eastern Paris, to free up more space for the vast collection. When it was finally finished, the Grand Louvre, already a vast museum, had doubled in size, making it the world's biggest.

The Pyramid

In 1989 the controversial Louvre Pyramid, designed by the Chinese-American architect I.M. Peï over the new main entrance, was opened. A celebration of angles, the pyramid's 666 panes of glass are held together with stainless steel nodes and cables. They reflect and, to some minds, complement the ancient curves of the surrounding main building. However, to traditionalists

Paris museum pass

If your plan is to visit as many museums as you can during your stay, it may be worth investing in a Carte Musées et Monuments. Valid for 1, 3 or 5 days, the Paris museum pass (www.intermusees.fr) gives free and no-waiting access to 70 museums and monuments. The advantages include skipping lines to get into permanent collections. The price is €15 for one day, €30 for two (consecutive) days, and €45 for three (consecutive) days. It is on sale at 70 museums, major Métro stations, tourist offices and FNAC tickets counters. Note that many museums are closed on Monday or Tuesday and on public holidays.

such modernism amid such historic beauty is a heresy – the same criticism that was levelled against the Parisians' beloved Eiffel Tower when it was first erected. The Pyramid also forms part of the Royal Axis, or Triumphal Way, an alignment of monuments, regal and triumphal, leading from the Louvre's Cour Carrée to the Grande Arche in La Défense.

Of course, it was not just designed to dazzle. The Pyramid also serves a practical purpose as it allows light to flood into the new sunken court where you buy your ticket, and along with three smaller pyramids illuminates the area where shops, restaurants, cafés and an exhibition area are situated. The exhibition area, called the Medieval Louvre, shows the palace at different stages of its development. It is also the new location for the Paris fashion shows.

However, the Pyramid entrance does become very congested, so try to avoid peak times such as Sundays or after 3pm, when ticket prices are reduced. There are alternative entrances at 99 rue de Rivoli, which takes you in via the Carrousel du Louvre shopping centre, or you can enter directly from the Palais-Royal-Musée-du-Louvre Métro. There are special queues for museum pass holders (Carte Musées; *see page 98*) who can also use the Porte des Lions entrance.

A tour of the treasures

From the central Hall Napoléon, escalators whisk visitors off to various parts of the complex, which is divided into three separate sections: Sully (east wing), Denon (south wing) and Richelieu (north wing), with the exhibits on three levels. Although star attractions are well signposted, the free map provided is essential.

A good exhibition to start with is the Medieval Louvre en route to the Crypte Sully under the Cour Carrée, where the remains of Philippe-Auguste's fort and keep, and some of the artefacts discovered in the recent excavations to build the underground complex, can be seen. Pieces of Charles VI's parade

Map on pages 94–95

Michelangelo's The Rebellious Slave.

BELOW:
the Pont des Arts.

Autumn (c. 1640) by Nicolas Poussin, one of a series of four seasonal paintings illustrating episodes from the Bible.

BELOW: light floods into the sunken court through the glass Pyramid.

helmet were found at the bottom of the well in the keep in 1984 and a replica of the helmet is now on display in the Salle St-Louis.

Up on the ground floor of the Sully and Richelieu wings are the Oriental Antiquities, including the Mesopotamian prayer statuette of Ebih-il (dating from around 2400 BC), which has striking lapiz lazuli eyes, and the black basalt *Babylonian Code of Hammurabi* (1792–50 BC), one of the world's first legal documents.

On the south side of the Sully Wing you will find the graceful Hellenic statue *Venus de Milo* (2nd century BC), purchased by the French government for a thousand euros in 1820 from the Greek island of Milos. From here, head on into the Denon Wing to see the Etruscan Sarcophagus of the *Reclining Couple*. Continuing along the ground floor level, you will reach the Italian sculpture section and its famous masterpieces, such as Michelangelo's *Slaves* (1513–20), sculpted in marble for Pope Julius II's tomb but never finished, and Canova's

neoclassical *Psyche Revived by the Kiss of Cupid* (1793).

In the Denon Wing, on the first floor, is the work of art that everyone wants to see for themselves, the *Mona Lisa* (1503) – La Joconde in French. The first incumbent in the Louvre, Leonardo da Vinci's small painting of a Florentine noblewoman rests securely behind glass since her knife assault in the 1980s. But don't ignore the many other masterpieces hanging in this gallery, including more by Leonardo and works by Raphael, Titian and Veronese, as well as Caravaggio's *The Fortune Teller* (about 1594).

On the same floor is the Grande Galerie, starting at the top of the Escalier Daru opposite the *Winged Victory of Samothrace* (2nd century BC), the Hellenistic stone figurehead commemorating a victory at sea. Here hang 19th-century French paintings, with Delacroix's *Liberty Leading the People*, Géricault's *Raft of the Medusa* and David's *Sabine Women*. The Spanish School, with masterpieces by El Greco and Goya, can be found close by.

Map on pages 94–95

The second floor of the Richelieu and Sully wings are completely given over to paintings and include Rembrandt's masterpiece of his second wife, *Bathsheba Bathing* (1654), and the Dutch painter Jan Vermeer's telling portrayal of domestic life in the 1660s, *The Lacemaker*. The beautifully renovated Richelieu Wing houses a vast collection of French sculpture on the ground floor and is focused around two splendid sculpture courts, starring Guillaume Coustou's two giant Marly Horses.

Housed in a separate wing (entrance at 107 rue de Rivoli) are three other collections. The **Musée des Arts Décoratifs ❷** (tel: 01 44 55 57 50; www.ucad.fr; open Tues–Fri 11am–6pm, Wed until 9pm, Sat–Sun 10am–6pm, entrance fee) complements the Louvre's Objets d'Art collection. The museum presents an exhaustive survey of interior design, from medieval tapestries to extravagant Empire furniture and 20th-century design, including Art Nouveau and Art Deco. Currently, only the newly renovated Renais-sance and Middle Ages galleries are open. The remaining period rooms are due to be renovated by 2005.

In the same wing, the **Musée des Arts de la Mode et du Textile ❸** covers Paris fashions and textiles from the 16th century until today. Each year it mounts a big display focusing on a different aspect of its collection, from the earliest existing dresses to the ground-breaking designs of the big-name couturiers of the 20th century, such as Christian Dior and Yves Saint-Laurent.

Upstairs, the **Musée de la Publicité** (tel: 01 44 55 57 50; www. museedelapub.org; opening times as above) was designed for the millennium celebrations by architect Jean Nouvel, who turned to the city for his inspiration. It is home to a rich collection of posters – around 100,000 in all, starting from as early as the Middle Ages – newspaper and radio advertisements, and other promotional memorabilia, complemented by interactive displays, slide shows and videos. Only a fraction of the vast collection can ever be exhibited at one time.

Aristide Maillol (1861–1944) started sculpting at the age of 40, concentrating his efforts on large, bronze, nude women – 20 of which adorn the Tuileries.

BELOW: stone drama in the Jardin des Tuileries.

A walk in the Tuileries

The **Jardin des Tuileries** ❹ offers shade, statues, fountains and a place to relax and pretend to read *Le Monde*. Once a rubbish tip and a clay quarry for tiles (*tuiles*, hence the name), the garden was initially created, in 1564, for Catherine de Médicis in front of her palace, to remind her of her native Tuscany. In 1664, Louis XIV's celebrated gardener, André Le Nôtre, redesigned the park with his predilection for straight lines and clipped trees.

It was then opened to the public and quickly became the first fashionable outdoor area in which to see and be seen, triggering the appearance of the first deckchairs and public toilets. One of the earliest hot-air balloon flights was launched from here in 1783.

In the 1990s the Tuileries were renovated, restoring Le Nôtre's original design and incorporating a new sloping terrace and enclosed garden. The Passerelle de Solférino, a footbridge across the Seine opened in 1999, links the gardens to the Left Bank and the Musée d'Orsay.

Approaching the gardens from the Louvre, you pass through the Arc de Triomphe du Carrousel, the smallest of the three arches (the others being the Arc de Triomphe and the Grande Arche at La Défense) on the Triumphal Way. Erected in 1808 by Napoleon to commemorate his Austrian victories, this arch is a garish imitation of the great triumphal arches built by the Romans, and the four horses galloping across its top are copies of four gilded bronze horses, stolen by Napoleon from St Mark's Square in Venice to decorate his memorial. After his downfall in 1815, the originals were returned.

In front of the arch, where the Tuileries Palace used to stand linking the Pavillon de Marsan and the Pavillon de Flore, is a collection of sculptures of sensuous nudes, produced between 1900 and 1938 by Aristide Maillol, adorning the ornamental pools. More works by sculptors such as Rodin and Le Pautre, along with copies of ancient works and late 20th-century sculpture added for the millennium, can be found scattered around.

André Le Nôtre (1613–1700) is France's most celebrated gardener. Creator of the French formal garden, he designed those at Versailles, the Champs-Elysées and the Tuileries, where his family had gardened for three generations.

BELOW: relaxing by an ornamental pool in the Tuileries.

Continue westwards along the Terrasse du Bord de l'Eau, where Napoleon's children played under the watchful gaze of their emperor father, to the hexagonal pool – still a favourite spot for children with boats, and ducks with attitude. Here, facing each other, are the twin museums of the **Galerie Nationale du Jeu de Paume** ❺ (tel: 01 47 03 12 50; open Tues noon–9.30pm, Wed–Fri noon–7pm, Sat–Sun 10am–7pm; entrance fee) and the **Musée de l'Orangerie** ❻ (closed for renovation until 2005). These buildings are all that remain of the Palais des Tuileries, burnt down during the Paris Commune of 1871.

When the Impressionist collection moved from the Jeu de Paume to the Musée d'Orsay *(see pages 169 and 172)*, the former royal "real" tennis court of the Tuileries palace was redesigned to house contemporary art. The two-storey space is particularly suited to installation and sculpture.

The list of canvases in the Orangerie's collection is impressive: 22 Soutines, 14 Cézannes – including one of *The Bathers* which was cut into three, then stuck back together again (look for the joins) – 24 Renoirs, 28 Derains and a pile of Picassos, Matisses and Utrillos. The highlight, though, is the unforgettable and extraordinarily fresh series of waterlilies by Claude Monet, conceived especially for two oval rooms downstairs. Donated by the artist to the state in 1918, the eight vast curved panels hover between abstraction and decoration.

During renovations on the Orangerie, workers uncovered a wall dating from Charles IX's reign (*c.* 1566). The reopening of the museum, scheduled for 2004, will be delayed while the Minister of Culture decides what to do with the historic find.

Rue de Rivoli

The long, arcaded Rue de Rivoli, topped with neoclassical apartments, runs from the Louvre along the Tuileries to place de la Concorde. It was built to commemorate Napoleon's victory over the Austrians at Rivoli, north of Verona, in 1797 but was completed well after

Map on pages 94–95

TIP

The Hôtel Meurice (228 rue de Rivoli), overlooking the Tuileries gardens, has been gloriously restored to its glittering best. The Michelin-starred restaurant, with celebrated chef Yannick Alléno at the helm, offers a memorable (and expensive) dining experience.

BELOW: Galerie Nationale du Jeu de Paume.

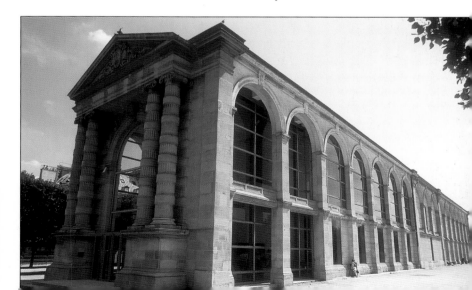

A bird in the hand – and just about everywhere else – in the gardens of the Palais Royal.

BELOW: arches, Palais Royal.

the Emperor's demise. Amid the souvenir shops, the presence of English language bookshops and shirtmaker Hilditch & Key are a legacy of the English, who often stayed here around the 19th and early 20th centuries, notably at the Hôtel Meurice. Nearby is Angélina, a late 19th-century Viennese *salon de thé* famous for its hot chocolate.

Parallel to Rue de Rivoli is the ancient street of Rue St-Honoré. Once full of noble residences, it still has some elegant façades and several ornate period shopfronts. However, the area, long considered rather staid and straight-laced, has been transformed by the arrival of influential designer boutiques and so-called concept stores.

Halfway along the street stands the Baroque church of **St-Roch** ❼ which contains the tombs of royal landscape gardener, Le Nôtre, the playwright Corneille and philosopher Diderot. In 1795, Royalist insurgents were shot dead on the church steps on the orders of a young brigadier general named Napoleon Bonaparte (the bullet holes are still visible).

On the nearby Place des Pyramides is a statue of Joan of Arc (one of four statues of the Maid of Orléans in the city), wounded here in battle when fighting against the English in 1429.

The French national theatre, **Comédie Française** ❽, overlooks two squares named after the writers Colette and Malraux. The company which started life with Molière and his acting troupe *(see below)* was officially founded in 1680 by Louis XIV. It has been in the present building since 1799, and the plays of Racine, Molière, Corneille and Shakespeare form the backbone of its classical repertoire.

Palais Royal

Palais Royal ❾ is a timeless and tranquil spot. The palace was built on the site of a Roman bath house for Cardinal Richelieu, who became prime minister in 1624. On his death in 1642, it was passed to the Crown and became the childhood home of Louis XIV. At the beginning of the 18th century, the dukes of Orléans took up residence and the palace

Master of Comedy

Born Jean-Baptiste Poquelin in Paris in 1622, Molière, playwright, actor, director and stage manager, created 12 enduring satirical comedies, including *Tartuffe* (1669) and *Le Bourgeois Gentilhomme* (1671). After studying law, he formed an acting troupe called The Illustrious Theatre with members of the Béjart family (whose daughter, Madeleine Béjart, he was in love with). It was around this time he changed his name to Molière, possibly to spare his father the embarrassment of having an actor in the family. The troupe had an unsuccessful start, but after Molière polished up his act in the provinces, they became Louis XIV's official entertainers.

In 1673, at 51, Molière collapsed on stage with a haemorrhage while acting the title role in his play *Le Malade Imaginaire*, in which an old man feigns death; he died a few hours later. In 1680 the King merged his company with a rival's, creating a united Parisian theatre called the Comédie Française. The great thespian lived at 40 rue de Richelieu and is commemorated by the Molière Fountain close by.

turned into a den of debauchery, as a result of the infamous "libertines' suppers" regularly thrown by the Regent, Philippe d'Orléans. The dukes forbade the police entrance to the palace precincts and gambling and prostitution were rife. In 1780, to compensate for his family's profligate spending, Louis-Philippe built shops around the palace, which were let at exorbitant prices.

After the Revolution, this complex with its restaurants and casinos became the focal point of Parisian life, until the Palais fell to the Orléans once again after the demise of Napoleon. The Palais Royal was seriously damaged during the Paris Commune (1871), but was faithfully reconstructed in the following years.

Today, the Palais Royal houses the Ministry of Culture. In the main courtyard stand 250 black-and-white striped columns of varying heights, erected by artist Daniel Buren in 1986. On weekends it echoes with the squeals of delighted children who love to play around them. The garden, which was once a meeting place for some of the

most important protagonists of the Revolution, is now a tranquil oasis while the eccentric mix of shops in the arcades ranges from old-fashioned specialists in medals and lead soldiers to make-up, vintage couture and upmarket interior design.

Bibliothèque Nationale

North of the Palais Royal, at No. 58 rue Richelieu is the **Bibliothèque Nationale de France (Richelieu)** ❿ (tel: 01 53 79 59 59; www.bnf.fr; open Mon–Fri 9am–6pm, Sat 10am–5pm; closed public holidays and for two weeks in Sept). This was formerly home to every book published in France since 1500, but most of the collection was transferred to the massive building at Tolbiac *(see page 57)* – the last (and least successful) of Mitterrand's *grands projets*. The book collection is one of the biggest in the world and includes Charlemagne's illuminated bible as well as original manuscripts belonging to Villon, Rabelais, Hugo and Proust. The Richelieu building now houses the collection of prints, drawings, maps, music and manu-

Map on pages 94–95

TIP

Sip a strong coffee at the expansive copper counter of the refurbished Le Grand Colbert, an 1830s brasserie at 4 rue Vivienne, and pop into No. 6 to check out Jean-Paul Gaultier's latest creations. Tea addicts will find a welcome repose at A Priori Thé, in the Galerie Vivienne, a *salon de thé* which spreads out into the gallery.

BELOW: Daniel Buren's columns in the Palais Royal courtyard.

Map on pages 94–95

Jean-Paul Sartre sculpted outside the Bibliothèque Nationale de France (Richelieu).

BELOW: the stylish 19th-century Galerie Colbert.

scripts. The main reading room, designed by Henri Labrouste in 1863, is an architectural masterpiece. Downstairs, the permanent museum, the **Cabinet des Médailles** (open afternoons; entrance fee), contains objets d'art from the royal collections seized during the Revolution.

Opposite the library, across Rue de Richelieu, the charming **Square Louvois** contains one of the most beautiful fountains in Paris, which represents the four "female" rivers of France – La Loire, La Seine, La Garonne and La Saône.

Grands Galeries

The area between the Palais Royal and rue du Faubourg-Montmartre is laced with picturesque shopping arcades. The 20 or so *galeries* represent a fraction of the number that existed in the early 19th century. By the 1840s there were over 100 passages built by speculators who snapped up the land of the dispossessed aristocracy that came on to the market after the Revolution. They became the places to discover novelties, inventions and the latest fash-

ions, while keeping out of the mud-splashed, carriage-laden thoroughfares. The best preserved of these latterday shopping malls is **Galerie Vivienne** ⓫, which has a fine mosaic floor, intricate brass lamps, graceful glass canopies and restored wooden shopfronts. It has been colonised by art galleries and upmarket clothes designers. The adjoining **Galerie Colbert**, formerly an annexe of the Bibliothèque Nationale, has a spectacular glass dome.

Adjacent to these galleries is the **Place des Victoires** ⓬, an archetypal royal square designed in 1685 by Louis XIV's architect Jules Hardouin Mansart as a backdrop for the equestrian statue of his patron (a bronze copy – revolutionaries destroyed the original), the Sun King. The square became a model for squares across France. Many of its surrounding mansions are now occupied by designer boutiques (Thierry Mugler, Cacharel, Kenzo, etc.).

Heading south down Rue Croix-des-Petits-Champs for about five minutes, you reach the most beautiful and atmospheric passageway in Paris, **Galerie Véro-Dodat** ⓭ (opposite Rue Montesquieu), with polished mahogany facades, brass lamps and skylights all beautifully preserved. It is named after the duo of wealthy pork butchers who financed the arcade's construction in 1826, fitting it with the new technology of the day: gas lighting. One of its main attractions is the vintage Café de l'Epoque, a good lunch spot.

A little further south, on Place du Palais-Royal, is the massive **Louvre des Antiquaires** ⓮, home to some 250 antique dealers. This area was cleared by Napoleon following an attempt on his life in 1800. Two Royalists planted explosives in a cart, but the bomb missed his carriage. Not wishing to repeat the experience, when he became emperor, Napoleon razed 50 houses. ❑

RESTAURANTS & CAFÉS

Restaurants

L'Absinthe
24 place du Marché, 1st.
Tel: 01 49 26 90 04. Open:
L Mon–Fri, D Mon–Sat. €€€
www.michelrostang.com
Although they don't
serve absinthe here and
it is more chic than
bohemian, it is still a lot
of fun. The terrace is one
of the best in Paris and
there are exhibits of contemporary artists (works
for sale).

Café Marly
Palais du Louvre, cour
Napoléon, 93 rue Rivoli.
Tel: 01 49 26 06 60. Open:
L & D daily (until 2am). €€€
With views of the Louvre
pyramid, this designer
museum café is perpetu-
ally abuzz with Parisians
and tourists. The food,
which is modern and
light, is prepared to a
high standard, but
steeply priced.

Hôtel Costes
239 rue St-Honoré, 1st.
Tel: 01 42 44 50 25. Open:
L & D daily (until 1am). €€€
The ultra-hip restaurant
of the Hôtel Costes is a
playpen for people from
fashion and film. Prices,
except for cocktails, are
only a little above
average.

L'Estaminet Gaya
17 rue Duphot, 1st. Tel: 01
42 60 43 03. Open: L & D
Mon–Fri. €€€
A fish bistro where the
menu changes every day
depending on the *marché*

du jour. The *bouill-
abaisse* is superb. Ask
for a table on the ground
floor – the colourful tiles
are a remnant of its for-
mer life as turn-of-the-
century Portuguese bar.

La Ferme
55-57 rue Saint-Roch, 1st.
Tel: 01 40 20 12 12. Open:
L & D Mon–Sat. €
A self-service *bio bou-
tique* for delicious sandwiches – free-range
chicken on bread from a
top baker (Kayser) and
salads. No credit cards.

Le Grand Véfour
17 rue de Beaujolais, 1st.
Tel: 01 42 96 56 27. Open:
L Mon–Fri, D Mon–Thur.
€€€ Hiding under the
arches of the Palais
Royal is one of the most
beautiful restaurants in
Paris. Le Grand Véfour
opened its doors in
1784 and has fed the
likes of Revolutionary
Camille Desmoulins, the
Emperor Napoleon and
writers Alphonse Lamar-
tine and Victor Hugo.

Juvénile's
47 rue de Richelieu, 1st. Tel:
01 42 97 46 49. Open: L & D
Mon–Sat (until 11pm). €€
Popular wine bar run by
British ex-pat, Tim John-
ston, who offers a truly
special – and personal –
selection of wines as
well as tapas and simple
plats du jour.

Macéo
15 rue des Petits-Champs,
1st. Tel: 01 42 97 53 85.
€€€ www.maceorestaurant.com

The modernised Second
Empire dining room is
cool, casual and elegant.
The restaurant is under
the same management
as Willi's Wine Bar next
door, so the excellent
wine list comes as no
surprise; the food to go
with it is underwhelming
however. Lots of Ameri-
can tourists. Bilingual
service.

Restaurant du Palais Royal
43 rue de Valois, 1st. Tel: 01
40 20 00 27. Open: L & D
Mon–Fri, D only Sat. €€
The most attractive ter-
race on the Palais Royal
and the finest of the
restaurants circling the
inner gardens. The food,
without being wildly
imaginative, lives up to
the view.

Le Rubis
10 rue du Marché St-
Honoré, 1st. Tel: 01 42 61 03
34. Open: L & D Mon–Fri,
L only Sat. €€
This wine bar/bistro is a
great spot for a glass of
Beaujolais and a slice of
pâté. Several plats du
jour are served, ranging
from bœuf bourguignon
to lentils with salt pork.
Informal and crowded,
the nicotine-stained
walls and half-barrel
decor are comfortingly
provincial. No credit
cards.

Scoop
154 rue Saint-Honoré, 1st.
Open: daily (until 7pm). €
A narrow lunch café that

is fun and funky. The old
stone walls abut where
you least expect them
and crooked beams come
out of nowhere. There are
love seats upstairs for
lounging. Choose from an
all-day menu of home-
made soup, sandwiches
and salad (smoked duck
breast, roast chicken,
etc.).

Willi's Wine Bar
13 rue des Petit-Champs, 1st.
Tel: 01 42 61 05 09. Open:
L & D Mon–Sat (until 11pm).
€€ www.williswinebar.com
One of the classic wine
bars in Paris. It's worth
elbowing your way
through the crowd to
sample the extraordinary
wine list, which includes
New World wines.

L'Ardoise
28 rue du Mont-Thabor, 1st.
Tel: 01 42 96 28 18. Open:
L & D Wed–Sun. €€€
A successful, modern
bistro, which offers a
good-value blackboard
menu. The typical bistro
cooking is careful, even
if the surroundings are
rather utilitarian, but the
position near the
Tuileries gardens makes
it a convenient choice.

PRICE CATEGORIES

Prices for three-course
dinner per person with a
half-bottle of house wine:
€ = under €25
€€ = €25–40
€€€ = €40–60
€€€€ = over €60.

THE LOUVRE

The largest palace in Europe, the Louvre has an incomparable collection of old masters, sculptors and antiquities

The Musée National du Louvre has something to interest everyone. It is also a building of breathtaking beauty and a labyrinth. Although getting lost is one way to discover the unexpected, wander round too long without direction and it's possible to miss even the major collections. Either use the plan opposite or pick up one showing current exhibitions on your way in at the information desk. If it all gets too much you can leave the museum and return on the same day or you can get a bite to eat and rest at one of the museum's cafés and restaurants (one of the best is the terraced Café Marly which overlooks the pyramid). The museum also has some excellent shops to buy souvenirs of your visit but don't to try to see everything in one day – return again and get lost in a different place.

LEFT: Dating from the 2nd century BC, the *Venus de Milo* with its serene gaze and soft curves rivals the *Mona Lisa* as an icon of female beauty.

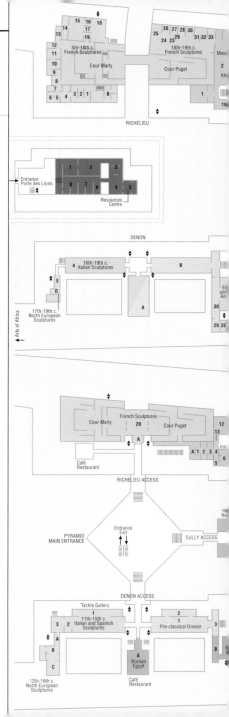

Ground Floor

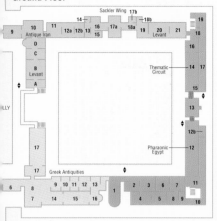

Oriental Antiquities and Islamic Art

Sculptures

Egyptian Antiquities

Greek, Etruscan and Roman Antiquities

History of the Louvre, The Medieval Louvre

Arts of Africa, Asia, Oceania and the Americas

Lower Ground Floor

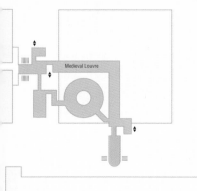

THE HIGHLIGHTS

Leonardo da Vinci's *Mona Lisa* (1503–6)
The most famous High Renaissance enigmatic smile can be found in the new Mona Lisa room.

The *Venus de Milo* (c.2nd century BC)
The mythical statue can be seen in a parallel gallery to the Galerie des Antiquités.

***Raft of the Medusa* by Géricault (1816)**
A stirring vision of suffering based on the real tale of a shipwreck and cannibalism (Grande Galerie).

***Liberty Leading the People* by Delacroix (1830)**
Iconic painting of the Revolution by the leader of Romanticism (Grande Galerie).

***The Card Cheat* by Georges de la Tour (c.1635–40)**
A young woman succumbs to the temptations of gaming, wine and luxury (French 17th-century painting).

***The Bather* by Ingres (1808)**
This celebrated figure was re-used by the painter fifty years later for his painting *The Turkish Bath* (French 19th-century painting).

***Virgin and Child in Majesty* by Cimabue (c.1270)**
This Early Renaissance masterpiece was acquired by Napoleon (Denon wing,1st floor).

***Venus and the Graces Presenting Gifts to a Young Woman* by Sandro Botticelli (c.1483)**
This is one of a pair of frescoes from the Villa Leman near Florence, thought to have been commissioned for a wedding (Denon wing, 1st floor).

***The Astronomer* (1668) and *The Geographer* (1668–9) by Vermeer**
Painted by Vermeer to celebrate the progress of science in Europe in the 17th century (Richelieu wing, 2nd floor).

***The Rebellious Slave* by Michelangelo (1513–15)**
one of a pair of unfinished sculptures intended for the tomb of Pope Julius II (Denon, ground floor).

***The Seated Scribe* (2500–2350 BC)**
This famous figure is made from painted limestone and alabaster, with eyes of rock crystal (Sully, 1st floor).

The Persian *Winged Bull* glazed tiles (c.500 BC)
This glazed, molded relief formed part of the palace of the Persian king Darius I at Susa (present-day Iran).

THE MAIN COLLECTIONS

French painting 17th–19th century
Works are arranged in chronological order from
the late Gothic period to the mid-19th century.

The Grande Galerie
This gallery contains large Neo-classical and
Romantic canvases painted for political ends.

Italian and Spanish painting
The Italian department contains early masterpieces, while the Spanish collection is patchy.

Northern Schools
Six new rooms show northern European
paintings of the 18th and 19th centuries.

French sculpture
French sculpture dominates the collection in
the courtyards of the Richelieu wing.

Decorative arts
One of the least known aspects of the Louvre,
the decorative arts collection is extensive.

Greek, Roman & Etruscan antiquities
A comprehensive collection which includes the
mythical *Venus de Milo* and the *Three Graces*.

Egyptian antiquities
The collection spans over from the fourth-
millennium BC to the 4th–6th centuries AD.

Oriental antiquities and Islamic arts
The collection is mainly from the eastern
Mediterranean and holds the oldest item in the
museum – a 7,000-year-old neolithic statue
from Ain Ghezal.

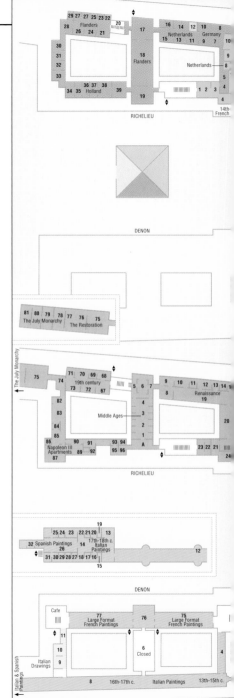

Second Floor

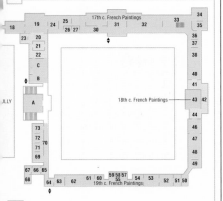

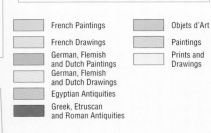

French Paintings

French Drawings

German, Flemish and Dutch Paintings

German, Flemish and Dutch Drawings

Egyptian Antiquities

Greek, Etruscan and Roman Antiquities

Objets d'Art

Paintings

Prints and Drawings

First Floor

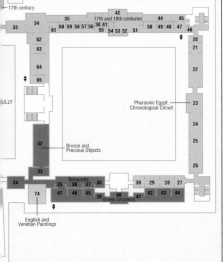

EGYPTIAN ANTIQUITIES AND ISLAMIC ARTS

The museum's spectacular Egyptian collection is very popular. Its core originates from the victory spoils of Napoleon's Egyptian campaign of 1798. The collection was subsequently expanded, largely through the efforts of the famous Egyptologist Jean-François Champollion (1790–1832), the first person to decipher hieroglyphics. Beyond the pink granite *Giant Sphinx*, insights into Egyptian life and the Nile culture are given through a thematic presentation on the ground floor, followed by a chronological presentation on the first floor. The later rooms follow religion and funerary rites.

The Oriental antiquities collection (essentially from the Eastern Mediterranean) may be overshadowed by the Egyptian collection, but it is no less important. The most spectacular items are the reconstructions of palaces at Susa and Khorsabad. The palace of Persian king Darius I at Susa (in present-day Iran) was constructed in around 510 BC. Other highlights include Cypriot terracotta figures and stag-shaped vessels, Mycenaean pots with geometric decoration, carved ivory, chalcolithic vessels from the Negev and the neolithic statue from Ain Ghezal, discovered in 1985.

ABOVE: female figurine (*c*. 4500 BC) in terracotta from Mesopotamia (Northern Syria).
BELOW: an Egyptian relief.

GRANDS BOULEVARDS AND CHAMPS-ELYSÉES

The Grands Boulevards are crowded with one-stop shoppers by day and cinema-goers by night. The Champs-Elysées has broken ranks with its brashly commercial neighbours and is regaining a reputation as a cool and stylish place to hang out.

North of the Palais Royal lie the Grands Boulevards, a string of wide avenues running from west to east. The boulevards date from the 17th century when Louis XIV tore down the medieval walls around Paris and created wide, open spaces bordered with trees for his subjects. By the 19th century, the west end of the thoroughfare was the preserve of the rich, while the east had become the playground of the city's industrial workers, lined with vaudeville theatres, restaurants, bars and brothels, and later cinemas. Today the boulevards are dominated by mass-market clothing chains, discount outlets and chain restaurants, but if you look up, the plate glass traces of the Second Empire extravagance can be seen in the ornate balconies and facades.

Maintaining a haughty distance from the populist strip is the grandest of Parisian avenues, the Champs-Elysées, designed by Le Nôtre in 1667 as an extension of the Tuileries. Initially the promenade reached only as far as the Rond-Point des Champs-Elysées. Over a hundred years passed before the rest of the avenue, stretching up to the Arc de Triomphe, was completed. Its reputation has ebbed and flowed with the centuries. Growing numbers of contemporary restaurants, trendy cafés and stylish nightclubs are joining the fashion and luxury goods boutiques that appeared through the 1990s, heralding the monumental thoroughfare's comeback as one of the world's premier leisure destinations.

Map on pages 94–95

Waxworks and arcades

Going roughly from east to west, the first place of interest, especially if you have kids in tow, is the **Musée Grévin** (10 bd Montmartre; tel: 08 91 67 67, Fri 10am–6.30pm,

LEFT:
Place de la Concorde fountains.
BELOW:
Café Le Nôtre in the Pavillon Elysée.

Beneath the auditorium of the Opéra lies an underground lake, draining water from the foundations, which inspired the setting for Leroux's Phantom of the Opera.

BELOW: the resplendent Opéra Garnier's dome is painted by Chagall.

Sat–Sun 10am– 7pm; entrance fee), a light-hearted waxworks gallery, full of cheerfully incompatible figures – from Marie-Antoinette and Gandhi to virtual heroine Lara Croft and French goalkeeper Fabien Barthez – and a hall of mirrors. The lavish decor of this century-old museum is a confection of Venetian rococo, rosewood and marble, and the staircase by Rives is an architectural gem.

To the right of the museum is the **Passage Jouffroy**, with a shop for cinema buffs, antique silver and the old-fashioned Hôtel Chopin. Next door is the soothing **Café Zephyr**, one of the few cafés with style on the Grands Boulevards. Across the busy boulevard, the **Passage des Panoramas** is one of the earliest of the covered passages. Opened in 1800 on the site of a former aristocratic mansion, Parisians flocked here to see the giant painted panoramas of different cities that were exhibited in two great rotundas. The shop Stern Graveur has been engraving headed notepaper and wedding invitations since 1840. Other shops sell lingerie,

floaty clothes, vintage vinyl and old postcards; but above all this passage is a focus for philatelists with half a dozen specialist stamp dealers.

Bourse and Opéra

On emerging from the arcades head south towards the colonnaded **Palais de la Bourse** (tel: 01 49 27 55 55; www.euronext.com; guided tours Mon–Fri; entrance fee), the French stock exchange. Built in 1808, the grand building is one of the most distinctive of the Napoleonic era.

From here, the Rue du Quatre-Septembre leads to the Place de l'Opéra. This broad square is dotted with elegant shops, luxury hotels and cafés, notably the **Café de la Paix**, where you can join the chic clientele enjoying coffee and croissants for breakfast, afternoon tea, or a glass of wine and oysters later in the day.

Soaring over the north end of the square is the city's recently restored opera house, the **Opéra Garnier** (tel: 01 41 10 08 10; www.opera-de-paris.fr; open daily 10am–4pm, entrance fee). Architect Charles Garnier was commissioned in 1860 by

Napoleon III to build an opera house for the imperial capital, and his lavish designs were wholly in tune with the pomp and opulence that characterised the Second Empire. The profusion of marble and gilt that decorates the interior is almost oppressive in its excess, but the glamour of the building's various foyers is undeniable. The grand marble staircase was conceived by Garnier as the ultimate celebrity catwalk: "Everything is designed so that the parade of spectators become themselves a show." The five-tiered auditorium, dripping in red velvet and gilt, is dominated by a six-tonne chandelier, which famously crashed down on the audience during a performance in 1896. The ceiling of the auditorium was painted by Marc Chagall in 1964. On the Rue Scribe side of the building, the Emperor's Pavilion now houses a **library and museum** (open daily 10am–5pm, entrance fee), with a collection of scores, portraits, costumes and sets.

The dance tradition at the Palais Garnier is historically strong, and, with the appearance of the Opéra Bastille in 1989, it is now the principal stage in Paris for ballet.

Across the street from the Opéra, the **Musée du Parfum Fragonard** ⓲ (tel: 01 47 42 04 56; www. fragonard.com; open Mon–Sat 9am– 6pm, Sun 9.30am– 4pm; free) is one of two small museums tracing 5,000 years of perfumery. A heady fragrance permeates the air of this museum in a beautifully restored 19th-century town house in the Rue Scribe. The second museum is located in the **Théâtre des Capucines** ⓴, where legendary music-hall singer and actress Arletty began her career in the 1930s.

Grands Magasins

The area just behind the Opera House, along Boulevard Haussmann, is dominated by the *grands magasins* (department stores). **Galeries Lafayette** and **Au Printemps**, both established in the late 19th century, have remained rivals ever since. Galeries Lafayette is especially famed for its splendid art nouveau central hall topped with a vast coloured-glass dome.

Map on pages 94–95

The following statistics give an idea of the scale of the Opéra: it has 1,991 seats, 334 boxes, 1,606 doors, 7,593 keys, 450 fireplaces and 6,319 steps.

BELOW: Cartier, Place Vendôme.

Cour des Miracles

Place du Caire (which is off Rue d'Aboukir) is rich in mementoes of Napoleon's campaign in Egypt, including sphinxes and hieroglyphics. It was here that the Cour des Miracles was established in the 1600s. By day, beggars went out on the streets, convincingly handicapped, blind and deaf. At night, they returned and shed their wooden legs and eye patches – hence the miracles. Not until 1667 did the police dare clear out this criminal enclave. Today, the square, just across from Métro Sentier, is the centre of a clothes manufacturing area, with numerous low-cost clothing shops.

Pont Alexandre III, south of the Grand Palais and Petit Palais.

Place Vendôme

With a grand vista between Palais Garnier and the Rue de Rivoli, octagonal **Place Vendôme** ㉑ is perhaps the smartest square in Paris. Laid out in 1699 by Colbert to glorify Louis XIV (whose equestrian statue was subsequently replaced in the centre by an imitation of Trajan's column featuring Napoleon's military exploits), it is now home to luxury jewellers and designers, such as Boucheron, Van Cleef & Arpels, Bulgari, Cartier, Chaumet and Dior. Here, too, are a number of big financial institutions such as the J.P. Morgan merchant bank, and, of course, there's the Ritz at No. 15. This luxury hotel is now most famous for being the place where Princess Diana had her last meal before being killed in a car crash.

Eglise La Madeleine and Place de la Concorde

Close to Place Vendôme and reached via the chic, boutique-laden Rue du Faubourg St-Honoré, **Sainte-Marie-de-la-Madeleine** ㉒

rises from the midst of the roaring traffic and expensive shops. The neoclassical church was built as a self-aggrandising exercise by Napoleon and is a favourite venue for celebrity weddings and funerals. In the square the mouth-watering displays at foodstores **Fauchon** and **Hédiard** are tourist attractions in their own right.

From La Madeleine, Rue Royale runs to Place de la Concorde, passing the Hotel de Crillon, where Benjamin Franklin signed the Treaty of Friendship between the newly formed United States of America and King Louis XVI in 1778.

The **Place de la Concorde** ㉓ has been the site of many major historical events since its completion in 1763, most importantly, the decapitation of Louis XVI by Revolutionaries in January 1793. Standing majestically in the middle of the traffic chaos, the central obelisk was a gift from the Viceroy of Egypt in 1829. The 3,300-year-old column, weighing 220 tonnes, took four years to reach Paris.

The Champs-Elysées

First initiated by Louis XVI in 1667, the Champs-Elysées was originally laid out by landscape architect Le Nôtre to create a visual prolongation of the Tuileries gardens running west from the Louvre palace. The wide street, lined with elegant gardens and rows of trees, was continued after the completion of the Arc de Triomphe in 1836 (*see opposite*). By the turn of the 20th century the Champs, in contrast to the rather common Grands Boulevards, had reached a zenith of popularity and elegance, attracting stylish and monied types from all over the world to linger on its animated café terraces.

The sophisticated spectacle on the avenue evaporated during World War I, but made a brief and giddy

comeback during the 1920s. This was followed by the Depression, World War II and, with the post-war popularity of the automobile, growing traffic problems, as the Champs shifted from a luxury address to a commercial one distinguished by numerous cinemas and airline offices during the 1950s, '60s and '70s. By the 1980s it had become quite dumpy, with an atmosphere comparable to a tatty shopping mall.

Determined to resurrect the area, Jacques Chirac, then mayor of Paris, budgeted 75 million euro to renovate, modernise and beautify the Champs: street parking was replaced by underground car parks; new street furniture was added, including handsome teak benches and retro Art Nouveau newspaper kiosks; dove-grey granite paving stones were laid; and the number of trees doubled. Not surprisingly, Parisians gave the avenue a second look. A turning point occurred in 1999 when Ladurée, the venerable Parisian tearoom in rue Royale, opened a second branch at No. 75. Today, the Champs is considered not only elegant again, but a cool place to hang out.

The commercial stretch of the Champs-Elysées runs from the Rond-Point to the Arc de Triomphe. The landmark stores are the Virgin Megastore at Nos 52–60, where you can sample CDs until midnight; Guerlain at No. 68, with its rococo-style façade and sumptuous interior; the Aladdin's cave of beauty products, Sephora, at No. 70; and Louis Vuitton at No. 101. The majority of the designer shops are concentrated around the avenue Montaigne, avenue George V south, and the rue du Faubourg St-Honoré. This is fashion land, where prices for the majority are prohibitive, but window shopping is free. Fashionable bars and restaurants have mushroomed in the surrounding streets with popular new places including: Senso, Tanjia, Spoon and Market to name but a few (*see page 119*).

On the south side of the Champs, between place Clémenceau and the river, is the glass-domed **Grand Palais ㉔** built for the 1900 World Fair. It hosts major art exhibitions

Map on pages 94–95

Guarding the Palais de l'Elysée.

BELOW: the Arc de Triomphe.

Where Gourmets Gather

The Place de La Madeleine has shops devoted to mustard (**Boutique Maille**, No. 6), caviar (**Caviar Kaspa**, No. 17), truffles (**La Maison de la Truffe**, No. 19) and the famous delicatessen, **Fauchon** at Nos 26 and 30. Prices and service are usually better elsewhere but it's fun to look around. The cheese shop **La Ferme Saint-Hubert**, on one of the square's tributary streets (21 rue Vignon), is famous for aged cheeses. Across the street is **La Maison du Miel** (No. 24) devoted to honey. **La Maison du Chocolat** (nearby at 8 boulevard de la Madeleine), is one of three outlets for Robert Linxe, the city's most renowned chocolatier.

Map
on pages
94–95

*Les Caves Augé (116
boulevard Hauss-
mann, tel: 01 45 22
16 97) is the oldest
wine shop in Paris
(since 1850). Marcel
Proust once browsed
the bottles.*

BELOW: Majorelle's
splendid Art
Nouveau interior
at Lucas-Carton.

and contains the science museum, **Palais de la Découverte** (tel: 01 56 43 20 20; www.palais-decouverte.fr; open Tues–Sat 9.30am–6pm, Sun until 7.30pm, closed public holidays; entrance fee). Its sister building, the **Petit Palais** houses the **Musée des Beaux-Arts de Paris** (closed for renovation until 2005) which has a permanent collection of 19th-century French art.

Arc de Triomphe

Crowning the Champs-Elysées is a memorial to megalomania, the **Arc de Triomphe** ❷⑥ (tel: 01 55 37 73 77; www.monum.fr; open Apr–Sept daily 10am–11pm; Oct–Mar 10am–10.30pm; closed public holidays; entrance fee). Commissioned by Napoleon in 1806, the ornately carved arch wasn't completed until after his death. Napoleon's chance to pass under the real thing came when his body was triumphantly returned to Paris for reburial in Les Invalides in 1840, 19 years after his death. Beneath the arch, the Unknown Soldier was laid to rest in 1920 and, in 1923, the eternal flame was lit. It is rekindled each evening at 6.30pm, with a wreath-laying ceremony. The platform above the arch can be reached via a lift and offers one of the finest views of Paris.

Belle Epoque mansions

Much of medieval Paris was swept away in the 19th century by Haussmann to make way for grand boulevards and Belle Epoque mansions, like the one that now houses the **Musée Jacquemart-André** ❷⑦ (158 boulevard Haussmann, tel: 01 42 89 04 91, www. jacquemart-andre.com, Métro: Miromesnil; open daily 10am–6pm; entrance fee).

The museum displays a collection of art and furniture that once belonged to wealthy collector, Edouard André and his wife, erstwhile society portrait painter, Nélie Jacquemart. Its fine art collection includes a small Uccello masterpiece, *St George and the Dragon*, as well as works by Bellini, Donatello, Rembrandt, Titian, Boucher and David. It is worth a detour.

Haussmann also built city parks like **Parc Monceau** ❷⑧, the 19th-century version of a theme park with an English-style garden and lake, a fake Egyptian pyramid, Venetian bridge, Greek colonnade and ancient tombs. The apartments surrounding it are among the most expensive in Paris.

Overlooking the park, the **Musée Nissim de Camondo** ❷⑨ (63 rue de Monceau, tel: 01 53 89 06 40) is a stately home built by a wealthy Jewish banking family, modelled on the Petit Trianon at Versailles. The remarkable collection of tapestries, carpets, porcelain, Oriental objets d'art, furniture and paintings all dating from the 18th century, were bequeathed to the state in 1935 by the passionate art collector, Count Moïse de Camondo, in memory of his son, Nissim, who was killed in action in 1917. ❏

RESTAURANTS & CAFÉS

Alain Ducasse au Plaza Athénée

25 avenue Montaigne, 8th. Tel: 01 53 67 65 00. Open: L Thur–Fri, D Mon–Fri. €€€€ (set menu) €€€€ (à la carte). www.alain-ducasse.com

Cooking elevated to art from France's first recipient of six Michelin stars (three apiece for two restaurants). According to Ducasse, his meals are not about fancy presentation but purity and essence of flavour. Expect truffles in abundance but also superb ingredients from his native Provence. The decor is a cross between Louis XV and Philippe Stark. Reservations essential.

Le Bistro de L'Etoile

19 rue Lauriston, 16th [map]. Tel: 01 40 67 11 16. Open: L Mon–Fri D Mon–Sat (until midnight). €€€ (set menu) €€€ (à la carte). This is not really a bistro but a fully fledged restaurant run by Guy Savoy. The vegetables and fish are particularly good. Wines are reasonably priced.

Café Jacquemart-André

158 boulevard Haussmann, 8th. Tel: 01 45 62 04 44. Open daily, 11.45am–5.30pm. €

This sumptuous café pulls in local residents as well as museum-goers. While waiting for your lunch salad to arrive (served with smoked salmon, breast of duck, etc.), look up at the *trompe l'œil* ceiling by Tiepolo, and a gallery of 17th-century faces staring down at you from the painted banister.

Guy Savoy

18 rue Troyon, 17th. Tel: 01 43 80 40 61; 01 46 22 43 09. Open: L Tues–Fri & D Tues–Sat. €€€€

It took some time for Savoy's imaginative haute cuisine to finally earn the highest Michelin rating, belated recognition of Paris's most inventive chef. The son of a gardener, Savoy has an obsession with vegetables and greens that anticipated the recent trend by more than a decade. He doesn't hesitate to pair truffles with lentils or artichokes. Savoy regularly makes the rounds to greet his guests.

Ladurée – Salon de Thé

16 rue Royale, 8th. Tel: 01 42 60 21 79. €

This oh-so civilised tea-room is a Parisian institution and a wonderful place to start the shopping day. Famous for its melt-in-the-mouth macaroons; the *pain au chocolat et pistache* is also a rare treat.

Lavinia

3–5 boulevard de la Madeleine, 1st. Tel: 01 42 97 20 27. €€

A restaurant/bar on the first floor of Paris's largest wine emporium. You can drink anything you buy with no corkage fee. The best approach is to order the simpler dishes and select a different glass of wine for each one with a little help from the expert house sommeliers.

Lucas Carton

9 place de la Madeleine, 8th. Tel: 01 42 65 22 90. Open: L Tues–Fri, D Mon–Sat. €€€€

Alain Senderens is one of the most exciting chefs in France and gastronomic sparks fly here amid the magnificent Art Nouveau decor. A jolting culinary experience and a bill to match.

Market

15 avenue Matignon, 8th. Tel: 01 56 43 40 90. Open: B & L Mon–Fri, D daily, Br Sat–Sun. €€€

Popular contemporary restaurant, run by globe-trotting star chef, Jean-Georges Vongerichten, next to the glamorous new Parisian head-quarters of Christie's auctioneers. East-meets-west style preparations and an international crowd against a slick backdrop.

Spoon

14 rue du Marignan, 8th. Tel: 01 40 76 34 44; fax: 01 40 76 34 37. Open: L & D Mon–Fri. €€ (set menu) €€€ (à la carte).

France meets the Pacific Rim in a mix-and-match menu from superchef Alain Ducasse. You choose a main course of fish or meat and then decide on sauces and side dishes. The wine list is packed with New World vintages. Reservations essential.

Mollard

115 rue Saint-Lazare, 8th. Tel: 01 43 87 50 22. Open: L and D daily. €€

The stunning Art Nouveau ceramic decor of this quiet, old-fashioned brasserie is as much of an attraction as its traditional menu, which runs to oysters, steaks, calf's liver with endives and *crêpes suzette*. The service can be doddery and the clientele is decidedly mature, but it's fine for a quiet meal and a glimpse of a quickly vanishing Paris.

Café Le Nôtre

Pavillon Elysée, Carré Marigny, 10 avenue des Champs-Elysées, 8th. Tel: 01 42 65 85 10. Open: B, L and D daily. €€–€€€

This pretty, wedding-cake-style pavilion in the gardens of the Champs-Elysées is famous for its pastries.

Prices for three-course dinner per person with a half-bottle of house wine:
€ = under €25
€€ = €25–40
€€€ = €40–60
€€€€ = over €60.

MONTMARTRE

The bohemian Montmartre of writers and artists is long gone, but the maze of steep and narrow streets around Sacré-Cœur still hum with life, as do the bars and clubs of a now respectable Pigalle

The "village" of Montmartre occupies the highest point of Paris, nestling into a small hillside in the 18th *arrondissement*, north of the city centre. Extending from the sometimes seedy yet always vibrant Place Pigalle in the south to the sugar-white cupolas of Sacré-Cœur, this urban village is an alluring huddle of small, steep streets and hidden steps.

In parts, Montmartre resembles a country hamlet with ivy-clad cottages and cobbled squares. Elsewhere, neon, fast-food, sex shows and tourist buses set the tone. Follow the golf hats up to Place du Tertre, filled with tourist bistros, tatty gift shops and would-be artists and Montmartre will seem brash and commercial. Enter a narrow side street, veer down a deserted flight of steps and you will be alone, wandering in Paris's most charismatic quarter.

Montmartre's beginnings

Montmartre has always stood slightly apart from the rest of the city. Legend has it that in AD 287 the Romans decapitated St Denis, the first Bishop of Paris, and two priests on the hill. St Denis picked up his head and walked off with it to where the basilica of St-Denis now stands *(see page 194)*. The hill

became known as Mons Martyrium (Martyrs' Mound). As local bar owners point out, people have been picking their heads out of the gutters of Montmartre ever since.

In the 12th century, a Benedictine convent settled on the hill and 400 years later, Henri IV took shelter in it when laying siege to Paris in 1589. His only conquest of the campaign, it appears, was the 17-year-old abbess of the time. The last mother superior here was guillotined during the Revolution at the

Map on page 122

LEFT:
the Sacré-Cœur.
BELOW:
Art Nouveau
Abbesses station.

age of 82, despite her deafness and blindness, and the convent buildings were destroyed.

Revolution has been the district's speciality ever since. In 1871, its inhabitants seized 170 cannons to defend themselves after the fall of Paris to the Prussians. The Thiers' government sent in troops to recapture them but the generals were overwhelmed, lined up on the hill and shot – so beginning the Paris Commune (*see page 24*).

For much of the 19th century, Montmartre was mined for gypsum and still retained a country charm with its vineyards, cornfields, flocks of sheep and 40 windmills. This charm and the lofty isolation of the hill attracted artists and writers. Painters and their models frequented Place Pigalle, and people flocked to the Moulin Rouge. Impressionism, Fauvism and Cubism were conceived in the lofts, bars and dance halls of Montmartre.

Pigalle peddles its speciality with energy if not subtlety.

When the bohemians migrated to Montparnasse, the district was left to sex-shop owners, pawnbrokers and cheap hotels and, for many years afterwards, Montmartre was synonymous with sleaze. Yet, today, the village is fashionable once more. Dingy strip bars have been transformed into chic rock clubs, peep shows are becoming American-style diners and the narrow streets are lined with buzzing cafés, quirky design shops, off-beat second-hand shops and hippy-chic boutiques. A new generation of bohemians are reclaiming Montmartre.

The Moulin Rouge

The kitschy **Moulin Rouge** ❶ (82 boulevard de Clichy; tel: 01 53 09 82 82; www.moulin-rouge.com) with its signature neon windmill, still does a roaring trade as tourists flock to see the high-kicking cabaret girls in feathers strutting their stuff. Of all the glitzy Parisian floor shows it is

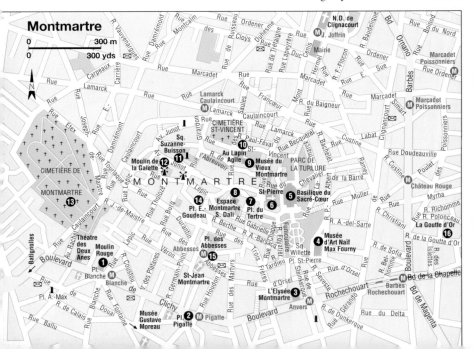

probably the most tame and traditional, but the club's history is gloriously scandalous. Toulouse-Lautrec sat here sketching the energetic cancan of working girls. In 1896, the annual Paris Art School Ball at the Moulin Rouge was the scene of the first fully nude striptease, by one of the school's prettiest models. She was arrested, and imprisoned and students went to the barricades in the Quartier Latin, proclaiming "The battle for artistic nudity" – two students died in subsequent scuffles with police.

Next door to the Moulin Rouge, teenagers and suburbanites gather at La Loco, a huge, train-shaped disco, pumping with the sounds of house, dance music and mainstream pop. And a few doors away, at No. 100 boulevard de Clichy, the Théâtre des Deux Anes offers another dose of typical Parisian cabaret.

Pigalle's changing face

A little further east along Boulevard de Clichy lies **Place Pigalle ❷**, the gateway to Montmartre. Less artistic attractions abound in Pigalle, or "Pig Alley", as it was once known to American soldiers, for it has been the core of the Parisian sex trade for several decades. Around the streets of Pigalle, tassled curtains provide glimpses of smoky interiors, slashed signs promote live sex shows and aggressive bouncers attempt to persuade tourists into "naked extravaganzas".

However, Pigalle's reputation is changing from sleaze centre to trendy night-spot. The cabarets, which once occupied half the houses along Rue des Martyrs in the 18th century, are being taken over by hip clubs, such as the Divan du Monde at No. 75, and trendy bars.

The **Elysée Montmartre ❸** concert hall has come out of retirement to host up-and-coming rock groups. The old hall greeted Russian soldiers during the Allied occupation of 1814. As they ordered their drinks (forbidden by the Russian military authorities) they shouted "bistro" meaning "quickly", thereby creating a Parisian institution. The Belle Epoque facade alone is worth the visit.

Map on page 122

The Musée de l'Erotisme (72 boulevard de Clichy, daily 10am–2am) exhibits 2,000 pieces of erotic art, from the precious to the tasteless.

BELOW: the Moulin Rouge still trades on the image of Toulouse-Lautrec.

Pigalle Nightspots

Popular venues include: **Elysée Montmartre** (72 boulevard de Rochechouart), a revitalised concert hall and dance club; **Folies Pigalle** (11 place Pigalle), a strip club turned hip club; **Le Moloko** (26 rue Fontaine), a hang-out for models, playboys and transvestites; **Le Divan du Monde** (75 rue des Martyrs), a cool, relaxed nightclub and music venue; **La Cigale** (120 boulevard de Rochechouart), an old vaudeville house with big-name acts; **Chez Madame Arthur** (75 bis rue des Martyrs), a transvestite version of the Folies Bergères; and **Le Bar Jaune** (6 rue Germain, tel: 01 42 58 03 05), a laid-back, bohemian hangout.

A call to arms at Sacré-Cœur.

Le Sacré-Cœur

The wide esplanade at the foot of the summit – or Butte Montmartre as it is known – is Square Willette. Here in front is the Halle St-Pierre, a former market hall designed by Baltard, the original architect of Les Halles *(see page 91)*, now a cultural centre housing the **Musée d'Art Naïf Max Fourny** ❹ (open daily 10am–6pm; closed Aug; entrance fee), a museum showcasing *art brut* and naïve art. The highly individual works are mostly produced by artists from around 30 countries, many of whom are self-taught and from humble backgrounds. There are numerous shops in the area specialising in cheap textiles that often attract professional designers.

Overlooking the tide of human activity that ebbs and flows beneath is the impressive white bulk of **Sacré-Cœur** ❺ (35 rue du Chevalier-de-la Barre, tel: 01 53 41 89 00; basilica open daily 6am–10.30pm; crypt 10am–5.45pm; entrance fee). To reach it, you can either walk up through the Square Willette, laid out in terraces in 1929, or take the *funic-ulaire* (cable car – Métro tickets are valid for travel) alongside the square.

The domed basilica was conceived by a group of Catholics in 1870 who vowed to build a church to the Sacred Heart if Paris was delivered safely from the Prussian siege – the heart of one of the men, Alexandre Legentil, has been preserved in a stone urn in the crypt. The Church took on the responsibility of the project in 1873 and work started two years later. Paul Abadie, the architect in charge of the project, based his design on the Romano-Byzantine cathedral of St-Front in Périgueux.

The bone-white colour of the building comes from its Château-Landon stone, which secretes calcite when it rains, bleaching the walls. Its mediocre architecture, added to its symbolic censure of a popular uprising, has rendered the Sacré-Cœur one of the Parisians' least favourite monuments.

Completed in 1914 but not consecrated until after the war in 1919, the dome offers a stunning view over Paris, up 237 narrow spiral steps (this is the second highest

vantage point over the city, after the Eiffel Tower). From the stained-glass gallery beneath there is a good view of the cavernous interior which, apart from the massive mock-Byzantine mosaic of Christ (1912–22) by Luc Olivier-Merson on the chancel's vaulted ceiling, has little else to offer.

Outside on the terrace, crowds gather together in the early evening to drink wine, strum guitars and watch the glittering lights of Paris, overlooked by statues of Joan of Arc and St Louis on horseback.

On the "butte"

Next to the Sacré-Cœur, the simple church of **St-Pierre de Montmartre ❻** is the second oldest in Paris (after St-Germain-des-Prés, *see page 151*), dating from 1133, and the only remaining vestige of the Abbey of Montmartre, where the Benedictine nuns used to live. After the Revolution, the church was abandoned, until it was reconsecrated in 1908. If you are here on Toussaint (All Saints' Day – 1 November), visit the small, romantic graveyard behind the church, because this is the only day of the year that it is open.

To the west, **Place du Tertre ❼** is the tourist trap of Montmartre, with kitschy, overpriced bistros, and craft shops selling junk. The square, once the site of the village hall, now throngs with coachloads of tourists. In the 19th century, artists began exhibiting their work here and now there are legions of mediocre artists on the square (two per square metre). This oppressive commercialisation makes it a place to avoid by day. It's more appealing at night, when the square is all lit up by fairy lights and it retains an animated charm.

Yet escaping the crowds is easy. From the Place du Tertre, quiet, winding Rue Poulbot leads through Place du Calvaire – the smallest square in Paris, which offers a spectacular view and is the intimate home of lovers and drinkers, to the **Espace Montmartre Salvador Dalí ❽** (11 rue Poulbot, tel: 01 42 64 40 10; www.dali-espacemontmartre.com; daily 10am–6.30pm,

Map on page 122

Street artists conjure up quick portraits in the Place du Tertre.

BELOW: archetypal Parisian café that inspired the film *Amélie*.

Salvador Dalí

A true eccentric, Catalan painter Salvador Dalí (1904–89) was desperate to go to Paris in the 1920s, for it was considered to be the art capital and already conquered by fellow Spaniards Picasso and Joan Miró. After studying art in Madrid and mixing with such Spanish modernists as film director Luis Buñuel, he finally reached Paris in 1929. With the help of the two established, older artists offering him introductions, and motivated by his "Catalan sense of fantasy", Dalí held his first Surrealist exhibition that very same year. Through Miró, Dalí met other Surrealists, many of whom he was to quarrel with later. Picasso once declared that Dalí's imagination reminded him of "an outboard motor continually running", and the painter himself wanted to "systemise confusion". In addition to his paintings, Dalí made films and wrote books, including an autobiography. "Every morning when I wake up," Dalí explained, "I experience an exquisite joy – the joy of being Salvador Dalí – and I ask myself in rapture, 'What wonderful things is this Salvador Dalí going to accomplish today?'."

Auguste Renoir (1841–1919) was an Impressionist who loved to paint the joyful and attractive sides of Paris, mainly using pretty girls in colourful clothes as subjects.

BELOW:
Au Lapin Agile.

9.30pm in July and Aug; entrance fee). A collection of 330 sculptures and drawings by the surrealist Catalan painter are exhibited in unusual settings here, including his famous clocks, intended to represent "the fluidity of time".

A few minutes' walk further on, Rue des Saules passes the top of Rue St-Rustique, a quiet, rustic street leading away from the buzz of the Place du Tertre, which contains the Auberge de la Bonne Franquette (tel: 01 42 52 02 42). This was originally called Le Billard en Bois, and was where Vincent Van Gogh and Auguste Renoir both painted. The crossroads outside the inn and other street scenes were immortalised by Maurice Utrillo in his paintings. Other frequent vistors to the auberge were artists Cézanne, Toulouse-Lautrec, Monet, Pissarro and Sisley, and novelist Emile Zola.

Old Montmartre
In Rue Cortot, the next street along, is the **Musée du Vieux Montmartre** ❾ (Tues–Sun 10am–

12.30pm, 1.30–6pm; closed Mon and public holidays; entrance fee), which chronicles the life and times of Montmartre and the artists' quarter in a 17th-century manor, the oldest house on the Butte.

Originally it was the country home of Rosimund, an actor in Molière's theatre company who suffered the exact same fate as his master: in 1686 he died during a performance of *Le Malade Imaginaire*, just as Molière had done 13 years earlier *(see page 104)*. Many artists had studios here, including Renoir, Dufy and Utrillo; the composer Erik Satie (1866–1925) lived in the same street. The museum is an evocation of past simplicity, gaiety and bohemian living, with pictures by Kees van Dongen (1877–1968) and Dufy, reconstructions of Utrillo's favourite café, complete with zinc countertop and absinthe bottles, and an artist's studio, with yellowing photographs and a wonderful view over Paris.

Nearby is the famous vineyard of Montmartre, cultivated since the Middle Ages. At the beginning of October, the grape harvest attracts hundreds of volunteers and the streets host processions and parties. Around 300 litres of wine are sold at auction, with the proceeds going to Montmartre pensioners.

Opposite the vineyard, at 22 rue des Saules, stands the legendary cabaret, **Au Lapin Agile** ❿ (tel: 01 46 06 85 87; www.au-lapin-agile.com; open Tues–Sun 9pm–2am; entrance fee). This was the avant-garde headquarters in 1900: a restaurant-cabaret, where Renoir and the symbolist poet Paul Verlaine (1844–96) laid tables, and Guillaume Apollinaire sang with fellow Surrealist poet Max Jacob. Picasso paid for a day's meals at the Lapin with one of his Harlequin paintings – now worth several million pounds. Now a tourist attraction, the smoke-

stained inn still has its old wooden tables, original paintings by Gill and Cubist Fernand Léger (1881–1955) – and cabaret in the evening.

Tranquil Montmartre

Far from the helter-skelter animation of Pigalle and Place du Tertre, the west of Montmartre, on the other side of St Vincent cemetery, is a puzzle of small old streets and tumbledown houses. Take the steps from Place Constantin-Pecqueur, off Rue Caulaincourt, to **Square Suzanne-Buisson** ⓫, one of the most romantic corners of Montmartre with a terrace and antiquated lamps. The square occupies the former garden of the Château des Brouillards, an 18th-century folly once inhabited by Renoir and the mad, symbolist poet Gérard de Nerval (who hanged himself in 1855, leaving a note saying, "Don't wait for me, for the night will be black and white"), and which was later turned into a dance hall. During the 19th century, the "château" could only be seen when the *brouillards* (thick fogs) of Montmartre lifted,

hence the name. In the middle of the square, a statue of St Denis washes the blood off his head while watching the old men playing boules.

From the square, Avenue Junot is one of the widest and most expensive streets in Montmartre. Constructed in 1910, the avenue cut through the ancient maquis scrubland that used to cover the hillside, where windmills turned their graceful sails and goats scampered among the trees.

The street's 1920s' Art Deco elegance has attracted the cream of Montmartre society – the singer Claude Nougaro lives in the big ochre house. Le Hameau des Artistes (No. 11) still provides artists' studios. Maison Tristan Tzara (No. 15) is named after the eccentric Romanian Dadaist poet who once lived here, and was designed especially for him by the Austrian architect Adolf Loos.

Below, on the corner of Rue Girardon and Rue Lepic, is the last of the great windmills of Montmartre, **Moulin de la Galette** ⓬. Built in 1604, the windmill became

Map on page 122

Au Lapin Agile where artists and intellectuals used to congregate.

BELOW: typical apartments in Montmartre.

Surreal sculpture of the writer Marcel Aymé (1902–68) in a square named after him in Montmartre. His short stories convey a vivid sense of the fantastic.

BELOW: Cimetière de Montmartre.

an illustrious dance hall in the 19th century. The artists and writers living in Montmartre often hosted parties here, and it was during one of these occasions that Auguste Renoir began sketches for his famous painting *Le Moulin de la Galette* (1866). Emile Zola held a party here to celebrate the success of his novel *L'Assommoir* (1877), set in La Goutte d'Or to the east of Montmartre. (The novelist lived just below the village on Boulevard de Clichy.)

Earlier, in the 1814 siege of Paris, the four Debray brothers had fought fiercely to save their windmill from the Russians – one of them was subsequently crucified on its sails. Today, the windmill is better protected, as a notice proclaims "Residence under electronic, radar and guard-dog surveillance".

Picturesque Rue Lepic, leading from the windmill and past the Moulin du Radet, descends to Place Blanche. The old quarry road housed Vincent Van Gogh and his brother Theo, an art dealer, at No. 54 for two years in the late 1880s. During that time, Van Gogh is said to have presented his paintings at Le Tambourin, a seedy cabaret on Boulevard de Clichy, until the owner demanded that he remove them, as they disturbed her customers.

Further down the hill, Rue Lepic turns into a quaint though slightly grubby market street, lined with mouthwatering shops selling pastries and exotic produce. Grab a drink at the picturesque Le Lux bar (No. 12) or across the street at Les Deux Moulins (No. 15) where Amélie Poulain worked as a waitress in the eponymous movie.

Just west of Rue Lepic, the artistic bias of the area is reflected in the **Cimetière de Montmartre** ⑬ (tel: 01 43 87 64 24; open Nov–mid-Mar Mon–Fri 8am–5.30pm, Sat–Sun from 9am; mid-Mar–Oct daily until 6pm). The tombs are elegantly sculpted and their inmates famous: here lie the 19th-century writer Stendhal, the novelist Alexandre Dumas, the poet and critic Théophile Gautier, the painter Edgar Degas, the dancer Waslaw Nijinsky, composers Hector Berlioz and Jacques Offen-

bach, and Emile Zola's bust (his body was moved to the Panthéon). The film director François Truffaut was laid to rest here in 1984.

On your way back to Pigalle, cut down Rue des Abbesses and turn left into Rue Ravignan, just before Place des Abbesses, for a detour to **Place Emile-Goudeau ⑭**, a particularly attractive square. At No. 13, modern art studios have replaced the wooden ramshackle building called Le Bateau-Lavoir, so named because it resembled a floating laundry. This artists' den housed Picasso and fellow Cubists Georges Braque and Van Dongen in the narrow ship-like corridors. Picasso painted *Les Demoiselles d'Avignon* (1907) in his chaotic studio, recalling the prostitutes of Barcelona, and Apollinaire and Max Jacob liberated verse-form in the rooms alongside. Unfortunately, the building burnt down in 1970 just as it was about to be renovated.

Turning left out of the square, take the Passage des Abbesses, a little further on, down to the pretty **Place des Abbesses ⑮** and the remarkable Art Nouveau Métro station, designed by Guimard *(see page 131)*. The rue des Abbesses is a focus of Montmartre life, with bustling cafés Le Sancerre and Le Chinon, grocery stores, wine merchants and trendy shops. The trio of streets east of the station – rue de la Vieuville, rue Yvonne-le-Tac, rue des Trois Frères – are lined with designer boutiques, offbeat second-hand shops, little galleries supporting local artists and boho bars, especially lively in the evenings.

La Goutte d'Or

To the east of Montmartre is the old working-class district of **La Goutte d'Or ⑯** centred around Barbès-Rochechouart Métro station. Vividly described by Zola in *L'Assommoir*, the district may still be one of the poorest in the city, but it

is also one of the liveliest. The conglomeration of Islamic butchers, African grocers, West Indian bakers, Jewish jewellers and Arab tailors is a never-ending spectacle of sight, sound and smell. Over 30 nationalities live side by side in the streets around Rue de la Goutte d'Or, Rue de la Charbonnière and Rue des Poissoniers. Cut-price clothes are sold at Tati on Boulevard Rochechouart.

Going up-market, the *Fédération Française du Prêt à Porter* (the ready-to-wear association) is transforming the Rue des Gardes into a new centre of fashion. Eight couture boutiques of "emerging talent" have opened in the street (Métro at Château-Rouge). Sylviane Nuffer's boutique (No. 6 bis) specialises in bustiers and corsets (in denim, cotton, leather, etc.).

La Nouvelle Athènes

South of Boulevard de Rochechouart and Boulevard de Clichy, the area known as La Nouvelle Athènes is being rediscovered. In the mid-19th century "New Athens" drew writers,

BELOW:
a good place for coffee or a snack.

Map on page 122

TIP

Tucked away among the atmospheric streets of Nouvelles Athènes is a hidden gem of a museum. The Musée de la Vie Romantique is a lovely and evocative museum, dedicated to the novelist Georges Sand and her intellectual circle of friends (Flaubert, Delacroix, Liszt and, of course, her lover Chopin). The museum has a lovely garden, open to the public for tea among the roses and wisteria.

artists and composers, among them Chopin and George Sand, as well as actresses and courtesans. The houses on Place St-Georges, the **Musée Gustave Moreau** (14 rue de La Rochefoucauld, tel: 01 48 74 38 50, www.musee-moreau.fr; open Wed–Mon 10am–12.45pm and 2–5.15pm; entrance fee), overflowing with fantastical paintings and drawings that the symbolist painter bequeathed to the state, and the **Musée de la Vie Romantique** (16 rue Chaptal, tel: 01 48 74 95 38; open Tues–Sun 10am–6pm; entrance fee; *see left*) and the exclusive private residential streets and villas off Rue des Martyrs give an idea of its rather grander past.

Rue Clauzel is an enclave of retro clothing outlets, bric-à-brac and "boho" clothes shops, including sister-act Hortensia Louisor; while the lower half of Rue des Martyrs has several good bakeries and delis.

Batignolles

West of Place Clichy, the area of Batignolles developed in the 19th century with a very different atmos-

phere from that of the grand mansions and apartment blocks of the western half of the 17th *arrondissement* around Parc Monceau. Sliced through by a huge area of railway depots that are due for redevelopment, it still retains its authentic urban fabric, with old working-class cafés, budget hotels, craft workshops and picturesque alleys and courtyards, but it is increasingly being colonised by quirky boutiques and arty bistros.

Two of the more unusual boutiques in Batignolles are L'Atelier de Maître (8 rue Brochant), an artisanal dollmaker, and Buteux (10 rue Brochant), the fine wigmaker who specialises in items for the theatre, but also rents out hairpieces for all occasions.

Parc des Batignolles was once an empty lot where the Fêtes des Batignolles were held. Transformed in 1862 into Napoleon III's idea of a London square, or park, it still has its 19th-century chalets, kiosks, glass-enclosed lookout and a miniature river and waterfall. Black swans cruise its little lake. ❏

Restaurants

Le Bouclard
1 rue Cavallotti, 18th. Tel: 01 45 22 60 01. Open: L & D Mon–Fri. € (set menu) €€ (à la carte). A shrine to the owner's grandmother Rosalie – everything is still cooked *her* way *(façon grand-mère)* from the macaroni with *foie gras* to a tarragon chicken *fricassée* and the classic chocolate fondant cake.

Casa Olympe
48 rue St-Georges, 9th. Tel: 01 42 85 26 01. Open: L & D Tues–Sat. €€. The fixed-price menus of chef

Patrice Gras are a culinary bargain and, unusually for a simple bistro, he offers an original selection of (affordable) wines by the glass for each course of the meal.

La Fourchette des Anges
17 rue Biot, Paris, 17th. Tel 01 44 69 07 69.
Open: D Mon–Sat. € (set menu) €€ (à la carte). "Angels' fork" is a soulful, cheap bistro on a quiet street just off the frenetic Place Clichy.

La Fourmi
74 rue des Martyrs, 18th. Tel: 01 46 06 15 11. Open: L & D daily (until 2am). €.

Despite its location near Pigalle, this designer café is anything but sleazy, drawing a late-night, young and dynamic crowd.

Au Grain de Folie
24 rue de la Vieuville, 18th. Tel: 01 42 64 70 35.
Open: L & D daily. €. This tiny restaurant, just off Place des Abbesses is one of the few vegetarian eateries in Paris. No credit cards.

Aux Négotiants
27 rue Lambert, 18th. Tel: 01 46 06 15 11. Open: L & D Mon–Fri (until 10.30pm). €€ A simple, rustic wine

bar/bistro. Try one of the well-prepared *plats du jour* with a wine from the Beaujolais region. Photographer Robert Doisneau was a regular.

Le Relais Gascon
6 rue des Abbesses, 18th. Tel: 01 42 58 58 22. €. This busy, good-value, bistro is a fine choice when you're on a Montmartre walkabout. Their speciality is a *salade géante* served in a big earthernware bowl.

● *Price categories:*
€ = under €25; €€ = €25–40; €€€ = €40–60; €€€€ = over €60.

The Métro

Deep beneath the streets of Paris there exists another city, a subterranean society with its own shops, cafés, market stalls, hairdressers, banking facilities, musicians, artists, beggars and pickpockets, even its own police force and its own micro climate. Temperatures here occasionally exceed 30°C (86°F), while wind speeds through the tunnels can reach up to 40 km (25 miles) per hour.

In Luc Besson's 1985 thriller, *Subway*, audiences had a glimpse of this surreal world and the eccentric characters who have made the Métro their home. In real life, it is a sad statistic that every night around 1,000 people take refuge underground, most because they have nowhere else to go.

Construction of the Paris Métro began in 1898. The first line, 10.3 km (6.4 miles) long, running between Porte de Vincennes and Porte Maillot, opened on 19 July 1900. Within a year it had carried over 15 million passengers. Since then, the Métro has extended its routes in every direction and, today, it is widely hailed as the world's cheapest, cleanest and most efficiently run underground system, carrying over 3½ million passengers daily along over 200 km (124 miles) of track to 370 stations on 14 Métro lines, 5 RER lines and 2 railway lines.

The massive station at Châtelet-Les Halles is the hub of the whole network. Five Métro lines and three RER commuter lines meet here, disgorging a quarter of a million passengers daily into its labyrinth of corridors. As you search this nightmarish warren for the exit, you may wonder if you will ever come up for air. Trudging the 75 km (47 miles) of corridors and 60 km (37 miles) of platforms, it seems unsurprising that the Parisian's average body weight is among the lowest in the industrialised world.

Métro stations abound in the city, with no point being further than 500 metres/ 550 yds away from one. Some entrances retain their elegant Art Nouveau features, designed by the late-19th century architect Hector Guimard, whose work is characterised by soft flowing lines and whiplash motifs, evoking the growth of plants. Two notable entrances that are still covered by his beautiful cast iron and glass pavilions are at the stations of Porte Dauphine and Abbesses.

Underground, the walls are mostly covered in white brick tiles, apart from a few stations such as St-Michel, which has a mosaic ceiling, and Bastille whose platforms are decorated with scenes from the Revolution.

In an attempt to make commuting slightly more bearable, the RATP (the organisation that runs both the Métro and the bus networks) organises a diverse programme of cultural events, from photography exhibitions to fashion shows, classical concerts to puppet theatre. Less organised but equally ubiquitous are the train-hopping buskers and beggars, hoping to profit from a captive audience – it is calculated that the average Parisian commuter spends a year and four months of his or her life below ground. ❑

RIGHT: the Métro is the cheapest and best method to get around after walking.

BASTILLE AND EAST PARIS

Head off the tourist-beaten track and explore the jumble of grand tree-lined avenues, grungy alleyways and bohemian-chic streets that reveal the soul of an old working-class district with a multicultural heart

Map on page 133

BELOW: Chez Prune, a cornerstone of trendy Canal St-Martin.

Traditionally, the capital has been divided into the Right and Left Banks (north and south) but these days the division between the east and west is more marked. The eastern side of Paris has long been associated with the workers and – unsurprisingly – social rebellion, beginning with that most famous revolutionary act of them all, the storming of the Bastille. This was the heartland of the Paris Commune, and today trade unions still begin their labour marches at Bastille.

Architecturally, the east of the city suffered under the reforming drive of the 1960s and 1970s. However, it is the tantalising whiff of a less salubrious past, of a grittier, less-conventional lifestyle, that makes the most appealing areas in the east – namely Bastille, Oberkampf and République – intriguing alternatives to the bourgeois conservatism of the western *arrondissements*. The east is certainly very run down in parts, but where sophistication and glamour may be lacking, creativity and youthful energy abound.

Bastille quartier

Once a fearsome bastion of royal strength, the Bastille quartier fell into disrepair and disrepute after the prison was destroyed during the Revolution. On 14 July 1789, when crowds stormed the prison, freeing the inmates – all seven of them – Louis XVI was unimpressed, recording in his diary, "Today – nothing." Following the dismantling of the Bastille, an enterprising workman made sculptures of the prison from the rubble and sold them to local councils, who were denounced as anti-Republican if they refused the high price demanded.

The medieval Bastille covered the present **Place de la Bastille** ❶

BISTROT
CHEZ PRUNE

and the Arsenal complex to the south, at the junction of the Seine with the Canal St-Martin. The modern square is a wide, busy thoroughfare with the Colonne de Juillet in the middle. The tall column was erected to commemorate the victims of the 1830 and 1848 revolutions, who are buried underneath.

Dominating the square is the city opera house, the **Opéra National de Paris Bastille 2** (box office at 130 rue de Lyon, tel: 08 92 89 90 90; guided tours Mon–Sat 10am, 1pm, 5.30pm or by reservation; tel: 01 40 01 19 70; www.opera-de-paris.fr). Its predecessor, the 19th-century Opéra Garnier, is now used to stage both ballet and opera performances. Ever since it was opened by Mitterrand in 1989, the "new" opera has been the object of much polemic from politicians, art critics and public alike. Aside from its appearance (half a goldfish bowl attached to a black triumphal arch), the opera house is actually coming apart and nets are in place to keep stone tiles from falling on people's heads.

The Bastille is one of Paris's most rapidly changing quarters. Old crumbling streets have been gentri-

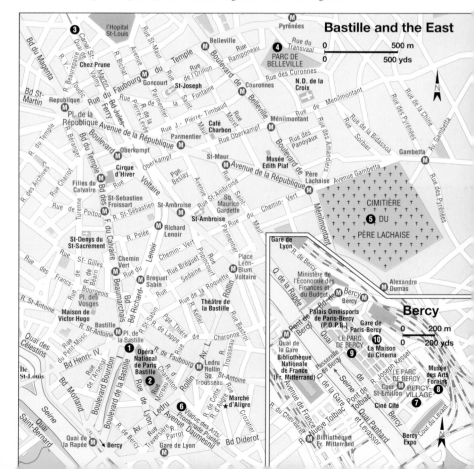

The **Marché d'Aligre**
(Rue d'Aligre,
Tues–Sun till 1pm) is
one of Paris's best and
cheapest open-air
food markets. On the
same square, the
covered market hall of
the **Marché Beauveau**
(Place d'Aligre,
Tues–Sun 8am–1pm
and 4–7pm) is the
place to stock up on
oysters and foie gras,
hundreds of cheeses
and, in season, wild
boar and venison.

BELOW:
Place de la Bastille.

fied and the old crumbling inhabitants are moving out. Some of the rebellious charm remains in streets such as Rue de Lappe and Rue de Charonne to the east of the square, yet the influx of the upwardly mobile has led to an epidemic of dimly lit bistro-bars that lure the in-crowd. Countless modern art galleries, small designer boutiques and trendy bars and cafés have sprouted up, particularly on Rue Keller, Rue de Charonne and Rue de Lappe. At night, Rue de la Roquette becomes a buzzing entertainment centre.

Le Balajo and La Chapelle des Lombards are two long-established Latin clubs on the Rue de Lappe that attract a mixed crowd of Latino locals and tourists. The Théâtre de la Bastille, on Rue de la Roquette (nothing to do with the Opéra – as the tatty decor proves), currently offers Paris's most challenging dance works.

At 17 rue de la Roquette, La Rotonde is a young, chic bar – a far cry from its past life as a brothel whose owner was shot dead by a blind accordion player. Off Rue du Faubourg-St-Antoine, you can wander through numerous passages of workshops manufacturing furniture, rugs and jewellery, as they have for centuries. Passage du Cheval Blanc leads off from the Bastille, with courtyards named after the months of the year. Passage de la Main d'Or, five minutes further on, is equally intriguing.

Oberkampf and République

As a rule, Paris is a city that doesn't change that quickly, but recent history has proved Oberkampf the exception. This area just north of Bastille has come a long way since the slums of Edith Piaf's childhood. Even six or seven years ago this was just another run-down district, but these days it is one of the hippest neighbourhoods in town – remember, though, this is the east so we're tallking urban rather than glamour. The vanguard may have moved on, but the bars, restaurants and clubs that make it so vibrant still remain.

Rue Oberkampf is the hippest limb of the 11th *arrondissement*,

especially at the upper end, east of Avenue de la République, where there's a high concentration of cafés and bars and some unusual shops. Look out for trendy bars Le Mécano and Café Charbon.

If you are looking for some of the old flavour of the area, wander down the side streets off Rue Oberkampf. Rue St-Maur, which crosses Rue Oberkampf, and Rue Jean-Pierre Timbaud are lined with tiny Middle Eastern food stores and cafés, retaining an aura of the area's Arabic inheritance.

Incorporating part of Rue Oberkampf, the eastern district of Ménilmontant is another hotbed of alternative culture. The area is home to many of the city's immigrants, forming an ethnic pastiche of cultures. It's not unusual to find a kosher butcher shop, Chinese DVD store and a Turkish snack kiosk on the same corner.

Canal St-Martin

The **Canal St-Martin ❸** begins at Pont Morland by the Seine, disappears undergound at Bastille (supposedly to allow troops faster access to subdue potential uprisings), then re-emerges in the 10th *arrondissement* at square François-Lemaître and leads up to Place de la Bataille-de-Stanlingrad. It was dug in 1821 as a transport link for the area's factories and warehouses. Many of these former factories are now art galleries and small shops.

The canal is shielded by trees, dotted with small public squares and crossed with iron bridges. It is a popular strolling and busking ground, particularly on balmy summer evenings. The bend in the canal is where you'll find the trendy Chez Prune café and a row of pastel-coloured shopfronts belonging to Antoine et Lili. On the opposite bank is the Hôtel du Nord, the subject and title of a 1930s French movie classic.

The old hotel now hosts anglophone stand-up comedy nights.

With its nine locks, the canal also makes for an attractive boat trip (Paris Canal, tel: 01 42 40 96 97).

Belleville and Ménilmontant

More than 60 nationalities make Belleville the melting pot of Paris. It is gradually becoming gentrified, which adds yet another layer of complexity. There are no major tourist attractions, five-star hotels or three-star restaurants. But it is a fascinating neighbourhood for an off-the-beaten-path excursion.

In the 19th century, Belleville was a fertile country village whose springs were tapped to channel water into Paris. There are still a few old stone *regards* left – control stations for the aqueducts, particularly in the little lanes that wind around **Parc de Belleville ❹**.

The park is a terraced crescent of green atop a high hill with a panoramic view of Paris. An "Air" museum occupies one of the terraces. The **Maison de l'Air** (27 rue Piat, tel: 01 43 28 47 63; entrance fee) is

Map on page 133

Belleville Insolite (1 rue Robert Houdin, 11th, tel: 01 43 57 09 20, www.belleville-insolite.org) is a non-profit organization of students who will take you on off-the-beaten-track tours around eastern Paris neighbourhoods such as Belleville, Ménilmontant, Charonne and Canal St-Martin. English-speaking guides are available. For information, send an email in English to belleville-insolite @wanadoo.fr.

BELOW: Canal St-Martin.

an air-measuring station hooked up to a weather satellite. A permanent exhibition demonstrates the alarming levels of air pollution in the city.

Legend has it that Edith Piaf was born under a lamp-post in the Rue de Belleville at No. 72. There is now a plaque over the doorway: *On the steps of this house, on 19 December 1915, was born, in the greatest poverty, Edith Piaf whose voice would later take the world by storm.*

The tiny **Musée Edith Piaf** (5 rue Crespin-du-Gast, tel 01 43 55 53 72, by appointment only) is a touching tribute to the diminutive queen of French chanson.

Cimetière du Père-Lachaise

The big tourist draw in the east is **Père-Lachaise cemetery** ❺ (Boulevard de Ménilmontant, tel: 01 55 25 82 10; open Nov–mid-Mar Mon–Fri 8am–5.30pm, Sat from 8.30am, Sun from 9am; mid-Mar–Oct daily until 6pm), an oasis of peace in Paris. The list of famous people buried here reads like a who's who of Paris's history – Abélard and Héloïse, Apollinaire, Balzac, Edith Piaf, Oscar Wilde, Molière, Proust, Gertrude Stein, Sarah Bernhardt, Chopin and, of course, Jim Morrison, the cemetery's most visited grave, manned by a stony-faced attendant. You can get a free map at the entrance or purchase a better one from shops that border the cemetery.

The cemetery was the site of the last battle of the Paris Commune *(see page 24)* against French troops from Versailles on 27 May 1871. At dawn the next day, the remaining Communards were lined up against a wall and shot. They were buried in a ditch where they fell, and the Mur des Fédérés (Federalists' Wall) has become a socialist shrine. Nearby are monuments to both world wars.

Viaduc des Arts

The area south of Bastille has become a potent symbol of urban regeneration in the 21st century. A disused railway viaduct and dilapidated wine warehouse district have been brought back to life, and are now thriving commercial and recreational centres.

Cimetière Père-Lachaise has a glittering cast of permanent residents.

BELOW: France's revered screen couple, Yves Montand and Simone Signoret, are buried in Père-Lachaise.

Map on page 133

Built in 1859, during the golden age of the railways, the Viaduc de Paris supported a railway from Bastille to Bois de Vincennes, at a time when the area between Gare de Lyon and Bastille was a thriving den of artisans. But, as the railways declined in the 20th century, the viaduct fell into disrepair. Thankfully, it was saved from demolition and reopened in 1998 as the **Viaduc des Arts ❻** (15–121 avenue Daumesnil). The arches beneath the viaduct have been converted into glass-fronted *ateliers* (workshops) and craft boutiques. The diversity of creativity here is impressive and from the street you can watch furniture makers, upholsterers, dress- and jewellery designers, and painters at work.

After exploring the shops under the viaduct you can take one of the city's unusual walks along the former tracks all the way across Bastille. The railway tracks on top of the viaduct have been replaced by the **Promenade Plantée**, a leafy walkway that provides a welcome green breathing space amongst the urban regeneration. Stretching for some 4 km (2½ miles) along the viaduct, and continuing at ground level through the Jardin de Reuilly and eastwards to the Bois de Vincennes, the promenade is accessible via staircases from the street.

Wandering among the rose bushes today it's hard to imagine the thunder of steam trains chugging their way to the Bois de Vincennes. It is a pleasant walk and an excellent way to see the city from a completely different angle.

Bercy

For centuries, wine was brought to Paris by boat from Burgundy, to the riverport of Bercy. Today, it is Paris's newest neighbourhood. The city is busy reclaiming the old riverport while creating a "New" Left Bank across the river, around the glass towers of the National Library *(see page 57)*. A fully automated, driverless "Meteor" line of the Métro (the first new line built since 1935) links both areas to central Paris (stops at Bercy and Cour St Emilion for the park and village, and the Bibliothèque Nationale de

The viaduct also houses the fashionable Viaduc Café (43 avenue Daumesnil, 12th, tel: 01 44 74 70 70), popular both for brunch and its late opening hours.

BELOW:
Bercy Stadium.

Map on page 133

France François Mitterrand for the New Left Bank; line 6 also goes to Bercy and Quai de la Gare on the Left Bank). The two areas will be joined in 2006 by a new footbridge, the Passerelle de Bercy.

Old stone-walled warehouses and cobbled streets have been given a new lease of life in the shape of **Bercy Village** ❼ (www.bercyvillage. com). The car-free village, centred on the Place des Vins de France, is full of boutiques, restaurants and cafés. Parisians visit its Club Med complex to enjoy a themed meal or drink designed to inspire them to book a holiday. The futuristic Ciné Cité is Paris's biggest multiplex cinema, with 18 screens showing both mainstream and arthouse films, usually in their original language with French subtitles.

Another less obvious attraction is the **Musée des Arts Forains** ❽ (Museum of Carnival Arts; 53 avenue des Terroirs de France, tel: 01 43 40 16 22; open by appointment only; entrance fee), a delightful collection of antique fairground attractions. The beautifully crafted carousels, amusements stalls, organs, stage sets and mechanical figures are displayed in the Pavillons de Bercy, a former wine depot.

Parc de Bercy

The long Quai de Bercy is backed by the vast **Parc de Bercy** ❾, graced by centuries-old chestnuts and plane trees. This riverside belt of green has nine themed sections, among them Le Jardin Romantique and Le Jardin du Philosophe. The Maison du Jardinage (House of Gardening) is an 18th-century building where green-fingered people share their secrets. The park has a lake filled with water from the Seine, neoclassical ruins and a trio of ornate bridges.

On the north side of the park, the former American Center juts out among the houses and offices overlooking the park. According to architect Frank Gehry, it expresses the spirit of a "younger country with fewer laws and fewer constraints" than Europe. It will house **La Maison du Cinéma** ❿, a film museum, research centre and film archive which is due to open in 2005 (www.51ruedebercy.com).

The reclaimed area is also the site of the vast new headquarters of the Ministry of Finance, whose edifice extends out over the Seine as if it were intended to be a bridge. Ricardo Bofil, its architect, claims it is "the monumental entrance which the east of Paris had always lacked".

The neighbouring structure, the pyramid-shaped Palais Omnisports de Paris-Bercy, is a state-of-the-art stadium seating 17,000 spectators, which offers a varied programme of concerts and sporting events from Thai boxing tournaments to opera recitals and reggae festivals. (For an up-to-date events programme and reservations see www.bercy.fr or tel: 08 96 69 70 73.) ❏

BELOW: a summer's day in Parc de Bercy.

RESTAURANTS & CAFÉS

Restaurants

Auberge Pyrénées-Cévennes

106 rue de la Folie Méricourt, 11th. Tel: 01 43 57 33 78. Open: L Mon–Fri D Mon–Sat. €€. Bring an appetite for French soul food like *caviar du Puy* (green lentils in vinaigrette) or Lyonnais-style endive salads topped with chunky bacon. The humble cassoulet and earthy Sabodet sausage are richly satisfying. Good value wines from Morgon. Among desserts, the tarte tatin takes pride of place.

Au C'Amelot

50 rue Amelot. Tel: 01 43 55 54 04; fax 01 43 14 77 05. Open: L Tues–Sat, D Mon–Sat. €€€. One long room with 10 tables, this bistro is the creation of the Michelin two-star chef Christian Constant. There is a daily menu reflecting his foray into the market. Choice is limited but when it is this good, who cares?

Bistrot à vins Mélac

42 rue Léon-Frot, 11th. Tel: 01 43 70 59 27. Open: L & D Mon–Sat (until midnight). € A wine bar/wine shop/ "vineyard" (there are a few vines on the exterior wall) just west of Place de la Bastille. Workers crowd the place at lunch time. Regional cheese and specialties from the province of Auvergne are paired with a wide choice of wines.

Bofinger

5 rue Bastille, 4th. Tel: 01 42 72 87 82. Open: L & D daily. €€ (set menu) €€€ (à la carte). A classic brasserie that claims to be the oldest in the city, with a stunning Art Nouveau interior. It serves excellent *fruits de mer* and one of the best Alsatian *choucroute* (sauerkraut) in Paris. The more creative dishes can sometimes disappoint.

Café Charbon

109 rue Oberkampf, 11th. Tel: 01 43 57 55 13. Open: L & D daily (until 6am, midnight for food). € The former coal *(charbon)* shop with its *fin de siècle* atmosphere – lofty ceilings, ornate mirrors and red-leather sofas – is a fixture of east Paris's café culture.

Chez Prune

71 quai Valmy, 10th. Tel: 01 42 41 30 47. € A cornerstone of the trendy Canal St-Martin area. This is still one of the better places in Paris to watch the world go by.

China Club

50 rue de Charenton, 12th. Tel: 01 43 43 82 20. This bar serves formidable cocktails from a long bar. The decor is supposedly reminiscent of colonial Hong Kong.

Le Pause Café

41 rue de Charonne, 11th. Tel: 01 48 06 80 33.

Open: L & D daily (Sunday until 8pm). € Hip and minimalist, located right in the trendy zone of the Bastille. Service is slow at peak times, but the heated terrace out front makes for a stylish place to sit and chat.

Comme Cochons

135 rue de Charenton, 12th. Tel: 01 43 42 43 36. Open: L & D Mon–Sat. €€ (lunch menu) €€ (à la carte) www.commecochons.com The big terrace is a great place for people-watching and browsing an honestly priced range of wines. Eat here before or after walking the nearby Promenade Plantée, elevated railway tracks now planted with roses and shrubs.

L'Oulette

15 place Lachambeaudie, 12th. Tel: 01 40 02 02 12; 01 40 02 04 77. Open: L & D Mon–Fri. €€€ www.l-oulette.com Marcel Baudis is equally at home with creative dishes and traditional fare. The fixed-price menu (lunch and dinner) is particularly good value, and during the winter months the grand menu provides the best glimpse of Gascon cooking in the city.

Le Passage

18 passage de la Bonne-Graine, 11th. Tel: 01 47 00 73 30. Open: L Mon–Fri, D Mon–Sat. €. Hidden in the elbow of an alley only

steps from a busy Bastille crossroad. The friendly staff pour out a vast selection of wine. There is grilled *andouillette* (chitterling sausage) as well as trendier things like seafood risotto or pasta. The trio of *pots de crème* makes a nice finale.

Le Square Trousseau

1 rue Antoine-Vollon, 12th. Tel: 01 43 43 06 00. Open: L & D Tues– Sat. €€. Spacious restaurant, with Art Deco ceiling lamps, colourful tiles, a glamorous bar and appetising menu of bistro classics. In summer, diners squeeze onto the terrace facing the leafy square.

Le Train Bleu

Gare de Lyon, 12th. Tel: 01 43 43 09 06. Open: L & D daily. €€€ www.le-train-bleu.com Go up the main staircase of the station, busy with commuters and pigeons, and suddenly you're in the glittering rooms of a fabulous Belle Epoque restaurant. The menu offers traditional dishes that are a bit pricey but for atmosphere it's hard to beat.

PRICE CATEGORIES

Prices for three-course dinner per person with a half-bottle of house wine:
€ = under €25
€€ = €25–40
€€€ = €40–60
€€€€ = over €60.

THE LATIN QUARTER AND ST-GERMAIN-DES-PRÉS

Writers, artists and thinkers have left their indelible mark on these areas since Roman times. Nowadays fashion, not philosophy rules on the Left Bank, but the literary legacy lives on in its historic buildings and cafés

The Latin Quarter and Saint-Germain-des-Prés, sitting side-by-side, make up the heart of the Left Bank. Once the home of artists and intellectuals, the district has changed over the past few decades, with high fashion replacing high art. Nevertheless, the Rive Gauche maintains its charm in the beautiful tree-lined boulevards, narrow streets, manicured parks and imposing monuments. This is the place in which to stroll, imbibe and look cool. Sit in the shaded parks and on café terraces by day and scan the menus in the fairylit streets by night.

What is generally referred to as the Latin Quarter lies to the east of Boulevard St-Michel, which runs from Place St-Michel on the banks of the Seine, crossing Boulevard St-Germain just in front of the ancient Roman baths of Cluny – a reminder that this was once the centre of the original Roman city of Lutétia. This maze of ancient streets and squares has been the stamping ground of students for nearly eight centuries, and Latin was virtually the mother tongue until Napoleon put a stop to it after the Revolution.

On the west side of the Boulevard St-Michel is St-Germain-des-Prés, the historical centre of literary Paris and existentialism, with the oldest church in Paris at its heart, now

chock-a-block with designer boutiques. If Saint-Germain's literary credentials remain intact it is thanks to Flammarion, Gallimard, Grasset and smaller publishers who have refused to be tempted by luxury groups' lucrative offers for their premises. As for the three monuments to the district's literary heyday – the Deux Magots, Café Flore and Brasserie Lipp – they are certainly thriving even if their clients are more likely to have Cartier than Camus on their minds.

Map on pages 142–43

LEFT: buskers outside St-Germain-des-Prés.
BELOW: breaking for lunch.

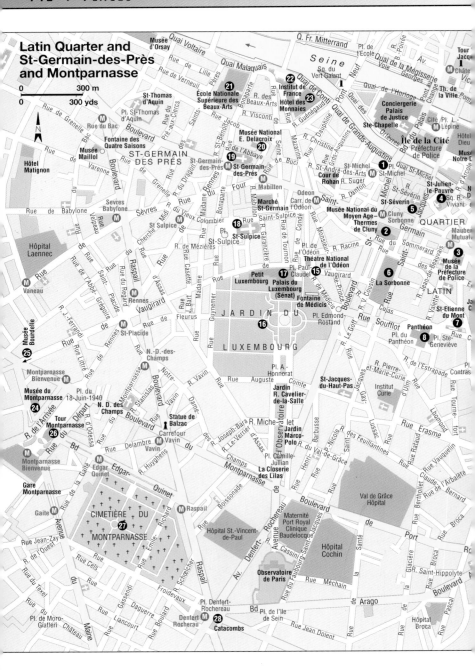

Latin Quarter and St-Germain-des-Près and Montparnasse

| 0 | 300 m |
| 0 | 300 yds |

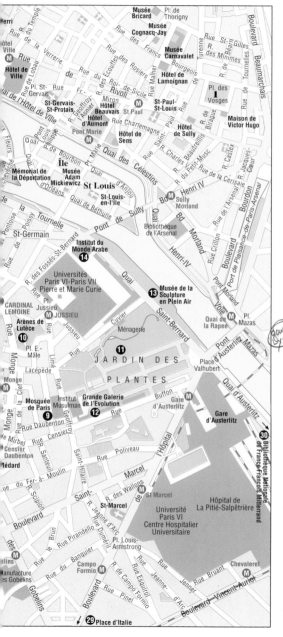

The Quartier Latin

Settled by the Romans in 53 BC and a cradle of philosophy and art since the Middle Ages, the Quartier Latin conjures up contradictions and delights in paradox, epitomised by the words of student and poet François Villon in 1456, who declared "I laugh in tears." Villon debated with professors at the Sorbonne by day and drank with thieves in the brothels of St-Michel by night. Villon's legacy of rebellion has survived. In 1871, the Place St-Michel was the headquarters of the 1871 Paris Commune. Then in May 1968 – regarded as a turning point in the history of post-war France – demonstrations against deteriorating conditions in the Nanterre faculty led to students tearing up the old cobblestones of Boulevard St-Michel to hurl at the riot police. Hundreds of students were arrested, the University of Paris was decentralised, and the ancient cobblestones were buried under concrete forever. Protests, albeit far more subdued these days, still take place, and roads are sometimes blocked by squatting students.

However, the Quartier Latin still remains a place of happy incongruity, where countless Greek souvlaki vendors stand amid traditional cafés spilling over the pavements, and new-wave cinemas front ancient academic façades.

Along the Boul' Mich

Across the river from the palaces of justice and salvation (the Préfecture de Police and Notre-Dame), **Place St-Michel ❶** revels in recklessness. The fountain depicting St Michael and a surprised dragon often seems buried under scooters, lip-locked lovers and the ubiquitous *clochards* (tramps), sitting philosophically amid youthful chaos. Extending south, the grand Boulevard St-Michel (Boul' Mich

A section of the six-panel, 15th-century tapestry, La Dame à la Licorne, *in the Hôtel de Cluny.*

BELOW: Shakespeare and Company.

to the initiated) will nourish the senses, the mind and the stomach, with an assortment of stalls, book-shops, alternative cinemas and fast-food joints.

By the crossroads of Boul' Mich and Boulevard St-Germain stands the fine 15th-century Hôtel de Cluny, which is home to the **Musée National du Moyen Age – Thermes de Cluny** ❷ (tel: 01 53 73 78 16; www.musee-moyenage.fr; open Wed–Mon 9.15am–5.45pm; closed public holidays; entrance fee). Once the residence of the Abbots of Cluny, these Gothic walls house one of the world's finest collections of medieval artefacts. Many of the treasures reflect life in the religious communities, such as illuminated manuscripts, embroideries, stained glass, liturgical vestments and various church furnishings.

Among the numerous tapestries is the exquisite, 15th-century *La Dame à la Licorne* (The Lady and the Unicorn) on the first floor of the rotunda. The six panels are beautifully worked in the millefleurs style of design, using rich, harmonious colours. The museum also holds 21 of the original heads of the Kings of Judah, sculpted in 1220 for Notre-Dame cathedral but vandalised during the Revolution.

Cluny's medieval garden is not a reproduction of a medieval garden but an imaginative modern evocation of the Middle Ages, taking its inspiration from objects in the collection and evoking the two spheres of the spiritual and the profane that governed the medieval world.

Next door are the remains of a huge **Gallo-Roman bath house** complex, which is believed to have been built in 200 AD by the guild of *nautes* (boatmen) – ships' prows are carved on the arch supports of the *frigidarium* (cold bath house). As elsewhere in their empire, the Romans living in Lutetia (their name for Paris) regarded bathing as the essence of civilisation.

Latin lanes

Heading east along Boulevard St-Germain you'll reach Place Maubert, a bustling market square at the centre of a network of small,

medieval streets lined with a jumble of boutiques revealing their shadowy interiors to the curious. The **Musée de la Préfecture de Police ❸** (1 rue des Carmes, tel: 01 44 41 52 50; open Mon–Fri 9am–5pm, Sat 10am– 5pm; free), on the second floor of the police station, houses an intriguing collection of macabre objects, weapons and documents.

Back on the banks of the Seine, quiet repose is to be found in the church of **St-Julien-le-Pauvre ❹**, (open daily 9am–1pm, 3–6.30pm; free) off Rue Lagrange, in the shadow of Notre-Dame. In the garden, you can sit under a 300-year-old false acacia. Behind is Rue du Fouarre, named after the bales of hay on which students used to perch during open-air lectures in the Middle Ages. The Italian poet Dante sat here in 1304.

Shakespeare and Company, at 37 rue de la Bûcherie, follows in the footsteps of Paris's most famous English bookshop, founded in 1921 by Sylvia Beach in Rue de l'Odéon, and frequented by Gertrude Stein, Hemingway and Ezra Pound. It closed during World War II and the present shop was founded in 1956 by American George Whitman. It contains a wide range of literature, from the Bard to the Beatniks and has attracted expatriate writers such as William Burroughs and James Baldwin. Today, it still stays open until midnight.

Le Petit Pont close by is a perfect spot from which to see the lights of the Seine shimmer at night. Here, the Quais St-Michel and Montebello offer picture-book views of the Ile de la Cité. By day, ancient bookstalls line the riverbanks, offering overpriced, antique volumes.

Trial by Revolutionary council has been replaced with trial by jazz at the **Caveau de la Huchette** (5 rue de la Huchette). Danton and Robespierre selected guillotine victims in the cellars where jazz musicians now jam. At No. 10, a young Napoleon dreamed of power.

The beautiful flamboyant Gothic church of **St-Séverin ❺**, on Rue St-Jacques, is famous for its vaulting, twisting spiral columns, mighty organ loft and ancient bell (1412).

The Sorbonne

Continue south along Rue St-Jacques and you'll come to the vast complex of the **Sorbonne ❻** (open 9am–4.30pm Mon–Fri; free; www.paris4. sorbonne.fr). Established in 1253 by St Louis and his confessor Robert de Sorbon, the oldest university in France has been rebuilt many times since its inception as a dormitory for 16 theology students, when it started to attract great thinkers from all over Europe.

In 1469, France's first printing press was set up by three Germans summoned here by Louis XI, which encouraged the growth of intellectual life. During the Revolution, the university was closed and became delapidated but Napoleon revitalised

Map on pages 142–43

TIP

Cinema buffs should pop into **Action Ecoles** or **Action Rive Gauche** (23 and 5 rue des Ecoles) for quirky film classics, both in English and French.

BELOW: Saint-Ursule-de-la-Sorbonne.

*In 1851 Leon Fou-
cault suspended a
steel, brass and lead
pendulum from the
top of the Panthéon's
dome, publicly prov-
ing that the world
was round and
rotated. The original
pendulum is dis-
played in the Musée
des Arts et Métiers
(see page 86), but a
fascinating recon-
struction of his
experiment can be
seen in the Panthéon.*

BELOW: wedding party
in Place du Panthéon.

and expanded it, and it once more became the most important university in France. Since decentralisation in 1970, there are 13 universities in Paris and the Sorbonne has lost its force but not its reputation.

Entering from Rue des Ecoles, you can wander through the corridors and galleries, which are lined with paintings that reflect the university's long history. The 17th-century chapel, commissioned by Sorbonne alumnus Cardinal Richelieu, containing his marble tomb, overlooks the university's main courtyard. Above the tomb, beautifully carved by François Girardon, hangs a hat believed to be the cardinal's. Legend has it that the hat will fall when Richelieu's soul is released from hell.

Across Rue St-Jacques, in the next block, is the **Collège de France** (open Oct–Jun Mon–Fri and Sat am; free), set up by François I in 1530 on the inspiration of the great humanist, Guillaume Budé, to offer an unexpurgated education, unfettered by the intolerance and dogmatism of the Sorbonne.

Today, the college still has its own say academically, although it is financially dependent on the state; lectures are open to the public without charge. Next door, the Lycée Louis-le-Grand is the school in which Jean-Paul Sartre taught and from which the 19th-century poet and art critic Charles Baudelaire was expelled.

The Panthéon

Climb up Rue St-Jacques, then follow the winding Rue de la Montagne-Ste-Geneviève to the church of **St-Etienne-du-Mont ❼** (tel: 01 43 54 11 79; open daily 8am–noon and 3–7pm, closed public holidays and Mon in Jul– Aug; free) where the remains of Ste-Geneviève are buried. The Parisians' most revered saint is credited with saving the city from Attila the Hun in 451 AD *(see page 18)*. Playwright Jean Racine (1639–99) and the scientist and philosopher Blaise Pascal (1623–62) are buried here, and a marble slab near the entrance marks the spot where the Archbishop of Paris was stabbed to death by a priest in 1857.

St-Etienne-du-Mont shares this commanding hilltop site with the monumental **Panthéon** ❽ (open Oct–Mar daily 10am–6.15pm; Apr–Sept 10am–6.30pm; closed public holidays; entrance fee). It was intended to be a church to Ste-Geneviève, rashly promised by Louis XV when he recovered from a serious illness in 1744. Money was short, however, and so public lotteries were organised to raise funds. Designed by neoclassical architect Jacques-Germain Soufflot (1713– 80), who drew inspiration from Rome's Pantheon, the building was finished just in time for the Revolution. In 1791 the church was designated a pantheon for the "Founders of Liberty", a monument to rival the royal mausoleum at St-Denis *(see page 194)*.

Thus Voltaire, who was transferred from the country, and Jean-Jacques Rousseau came to lie in the crypt and later Victor Hugo, Emile Zola and Louis Braille; Nobel prizewinning scientists Pierre and Marie Curie joined them in 1995. The body of the World War II Resistance hero Jean Moulin was reburied here in the 1970s.

After the Revolution, the use of the Panthéon yo-yoed from church to necropolis to church to headquarters of the Commune, until it finally became a civic building and lay temple in 1885. The interior is laid out in the shape of a Greek cross with the iron-framed dome towering above the centre. Frescoes depicting the life of Ste Geneviève line the south wall; her glorification is portrayed on the inside of the upper section of the dome.

Rue Mouffetard

Rue Mouffetard is one of the oldest streets in Paris; narrow, crowded, and full of cheap places to eat. In its lower half, there is a street market (Tues–Sat, Sun am) around the Gothic church of St-Médard. Walk there via the picturesque **Place de la Contrescarpe** (a few minutes from Place du Panthéon eastwards along Rue de l'Estrapade), a lively place to sit and people-watch with students skipping class, in a maze of surrounding streets.

BELOW: statue, Jardin des Plantes.

Ernest Hemingway's Paris

When the 22-year-old journalist Ernest Hemingway arrived in Paris in 1921, he spent his first night in room 14 of the Hôtel d'Angleterre. He rented his first apartment on the third floor of 74 rue du Cardinal Lemoine (near the Hôtel des Grandes Ecoles). He tried to write in the Café des Amateurs on the Place de la Contrescarpe until he decided it was the "cesspool of Paris" (it is now the seemingly harmless Café La Chope). Rue Mouffetard, on the other hand, was – and still is – a "wonderful narrow crowded market street".

He rented a garret hotel room at 39 rue Descartes to work in. On the Quai des Grands Augustins, he browsed the books of the *bouquinistes*, second-hand booksellers. He met Picasso for the first time in the artist's studio at nearby Rue des Grands Augustins (No. 7). The Café Pré aux Clercs (a stone's throw from the Hôtel d'Angleterre) was one of his favourite cafés. His last address in Paris was 6 rue Férou. By the time he left the city in 1926, leaving an enduring legend behind him, he was already rich and famous.

In the corner house (No. 1) Rabelais (1494–1553) composed his risqué rhymes, as did François Villon, the century before. At No. 122, towards the bottom of the hill, the well carved onto the façade dates from Henri IV's reign.

An Arab mosque and Roman ruins

The green and white **Mosquée de Paris ❾** (tel: 01 45 35 97 33; open Sat–Thur 9am–noon and 2–6pm, until 7pm in summer; entrance fee) was built in the Hispano-Moorish style in 1922 by three French architects to commemorate North African participation in World War I. Incorporating the Institut Musulman, the complex of buildings includes a museum of Muslim art, a large patio inspired by the Alhambra in Andalucia and an impressive selection of carvings and tiles. There is also a library, a restaurant, a salon de thé and a Turkish bath *(see opposite)*.

Behind a nondescript wooden doorway in the Rue Monge is the ancient gladiatorial arena, the **Arènes de Lutèce ❿**. The 15,000-

The guillotine, invented by Dr Guillotin near the Odéon.

BELOW: Grande Galerie de l'Evolution, part of the Muséum National d'Histoire Naturelle.

seat arena – destroyed by barbarians in AD 280 – was unearthed during the construction of Rue Monge in 1869; novelist Victor Hugo led the campaign to restore it. Today, where gladiator fights were once popular spectacles, the arena serves as a children's playground and on fine afternoons it echoes with the clink of *pétanque* balls.

Botanical Gardens

The **Jardin des Plantes ⓫** (open daily 7.30am–8pm in summer, 7.30am–5.30pm, until 8pm in summer; free; tel: 01 40 79 56 01) was opened in 1640 as a medicinal herb farm for Louis XIII. The oldest tree in Paris, a false acacia planted in 1635, is here. The garden expanded during the 1700s, with the addition of a maze, amphitheatre and exhibition galleries. In 1889, the Galerie de Zoologie was opened in the grounds, its object to display, conserve and study the millions of specimens brought back by globe-trotting European naturalists and explorers. The lavishly restored **Grande Galerie de l'Evolution ⓬** (open Wed–Mon

Exotic Imports

When the Jardin des Plantes was expanding in the early 18th century, the royal doctor, Fagon, and botanists such as Tournefort and the three Jussieu brothers travelled far and wide bringing back seeds from around the world. The wild and wonderful collection of flora that resulted includes a 2,000-year-old American sequoia, along with a Ginkgo biloba and iron tree from Persia. A laricio pine was grown from a seed brought back from Corsica in 1774 and the pistachio tree is almost 300 years old. The oldest Lebanese cedar in France, planted in 1734, was brought from Kew Gardens in England by the Jussieu brothers' nephew, Bernard de Jussieu. The story goes that after dropping and breaking the pot the young cedar plants were in, he nurtured the seedlings in his hat until he could return. The oldest tree in Paris, the false acacia or Robinia, brought back from America in 1635, is also here. The most attractive features for children are the 18th-century maze and the Grande Galerie de l'Evolution, part of the Muséum National d'Histoire Naturelle, set in the grounds of the garden *(see main text, above)*.

10am–6pm, Thur until 10pm, closed public holidays; entrance fee; www. mnhn.fr) is part of the **Muséum National d'Histoire Naturelle** (which includes galleries of palaeontology, mineralogy, geology and a microzoo). Its objective is to illustrate principles of evolution and dramatise the impact of human behaviour on the natural environment. The hall has retained elements of a 19th-century museum – parquet floors, iron columns, display cases – but has been completely modernised and equipped with interactive displays (mostly in French). The museum's *pièce de résistance* is the great herd of stuffed African animals that sweeps through the atrium.

For a riverside stroll, leave the gardens at Place Valhubert and head west to the **Musée de la Sculpture en Plein Air** ⑬ (open daily 10am–6pm; free), a park-cum-modern sculpture exhibition. Not the prettiest public space, and rather noisy by day, but it takes on a whole new character on summer evenings when it's used as a venue for free salsa and tango sessions.

One of the most striking buildings on the banks of the Seine is the high-tech **Institut du Monde Arabe** ⑭ (open Tues–Sun 10am–6pm; entrance fee; tel: 01 40 51 38 38; www.imarabe.org), a blend of modern Western and traditional Arab styles, symbolic of the institute's *raison d'être* – to create links and establish a deeper cultural understanding between the Western and Islamic worlds. It houses a cultural centre and museum of Arab-Islamic art and civilisation. The nine-storey palace of glass, aluminium and concrete was designed by Jean Nouvel . The southern façade is a flat patterned wall of gleaming symmetry that recalls traditional Arab latticework. The light sensitive steel and glass prisms open and close according to the movement of the sun. Views from the rooftop terrace (which has a restaurant) are breathtaking.

The Odéon

The Odéon district acts as a buffer zone between the boisterous Quartier Latin (5th *arrondissement*) and the more refined St-Germain-des-Prés

TIP

The minaret of the Paris mosque is a splendid 1920s' monument. The complex (1 place du Puits de l'Ermite, 5th) includes a tiled hammam (10am–9pm Mon, Wed, Sat for women; 2–9pm Tue for men, 10am–9pm Sun, tel: 01 43 31 18 14), and a Moorish tearoom, for mint tea and some sticky Middle Eastern pastries.

BELOW: the gleaming façade of the Institut du Monde Arabe.

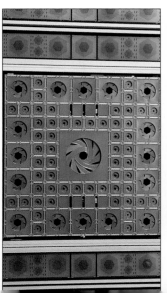

RIGHT: a quiet
moment in the Jardin
du Luxembourg.

(6th *arrondissement*). Walk along Rue St-André-des-Arts (Métro St-Michel) until you reach **Cour de Rohan**. It's worth popping in here to admire the picturesque courtyards with Renaissance façades. Turn left into Rue de l'Ancienne-Comédie, the next street along, where Le Procope, the first café to open in Paris and introduce coffee in 1686, is still doing good business.

Across Boulevard St-Germain, at the Carrefour de l'Odéon, the statue of the Revolutionary leader Georges Danton, marks the spot where his old house once stood. Fellow Revolutionary Camille Desmoulins lived at No. 2 before storming the Bastille in 1789. Others plotted in neighbouring streets to the north, which now shelter some of the most bourgeois boutiques and apartments in Paris.

From here, Rue de l'Odéon, the first street in Paris to have pavements and gutters, leads to Place de l'Odéon. Here the **Théâtre National de l'Odéon** ⑮ presents large-scale productions of foreign-language theatre, from leading playwrights such as Henrik Ibsen and Arthur Miller, while the smaller **Petit Odéon** within features avant-garde works.

Jardin du Luxembourg

The beautifully landscaped **Jardin du Luxembourg** ⑯ is the quintessential Parisian park. A haven of manicured greenery where young couples rendezvous under the plane trees by the romantic Baroque Fontaine de Médicis while children sail boats across the carp-filled lake in the middle. Statues of the queens of France gaze down from the terrace, while the thwack of tennis balls disturbs the reverie of sunbathers and smart nannies pushing babies in designer prams.

On Wednesdays and weekends, the famous Guignol puppet show is performed in the Théâtre des Marionettes. More serious entertainment is located at the corner with Rue de Vaugirard, where old men and young students play chess under the fragrant orange trees. There are 200 varieties of apple and pear trees in the garden and an apiary which produces several hundred kilos of honey

Left Bank Rendezvous

Cafés have played a huge part in the city's intellectual, political and artisic development for many years. Café Voltaire (1 place de l'Odéon), named after its most famous regular, was where, in the 18th century, Voltaire used to meet fellow philosopher Diderot to discuss their Enlightenment theories. The tormented 19th-century poets – Verlaine and Mallarmé – threw Symbolist ideas at each other here and, much later, in the 1920s, the American writers Ernest Hemingway and F. Scott Fitzgerald extolled the café's "sudden provincial quality". Other writers in Paris between the two world wars spent hours at their favourite tables in Le Procope (13 rue de l'Ancienne-Comédie), and the existentialist writer and philosopher Jean-Paul Sartre and his lover Simone de Beauvoir consolidated the highbrow reputation of Les Deux Magots (6 place St-Germain-des-Prés) in the 1950s. The Art Deco Café de Flore (172 boulevard St-Germain) was another of Sartre's favourites. Today, politicians congregate at Brasserie Lipp across the road.

a year. The **Musée du Luxembourg** in the former Orangery is used for temporary art exhibitions. most of which cover historical topics.

The **Palais du Luxembourg** ⑰ (guided tours by appointment, tel: 0142 34 20 00; www. senat.fr) was built for Marie de Médicis on the site of a mansion which belonged to Duke François of Luxembourg, following the murder of her husband Henri IV. Its Italianate style, modelled on the Pitti Palace in Florence, was intended to remind her of home. The widowed queen moved into the palais in 1625, but was forced into exile by Richelieu before it was completed, and died in Cologne, lonely and embittered. During the Revolution, the palace was used as a prison and in World War II the Germans made it their headquarters. Now it is the seat of the Sénat (the Upper House of Parliament). The adjacent Petit Luxembourg is the official home of the president of the Senate.

From Petit Luxembourg, the Rue Garancière leads north to the imposing church of **St-Sulpice** ⑱, a short walk away. Apart from one of the finest organs in Paris and Eugène Delacroix's *Jacob Wrestling with the Angel*, modelled on the painter's own struggle with Art, the great cavern of a church has little to offer. In front of the huge colonnaded façade, with mismatching towers, is a large square with an amusing fountain made by Joachim Visconti in 1844.

St-Germain-des-Prés

The historical heart of literary Paris, St-Germain-des-Prés covers an area stretching roughly from St-Sulpice to the Seine and bounded to the west by Boulevard St-Germain. Its elegant streets house chic boutiques, yet it still retains a sense of animation, with crowded cafés spilling out on to the pavements. In the 1950s the area became a fertile breeding ground for literature and ideas. Exis-

tentialists, led by Jean-Paul Sartre, Simone de Beauvoir and Albert Camus lived in cheap hotels and gathered in local cafés such as Les Deux Magots and Café Flore.

The days of black sweaters and beret-clad existentialists engaged in heated literary debate are well and truly over. The area has now been colonised by designers and antique dealers. The Marché Saint-Germain shows just how much it has changed. Following a tasteful restoration, the old market hall is now given over exclusively to fashion, surrounded by a very mixed bag of restaurants.

On the opposite side of the boulevard, the church of **St-Germain-des-Prés** ⑲ is the oldest in Paris, dating from AD 542 when it was built as a basilica for holy relics. It is named after St Germain, cardinal of Paris, who is buried here. Ransacked and rebuilt over centuries, the heavily restored 11th-century building is an unsubtle blend of simple Romanesque and pretentious Baroque. In the small square alongside, stands Picasso's tribute to his friend, the poet Apollinaire.

Map on pages 142–43

TIP

The best-known organic market in Paris is the Marché Biologique Raspail, between the Rue Cherche-Midi and the Rue de Rennes, which draws a chic crowd from all over Paris every Sunday morning.

BELOW: statue of St Sulpice, church of St-Sulpice.

Map
on pages
142–43

It was in the war years (1938–1946) that the Café de Flore, opposite its rival Les Deux Magots, came into its own. Boris Vian described its appeal: "Due to the black-outs writers didn't go far, so the Flore became like Suez, a necessary passage."

BELOW: detail from *Jacob Wrestling with the Angel*, one of three huge Delacroix frescoes in the church of St-Sulpice.
RIGHT: the Sorbonne.

Across the square, Les Deux Magots serves the best hot chocolate in Paris. Once the favourite haunt of the literati, the café is still popular – apparently, the waiters cover 12 km (7 miles) a day.

Heading east down the rue Jacob, filled with fascinating antiques and interior design shops, lies the elegant Place de Furstenburg, home of the **Musée National Eugène Delacroix** ❷⓪ (tel: 01 44 41 86 50; www.musee-delacroix.fr; open Wed–Mon 9.30am–5pm; entrance fee), where the Romantic painter Eugène Delacroix (1798–1863) spent the last few years of his life. He moved here in 1857 when he began painting the murals in the St-Sulpice church close by.

From Place de Furstenburg, narrow Rue Visconti leads to Paris's finest art school, the **Ecole Nationale Supérieure des Beaux-Arts** ❷❶ (tel: 01 47 03 50 00; www.ensba.f; open Tues–Sun 1–7pm; free), which occupies two *hôtels* fronting the Quai Malaquais. From 1608, the school was a monastery until the Revolution, when it was used to store pillaged works of art. In 1816, the School of Fine Arts moved in and today holds public exhibitions of students' work.

Close by stands the imposing **Institut de France** ❷❷, seat of the Académie Française, established in 1635. The select members of the illustrious institution, are guardians of the French language, protecting the dictionary from the insidious onslaught of English (*franglais*).

Next door is the 16th-century **Hôtel des Monnaies** ❷❸. When Louis XV installed the royal mint here, he commissioned the architect Jacques Antoine to build the workshops, completed in 1775. The hôtel now houses a museum of money and medallions, the **Musée de la Monnaie** (tel: 01 40 46 55 35; www.monnaiedeparis.f; open Tues–Fri 11am–5.30pm; Sat–Sun noon–5.30pm; entrance fee).

Along the Seine leading to St-Michel, the Quai des Grands-Augustins is the oldest quay on the river. It is lined with antiquarian bookshops and antique dealers. Picasso lived for 20 years on Rue des Grands-Augustins, which branches off the quay. ❑

RESTAURANTS & CAFÉS

Restaurants

Allard
41, rue St-André-des-Arts, 6th. Tel: 01 43 26 48 23. Open: L & D Mon–Sat. €€ (set menu) €€€ (à la carte). The dark Art Nouveau decoration makes this one of the loveliest bistros in Paris, with two intimate, atmospheric rooms evocative of Left Bank life. The traditional food – think duck with olives, roast lamb, etc. – is very good.

✓L'Alcazar
62 rue Mazarine, 6th. Tel: 01 53 10 19 99. Open: L & D daily, Br Sun. €€–€€€. Sir Terence Conran's contribution to the Paris restaurant scene was to transform this former music hall into a designer brasserie. It's been a hit with Parisians and tourists alike, thanks to the easygoing atmosphere and competitively priced menu, which includes an up-scale interpretation of British fish and chips.

✓Bistrot Côté Mer
16 boulevard Saint-Germain, 5th. Tel: 01 43 54 59 10. Open: L & D daily. €€. A Left Bank "seaside" bistro with affordable prices. From starters like ravioles de Romans au homard to a plump filet of Saint Pierre (John Dory). The tarte soufflée au chocolat amer is a superb finale.

Bouillon Racine
3 rue Racine, 6th. Tel: 01 44 32 15 60. Open: L & D daily. € (set menu) €€ (à la carte). This Art Nouveau monument historique is redolent with chandeliers and mirrored walls. A great place to sip a selection of Belgian beer as well as powerful monastery brews. For food, choose between the restaurant or the cheaper, more informal café. For the starving, there is suckling pig, roasted in beer.

Les Bouquinistes
53 quai des Grands-Augustins, 6th. Tel: 01 43 25 45 94. Open: L Mon–Fri, D Mon–Sat. €€€ (set menu) €€€ (à la carte). Under the general supervision of Guy Savoy, Chef William Ledeuil has demonstrated his powers of culinary imagination (sea bass tartare with bean sprouts, watercress and orange vinaigrette; langoustine tempura served with gazpacho) as well as a sense of fun. The romantic, mirrored decor on the Left Bank of the Seine is another plus.

Café des Délices
87 rue d'Assas, 6th. Tel: 01 43 54 70 00. Open: L & D Mon–Fri. €€ (set menu) €€€ (à la carte). A culinary virtuoso with a sense of adventure, Gilles Choukroun creates a new menu every few days in keeping with its sensual motto: Couleurs et Parfums. Visit the Luxembourg gardens before or after.

Chez Albert
43 rue Mazarine, 6th. Tel: 01 46 33 22 57. Open: L & D Mon–Sat. € (set menu) €€ (à la carte). An intimate family restaurant where fresh seafood lands on the table grilled, marinated or steamed. The rich paella for two comes heaped with fruits de mer.

Chez René
14 boulevard Saint-Germain, 5th. Tel: 01 43 54 30 23. Open: L Tues–Fri, Tues–Sat. €€ (set menu) €€€ (à la carte). Classic French bistro, two blocks from the Seine with a small outdoor terrace. It serves a savoury coq au vin and a perfectly aged entrecôte Bercy for two. The plateau de fromages is authoritative.

Lipp
151 boulevard Saint-Germain, 6th. Tel: 01 45 48 53 91. Open: non-stop daily 9am–2am. €€€. Brasserie Lipp remains the fashion barometer of Paris. To be offered a table on the first floor is social suicide, but swagger in on the ground floor nodding to passing celebs and the unthinkable ascent can be avoided. The rather dull brasserie food is variable, but nobody cares.

Moissonnier
28 rue des Fossés St-Bernard, 5th. Tel: 01 43 29 87 65. Open: L & D Tues–Sun. €€. A Parisian institution serving a mix of specialities from the Jura and the Rhône. Tempting dishes include a saladier lyonnais (salad served with crisp bacon, hard-boiled eggs and chicken livers) and quenelles de brochet (poached-pike dumplings).

Les Fontaines
9 rue Soufflot, 5th. Tel: 01 43 26 42 80. L & D Mon–Sat. €€€. Hidden behind a banal facade is one of the city's best-kept secrets. This is a bistro that takes food seriously, with huge portions of classic dishes, well cooked and with imaginative flourishes. On a good night, a noisy crowd of foodies is rarely disappointed.

Ze Kitchen Gallerie
4 rue des Grands-Augustins, 6th. Tel: 01 44 32 00 32. €€. One of the few really successful "fusion" restaurants in Paris with a menu of fish and vegetables cooked on a heated, flat-iron griddle; a variety of spices and condiments come from Asia as well as Europe.

PRICE CATEGORIES

Prices for three-course dinner per person with a half-bottle of house wine:
€ = under €25
€€ = €25–40
€€€ = €40–60
€€€€ = over €60.

MONTPARNASSE AND BEYOND

Between the wars, this neighbourhood was populated by revolutionaries and artists. Their legacy lives on, amid the modern tower blocks, in a thriving bar and café culture. Further south is the villagey Buttes-aux-Cailles quarter, Paris's Chinatown and the fast developing "New Left Bank"

Map on pages 142–43

BELOW: Tour Montparnasse.

The once rural area southwest of the Jardin du Luxembourg was christened Mount Parnassus (after the classical home of Apollo and his muses) by a local Dead Poets' Society in the 17th century, which gathered on quarry mounds to recite verse. Around the turn of the 20th century, the area became a magnet for artists, composers and revolutionaries, including Chagall, Léger, Soutine, Picasso, Modigliani, Lenin and Stravinsky. Some had decamped from Montmartre because of the inflated rents; others were emigrés in search of refuge or a new beginning, drawn to a city that embraced freethinkers and the avant-garde. They rented studios in a converted wine warehouse designed by Eiffel known as La Ruche (the beehive) on Rue de Dantzig, and gathered in the cafés and brasseries such as Le Select, Le Dôme, La Rotonde and La Coupole *(see page 159)*. Their bohemian lifestyle is as much a part of the Parisian myth as the era's legacy of artworks *(see page 156)*.

After World War II, writers and philosophers such as Jean-Paul Sartre, Simone de Beauvoir, Henry Miller and Louis Aragon moved in, patronising the same cafés clustered around the lively Carrefour Vavin, now Place Pablo Picasso, which still throbs with life well into the early hours. The Closerie des Lilas was among their favourite haunts *(see page 159)*.

On the artists' trail

Close by, on boulevard Raspail stands Rodin's dramatic **Statue de Balzac**. The sculpture so shocked the Société des Beaux-Arts when unveiled at the 1898 Salon that it was turned down, and only finally cast and installed here in 1939.

Tucked away down one of the small alleys of artists' studios that

previously littered Montparnasse, the **Musée du Montparnasse ㉔** (21 ave du Maine; tel: 01 42 22 91 96) was once a studio and art school run by Russian avant-garde artist Marie Vassilieff. Exhibitions here focus on different aspects of the area's artistic heritage, through photos and archive material as well as paintings.

Spread over the former apartment and studio of Antoine Bourdelle, the **Musée Bourdelle ㉕** (16 rue Antoine-Bourdelle, open Tues–Sun 10am– 5.40pm) is a showcase for the work of the modernist sculptor who was a pupil of Rodin. Bourdelle is best known for his friezes on the Théâtre des Champs-Elysées.

The Tour Montparnasse

The district, in fact the whole of the southern skyline, is dominated by the lumbering, 59-storey **Tour Montparnasse ㉖** (open daily; entrance fee). If you've a head for heights and the stomach for a lightening-fast lift, the roof terrace offers superb views of Paris. At the foot of the tower, facing an ugly shopping centre, is the **Place du 18 Juin 1940**, named in commemoration of the day on which General de Gaulle sent his famous BBC radio message, urging the French to carry on resisting German occupation: "We have lost a battle, but not the war."

Behind the tower is the Gare Montparnasse, which serves northwestern France. In the mid-19th century, thousands of Bretons emerged from this station, fleeing rural poverty and famine in Brittany, hence the many crêperies in the area.

Gravestones and old bones

On Boulevard Edgar Quinet, which has some nice cafés and a lively morning market (Weds and Sat), is the **Cimetière du Montparnasse ㉗** (tel: 01 44 10 86 50; open Nov–mid-Mar Mon–Fri 8am– 5.30pm, Sat from 8.30am, Sun from 9am; mid-Mar–Oct daily until 6pm). Among those buried here are the sculptor Antoine Bourdelle, composer Saint-Saëns and writers Baudelaire, Guy de Maupassant, Jean-Paul Sartre and Irish writer, Samuel Beckett who spent many years in Paris.

The Fondation Henri Cartier-Bresson opened in 2003. Its mission is "to preserve the independence and keep alive the spirit" of the photographer. The Fondation is located at 2 Impasse Lebouis, 14th arrondissement. Métro: Gaîté. Tel: 01 56 80 27 00; www.henricartier-bresson.org.

BELOW: Art Deco brasserie, La Coupole, is making a comeback.

L'Ecole de Paris

Today, the name Ecole de Paris still conjures up the incredible artistic momentum of Paris between the wars, the mood of intellectual ferment, of artistic and literary debate, and the arrival of cocktails, jazz and the tango. It was neither a school or a movement, nor an organised group or association of artists – rather it is an appellation that has come to designate those essentially foreign-born artists who congregated around Montmartre in the first decade of the 20th century, and later, after World War I, in the cafés and studios of Montparnasse.

Paris was an intellectual and cultural magnet; a bold city, where academic tradition had been challenged by the Impressionists, Cézanne and the Fauves; a city open to avant-garde currents like Cubism, Expressionism and Dadaism. As its reputation for free-thinking and artistic innovation spread, Paris also became a magnet for foreign artists in search of refuge or a new beginning, be they Jews escaping the ghetto, Russians fleeing the Revolution or Americans seeking adventure and an escape from Prohibition.

Although not a style, the Ecole de Paris is associated with figuration, not abstraction, marked by a form of expressionism and a certain relationship to the contemporary world, not Surrealism. At its centre were Chagall, Soutine, Modigliani, Foujita, Pascin, Kisling and Van Dongen. More peripheral figures include Picasso (although he's such a massive figure of modern art that he is hard to fix in any school) Chana Orloff, Marie Vassilieff, and Maurice Utrillo among others.

The Ecole de Paris, though, was as much to do with lifestyle as artistic style. These artists rented studios at La Ruche, Cité Falguière, Villa Seurat and countless others around Montparnasse. But exchanges also took place in the neighbouring cafés and brasseries, such as Le Dôme, La Rotonde and the glamorous La Coupole.

The artists painted each other, but also writers, critics and poets like Apollinaire, Max Jacob, Gertrude Stein and Henry Miller. Their paintings captured drinkers, dancers and prostitutes, Parisian icons like the Eiffel Tower, and themes like clowns and the circus.

Curiously, though, the figure who best epitomises the liberated spirit of artistic Montparnasse was not an artist, but model and muse Kiki de Montparnasse. Born Alice Prin in 1901, she arrived in Paris during World War I, and soon became part of the artistic circle who met at the Café de la Rotonde. Painted by Soutine, Van Dongen, Kisling and Foujita with her characteristic black fringe, she also entered the Surrealist pantheon, as mistress and model of Man Ray; she starred in several of his experimental films and in his photo *Le Violin d'Ingres*. Beautiful, charming, outrageous, Kiki painted, danced, sang lewd songs at Le Jockey and published her memoirs at the age of 28.

Perhaps, then, one should take Ecole de Paris literally, that it is Paris the city, not any particular academy or teacher, that was the inspiration, as place of liberty, cultural melting pot and school of life.

Work by the Ecole de Paris artists can be seen in many museums including the Centre Pompidou, the Musée d'Art Moderne de la Ville de Paris, the Musée de l'Orangerie and the Musée d'Art et d'Histoire du Judaïsme.

LEFT: La Rotonde in the 1930s, a popular hang-out for Montparnasse artists and writers.

If you're still in macabre mood after a walk through the graveyard pay a visit to the **Catacombs** ❷ (tel: 01 43 22 47 63; open Wed–Sun 9–4pm, Tues 11am–4pm; entrance fee) below Place Denfert-Rochereau, where the neatly stacked skulls, femurs and tibias of some six million departed souls line the long passageways. The former Roman quarries were converted into ossuaries in 1785, when cartloads of skeletons were removed from the overflowing cemeteries at Place des Innocents and other areas. Take a torch, and someone to hold your hand, as the inscription on the door reads: "Stop. You are entering the empire of the dead."

Around Place d'Italie

Place d'Italie ❷ is one of the main traffic nodes of the 13th *arrondissement*, a neighbourhood where historic districts alternate with soulless tower blocks thrown up in the 1960s. The square itself is dominated by the modern Centre Commercial Italie. More down to earth is the food market on Boulevard Auguste-Blanqui (Tues, Fri, Sun am).

Les Gobelins is the oldest part of the neighbourhood. Traces of a Gallo-Roman necropolis were discovered here last century as well as the tomb of the first archbishop of Paris, St-Marcel. The district owes its name to Jean Gobelin, a dyer from Bruges, and the **Manufacture Nationale des Gobelins** (42 ave des Gobelins, tel: 01 44 08 52 00; open Tues–Thur for tours in French, 2–2.45pm; entrance fee) a tapestry factory founded in 1662. Today visitors can still watch weavers at work.

Hidden just south of Place d'Italie is the tranquil villagey *quartier* of **La Butte-aux-Cailles**. Up until the last century, the hill was still covered with working windmills and water mills. The narrow, cobbled streets of this traditional workers' neighbourhood, where tourists rarely venture, offer some of Paris's friendliest, cheapest bars. The hub of activity is around the cobbled Rue de la Butte-aux-Cailles and the Rue des Cinq-Diamants. Though a few trendy restuarants have opened here, it's still unassuming and a delightful area to visit.

Map on pages 142–43

Mail man pictured at the Musée de la Poste at 34 Boulevard de Vaugirard (Mon–Sat 10am–6pm), which traces the history of carrying letters and of French philately.

BELOW: typical housing in the 13th *arrondissement*.

Map on pages 142–43

Chinatown is a close neighbour, roughly bordered by Avenue d'Italie and Avenue d'Ivry – a mini-city of skyscrapers where streets are lined with kitsch gift shops, Thai groceries, Vietnamese pho noodle bars and Chinese patisseries and tea rooms.

The "New" Left Bank

The "new" Rive Gauche (Left Bank) is the biggest urban renewal project since the mid-1850s, when Baron Georges Haussmann razed the city's medieval heart to carve out stately, tree-lined boulevards. Newly created streets and buildings are going up in a zone of rusty factories and disused railway tracks that extend south along the river from the Austerlitz railway station.

The area's architectural centrepiece is the **Bibliothèque Nationale de France** ③⓪ (tel: 01 53 79 59 59; www.bnf.fr; open Tues–Sat 9am–8pm, Sun noon–7pm) – or the TGB (Très Grande Bibliothèque), as Parisians have taken to calling it. Designed by architect Dominique Perrault, and opened in 1997, the library cost in excess of $1 billion and it is more expensive to maintain than the Louvre. Its 90-metre (300-ft) high glass towers are meant to evoke open books on end. They are set on top of a plank-covered plinth about 305 metres (1,000 ft) long. Below the towers is a sunken, glassed-in garden of pine trees. Whether or not you like it, the TGB is an undeniably impressive building.

Art galleries, upscale cafés, restaurants and boutiques have cropped up in the newly created streets. The **Rue Louise-Weiss** alone has 10 art galleries. Each gallery promotes its own stable of up-and-coming and established artists working in a wide-range of media. In an unusual display of solidarity, the galleries have synchronised openings.

Look out for Air de Paris (No. 32, www.airdeparis.com) that displays new conceptual art by young international artists, Galerie Jennifer Flay (No. 20), one of the best places for keeping track of trends in the rest of France, the UK and the US, Galerie Emmanuel Perrotin (Nos 5 and 30, www.galerieperrotin.com), with a focus on the young Japanese avant-garde, and Galerie Almine Rech (No. 24, www.galeriealminerech.com) which often features photography.

Nightlife on the Seine

This extension of the Left Bank is meant to have its own "Latin Quarter" with 30,000 students on a new Paris campus planned for 2006. There are also ambitions to install high-technology enterprises that will boost employment. The existing side streets have been extended to the banks of the Seine and the riverbanks have been landscaped.

The riverside here is Paris's hottest new area for nightlife, with a flotilla of barges where you can eat, drink and dance. The Batofar, the Guinguette Pirate, Péniche Blues Café and Péniche Makara, to

BELOW: corner café, La Butte-aux-Cailles.

RESTAURANTS & CAFÉS

Restaurants

L'Avant-Goût
26 rue Bobillot, 13th. Tel: 01 53 80 24 00. Open: L & D Tues–Fri. € (set menu) €€ (à la carte) The inventive cuisine of chef Christophe Beaufront draws an appreciative crowd. The house specialty is roast pork *pot-au-feu* or, in season, *sanglier* (wild boar) cooked for seven hours. The wine list is intelligent and affordable.

La Cagouille
10 place Constantin-Brancusi, 14th. Tel: 01 43 22 09 01; 01 45 38 57 29. Open: L & D daily. €€ (set menu) €€€ (à la carte) Gérard Allemandou learned to love seafood on the Atlantic coast where he grew up. His restaurant and cooking has much in common with the west coast of the USA. Grilled, roasted or fried, his seafood has an exquisite flavour. He also serves superb Cognacs from cellars in his native Charente.

La Closerie des Lilas
171 boulevard du Montparnasse, 6th. Tel: 01 40 51 34 50. Open: L & D daily (until 1.30am). €€ The historic brasserie retains its charm and offers richly satisfying fare though it does cash in on its reputation as a famous 1920s watering hole – tables are

inscribed with the names of Lenin, Modigliani and Surrealist poet André Breton and Hemingway's plaque rests on the bar. A pianist plays in the evening.

La Coupole
102 boulevard du Montparnasse, 14th. Tel: 01 43 20 14 20. Open: L & D daily (until 1am). €€ (set menu) €€€ (à la carte) This vast, legendary brasserie – the largest in Paris – is making a comeback. Waiters offer elegant service in a 1920s dining hall with food that is hit and miss.

L'Ô à la Bouche
124 boulevard du Montparnasse, 14th. Tel: 01 56 54 01 55; fax: 01 43 21 07 87. Open: L & D Tues–Sat. €€ Frank Paquier learned his trade from two of France's most talented chefs – Troisgros and Savoy. His ambitious menu includes signature salads and main courses like veal chops with *morilles* cooked in truffle oil. In the best bistro tradition, it is crowded and noisy.

Le Paradis Thai
132 rue Tolbiac, 13th. Tel: 01 45 83 22 26 Open: L & D daily. €€ The discreet décor offsets beautifully presented Thai and Vietnamese specialities and the varied menu considerately indicates levels of spiciness.

Le Parc aux Cerfs
50 rue Vavin, 6th. Tel: 01 43 54 87 83. Open: L & D daily. €€ (set menu) €€€ (à la carte) A former artist's *atelier* with a cosy mezzanine and interior courtyard. The Mediterranean menu is short but full of flair. The owner, an oenologue, offers an excellent, fairly priced wine list, and the ice creams and sorbets are home made.

La Régalade
49 avenue Jean-Moulin, 14th. Tel: 01 45 45 68 58; fax: 01 45 40 96 74. Open: L Tues–Fri, D Tues–Sat. €€ Classic bistro fare reinterpreted by a former chef of Le Crillon, one of the city's palatial hotel kitchens. Much praised and very popular, so reservations are a must.

Wadja
10 rue de la Grande-Chaumière, 6th. Tel: 01 46 33 02 02. Open: L Tues–Sat & D Mon–Sat. € (set menu) €€ (à la carte) The friendly owner serves a cheap market-fresh lunch menu with her own wine in a vintage 1930s dining room. A la carte takes over in the evening with imaginative starters such as terrine of wild duck and figues and hearty meat or fish mains.

RIGHT: Le Dôme, Boulevard du Montparnasse.

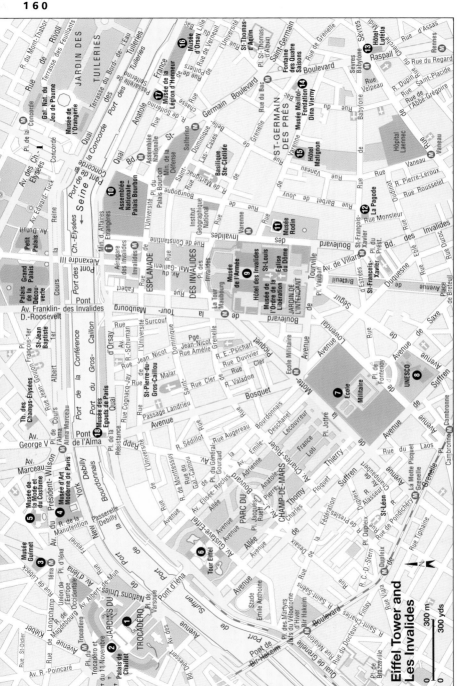

Eiffel Tower and Les Invalides

0   300 m

0   300 yds

THE EIFFEL TOWER AND LES INVALIDES

You can enjoy a bird's-eye view from the top of the tower and experience a rat's-eye view underground. At ground level, you can explore military splendour and the Musée d'Orsay's 19th-century art collection

Map on page 160

The Eiffel Tower looms above the Seine like a giant playing hide and seek among the grand apartment blocks of the 7th *arrondissement*. At the foot of the tower is the Champs de Mars. This stretch of parkland that was once a military exercise ground now teems with tourists all year round.

Facing the tower at the southern end of the Champs de Mars is the Ecole Militaire, the military academy where Napoleon trained. Glimpses through the shuttered security are rare, but occasional open doorways reveal fountains, statues and soaring stairways.

To the east, the Esplanade des Invalides is another splendid carpet of green that rolls from the gleaming gilt-domed church of the Hôtel des Invalides to the Seine and the Pont Alexandre III.

A chilly elegance prevails in the wide boulevards that link these great monuments and green expanses, but drift away from the crowd-filled Champ de Mars, and savour the gracious tree-lined streets bordered by *hôtels* (mansions), whose sumptuous apartments are occupied by senior civil servants, captains of industry and rich, retired Americans.

Across the river lies the 16th *arrondissement*. This area constitutes a sizeable slice of western

Paris and, like the 7th, it is full of smart residences occupied by wealthy inhabitants. Not for those in search of the arcane or the avant-garde, this is the bastion of BCBG *(bon chic, bon genre)*, a never-never land of big hair, Burberry plaid, diamond rings, pedigree dogs and Berthillon ice-cream. The reason most tourists and Parisians venture here is to visit one of the museums around the Place du Trocadéro, or to gaze at the magical views to be had across the Seine to the Eiffel Tower.

BELOW:
statue at the Trocadéro, Palais de Chaillot museum.

A gendarme keeping the peace.

Palais de Chaillot

Start by crossing the Seine to the Trocadéro. From here, framed by the cascading fountains and gold statues of the **Jardins du Trocadéro** ❶, the Eiffel Tower can be seen at its most magnificent. Dominating the Place du Trocadéro is the **Palais de Chaillot** ❷, built for the Paris World Fair of 1937. The imposing pseudo-Classical palace was designed in the shape of an amphitheatre, with its wings following the original outline of the old Trocadéro, built for the 1878 World Fair. The building holds three museums, but major restoration is ongoing and much of the complex is inaccessible.

In the west wing, one museum you can visit is the **Musée de la Marine** (tel: 01 53 65 69 53; www.musee-marine.fr; open Wed–Mon 10am–6pm, entrance fee) which charts the history of France as a seafaring nation. Hundreds of models, often of superb craftsmanship, cover everything from historic battleships and three-masted schooners to langoustine fishing boats and primitive canoes. A large window looks onto the restoration workshop where you can watch models being made and repaired. The development of modern marine warfare is traced from the first torpedoes to nuclear submarines. Other displays include navigational instruments, sections on ship-building and rope-making, carved whale teeth and giant lighthouse lenses.

Also in the west wing, the **Musée de l'Homme** (Museum of Mankind; tel: 01 44 05 72 72; www.mnhn.fr; open Wed–Mon 9.45am–5.15pm; entrance fee) has world-class African, Aztec and Mayan collections, but they are almost all now in storage, waiting to be moved to the new Musée du Quai Branly (www.quaibranly.fr), which will open in 2006.

The east wing, former home of the Musée des Monuments Français, is currently being renovated. A new **Cité de l'Architecture et du Patrimoine**, combining the original architecture museum with the Institut Français d'Architecture – an architectural exhibition centre currently at 6 rue de Tournon in the 6th arrondissement – is due to open

in 2005. The new institution will serve as both a public museum and a research centre for professionals.

The Musée du Cinéma, once housed in the east wing, is closed. Its collection will be moved to the new **Maison du Cinéma** located in the former American Center at Bercy (www.51ruedebercy.com) in 2005 *(see page 138)*. The **Aquarium du Trocadéro**, closed since 1985, is scheduled to reopen in 2005.

Against the backdrop of the Palais de Chaillot, the terraces and grassy banks of the garden play host to flamboyant skateboarders and rollerbladers. At night, when the ornamental pool's huge fountains are lit up, the sight is spectacular.

Place d'Iéna

The **Musée Guimet** ❸ (tel: 01 56 52 53 00; www.museeguimet.fr; open Wed–Mon 10am–6pm; entrance fee) in Place d'Iéna is one of the world's finest Asian art museums. Reopened in 2001 after five years of renovation, the once-dusty museum has been enlarged and rejuvenated with spacious day-lit galleries that give its collections new visibility. It is home to a superb collection of oriental art and statuary from China, Japan, India, Tibet and Nepal, Afghanistan and Pakistan, Korea and Vietnam – a reflection, in part, of France's colonial past. The prize exhibits are the Cambodian Buddhist sculptures from the temples of Angkor.

Back on the Avenue du Président-Wilson to the east, the Palais de Tokyo contains the underrated **Musée d'Art Moderne de la Ville de Paris** ❹ (tel: 01 53 67 40 00; open Tues–Fri 10am–5.30pm, Sat–Sun 10am–6.30pm; closed for renovation until the end of 2004, call for opening date; free). The museum gives a coherent survey of 20th-century art, in particular relating to the city of Paris, with strong holdings of the Fauves, Ecole de Paris *(see page 156)* and conceptual art from the 1970s. Its masterpieces include works by Picasso, Matisse (*La Danse*, 1932), Modigliani and Soutine, and the world's largest painting: Raoul Dufy's *Fée de l'Electricité* (*Electricity Fairy*), a celebration of light and energy com-

Map on page 160

BELOW: Musée Guimet, one of the best museums of Asian art in the world.

In 1784 Napoleon entered the Ecole Militaire as a cadet. He left as a sub-lieutenant a year later, with the recommendation: "He will go far, circumstances permitting."

BELOW:
the Eiffel Tower.

missioned for the 1937 World Fair. The museum is particularly well known for its temporary exhibitons.

Housed in the opposite wing of the Palais de Tokyo, the **Site de Création Contemporaine** (tel: 01 47 23 54 01; www.palaisdetokyo.com; open Tues–Sun noon–midnight) is a state-funded venture, intended to serve as a sort of laboratory for current art production. An adventurous, multi-disciplinary programme focuses on young artists through exhibitions, performances and workshops.

On the north side of the Avenue President Wilson, the imposing Italianate Palais Galliera is hard to miss. It houses the **Musée de la Mode et du Costume ❺** (tel: 01 56 52 86 00; open Tues–Sun 10am–6pm during exhibitions; entrance fee), which has 12,000 outfits and 60,000 accessories dating from the 18th century to the present day. To rotate this rich collection, only a fraction of which can be displayed at one time, the museum holds two exhibitions a year focusing on either a historic period, a theme or a designer.

The Eiffel Tower

It's a short walk from the Trocadéro gardens across the Pont d'Iéna (built by Napoleon to celebrate another of his victories) to the **Tour Eiffel ❻** (www.tour-eiffel.fr; open Sept–mid-Jun daily 9.30am–11pm, Jul–Aug till midnight; entrance fee). When Gustave Eiffel's icon of iron girders was chosen as the centrepiece to the World Fair of 1889, he claimed enthusiastically, "France will be the only country with a 300-metre flag-pole!" But his designs were met with a barrage of opposition. The Opéra architect Charles Garnier and the novelist Guy de Maupassant were the most vocal opponents; Maupassant organised a protest picnic under the tower's four legs – "the only place out of sight of the wretched construction".

However, the Parisian public loved their new tower and only a few years later it was being lauded by writers and artists such as Apollinaire, Jean Cocteau, Dufy and Utrillo. Surviving a proposal for its dismantlement in 1909, when the placing of a radio transmitter at the

Vital Statistics

At 321 metres (1,054 ft) high, including the masts, the Eiffel Tower was the tallest building in the world until the Empire State Building was constructed in New York in 1931. On hot days, the ironwork expands, enabling it to grow as much as an incredible 15 cm (6 inches).

A masterpiece of engineering, Gustave Eiffel's tower, the world symbol of Paris, is held together with 2.5 million rivets and the 10,100 tonnes of iron exerts a pressure of 4 kg per sq cm (57 lb per sq inch), the equivalent of the weight of a man sitting on a chair. Even in the strongest of winds, the tower has never swayed more than 12 cm (4 inches). Up to 40 tonnes of paint has to be used when it is painted every seven years. There are 360 steps to the first level, where there is an audio-visual presentation of the tower's history, and another 700 to the second. There is always a queue for the tower's lifts, which travel 100,000 km (62,137 miles) a year. On the third level is Gustave Eiffel's sitting room. On a clear day panoramas of over 65 km (40 miles) can be seen.

top saved the day, the tower is now swarmed over by some six million visitors a year.

The first two floors are negotiated on foot or by lift, and then another lift goes up to the top which, apart from being a meteorological station and aircraft navigation point, is an observation point that can accommodate up to 800 people at a time. The view from here is awesome. At night, the tower is transformed into a skeletal tableau, lit up by arc lights.

Ecole Militaire

Stretching beneath the Eiffel Tower, are the ever-crowded gardens of the **Champs-de-Mars**. For centuries this was the site of a market garden supplying vegetables to Parisians. After the Ecole Militaire was built in 1752 the area was turned into a military exercise ground with a capacity for 10,000 men. The first balloon filled with hydrogen rather than hot air was launched from here in 1783, and it was the venue for the first anniversary celebration of the storming of the Bastille – a miserable Louis XVI was forced to attend.

At the far end of the gardens is the imposing **Ecole Militaire ❼** (closed to the public). Louis XV commissioned the military college to help men of little means learn the art of soldiering. Bonaparte studied here for a year in 1784. The splendid 18th-century academy, designed by Jacques-Ange Gabriel, is still the centre of French military expertise. The main façade, with its Cour d'Honneur enclosed by colonnades, borders Avenue de Lowendal.

Behind this university of war is the foundation for reconciliation and understanding, the headquarters of **UNESCO ❽** (tel: 01 45 68 16 42; www.unesco.org; open Mon–Fri 9am–6pm; closed during conference sessions; free). The graceful, Y-shaped building was designed by an alliance of American, French and Italian architects, and engineers led by Bauhaus member Marcel Breuer. Inside, 142 countries cooperate in educational, scientific and cultural projects. A temple of modern art, its decoration is equally cosmopolitan: Joan Miró ceramics, Henry Moore sculptures, an Alexander Calder

Map on page 160

In the Eglise du Dôme, Napoleon's remains lie in six coffins, one inside the other. The last giant coffin, made of oak, is elevated on a base of green granite and surrounded by 12 damsels representing his 12 military campaigns.

BELOW: Trocadéro sculpture.

mobile and a huge Picasso mural. The Japanese garden displays a spine-chilling relic of war – a stone angel found after the atomic bomb blast at Nagasaki in 1945.

Hôtel des Invalides

The gleaming dome of the **Hôtel des Invalides** is a masterpiece of French Classical architecture and one of Paris's most prominent landmarks. Behind it is a remarkable 17th-century set of buildings commissioned by Louis XIV to house and care for retired and wounded soldiers. It also served as the royal arsenal, and it was from here, in 1789, that revolutionaries comandeered 30,000 rifles for the storming of the Bastille. Napoleon, whose wars kept the hospital full, restored the institution to its former glory, making the church a necropolis and regilding its dome. The **Eglise du Dôme** (tel: 01 44 42 54 52; open daily 10am–6.45pm; closed public holidays; entrance fee) contains the tomb of Napoleon. The Emperor's body was returned to the city from St Helena in 1840 with much pomp

A sculpture of Auguste Rodin, whose career took off after a visit to Italy in 1876, where he discovered Michelangelo.

BELOW: Rodin's *The Thinker.*

and ceremony, and eventually laid to rest in the church crypt. The emperor's mausoleum is fittingly overblown *(see page 165)*.

Spread across either side of the Cour d'Honneur the large **Musée de l'Armée** (tel: 01 44 42 37 72; www. invalides.org; open Apr–Sept daily 10am–5.45pm, Oct–Mar 10am–4.45pm; combined entrance fee for tomb and museum) offers an extensive view of man's inhumanity to man, and skill at warfare, from the Stone Age to Hiroshima, with a terrifying selection of weapons, armour and poignant displays of the two world wars.

In a separate wing, the **Musée de l'Ordre de la Libération** (open Mon–Sat 2–5pm; closed Sun and public holidays; entrance fee) commemorates the Resistance fighters who received the Order of Liberation, France's highest honour created by Charles de Gaulle in 1940.

Stretching to the Seine, the beautiful **Esplanade des Invalides** is another symmetrically designed garden much loved by strollers, joggers, dog-walkers and roller-

Auguste Rodin

One of the world's smallest artists (at 1.65 metres/5 ft 4 in), Auguste Rodin was born in the Quartier Latin in 1840 and grew up wandering the markets of Rue Mouffetard *(see page 61)*. Rejected by the Ecole des Beaux-Arts, he trained himself, visiting the zoo at the Jardin des Plantes and the horse markets on the Boulevard St-Michel for inspiration. A trip to Italy in 1876, where he discovered Michelangelo, transformed his career.

Further stimulus came from his incessant love affairs, which were interrupted only for a short while when the sculptor took holy orders. This was a reaction to the death of his sister in a convent, after she had been rejected in love by one of Rodin's close friends. Chastity did not suit him, however, and a year later he returned to his mistresses and his art. Among his most famous works are *The Kiss, The Thinker, The Burghers of Calais, God's Hand* and the unfinished *Gates of Hell*, on which he worked from the 1880s until his death in 1917. He was honoured with a pavilion by Pont de l'Alma for the Exposition Universelle, where he exhibited hundreds of his small groups.

bladers. Along the west side is a series of boules courts. Opposite is a small airport coach terminal which doubles as a metro and RER station. From here, you can either head west along the Seine to the Place de la Résistance and the sewers *(see page 170)* or east to the Musée d'Orsay *(see page 169)*.

Heading east, you pass the colonnaded **Assemblée Nationale (Palais Bourbon)** ⑩ (tel: 01 40 63 69 81; www.assemblee-nationale.fr; open Sat at 10am, 2pm, 3pm; closed during sessions; passport required), which is the Lower House of the French Parliament. The extravagant columns were grafted onto an 18th-century facade by Napoleon to complement La Madeleine across the river and now shelter an armed guard, protecting the 491 *députés* (Members of Parliament).

Musée Rodin

At the end of Rue de Varenne, next to Les Invalides, is the Hôtel Biron which houses the **Musée Rodin** ⑪ (tel: 01 44 18 61 10; www.musee-rodin.fr; Apr–Sept Tues–Sun 9.30am–5.45pm, Oct–Mar until 4.45pm; entrance fee). Auguste Rodin's first critically acclaimed sculpture was *The Age of Bronze* (1877), depicting a naked youth caressing his hair, modelled by a Belgian soldier. The establishment was shocked, maintaining that the statue was too lifelike to be regarded as art. A card stuck to the work at the Paris salon read: "Beware – moulded from the body of the model." Eventually, the French government bought the statue and Rodin's reputation was confirmed.

Rodin came to live in the Hôtel Biron in 1908 and stayed there until his death in 1917. He paid his rent with his best works which form the basis of the museum's exquisite collection. Here you can admire *The Kiss* (removed from the Chicago World Fair of 1893 for being too shocking), *The Thinker* (reputedly Dante contemplating the Inferno), *The Burghers of Calais, The Hand of God* and many other works.

Recently restored to their white marble finish, the statues ripple with life; many of the bronzes are outside in the beautiful rose garden. Bronze

Map
on page
160

TIP

Maison Poujauran (18–20 rue Jean-Nicot) is a tiny, late 19th-century boulangerie, but behind its old-fashioned pink façade you'll find some of the best *baguettes* and *sablés* (biscuits) in town (the shop is the official supplier to the Elysée Palace).

BELOW: Musée Rodin in the Hôtel Biron, where the artist lived from 1908.

casts of several of Rodin's major works are displayed amid the large lawns, hedged enclosures, pools, mature trees and topiaried yews providing a context for the studies and smaller works around the house.

Also included in the exhibition are works by Camille Claudel, the most famous of Rodin's mistresses and a gifted artist in her own right.

Around Les Invalides

The area around Les Invalides is well worth exploring: start with Paris's most interesting cinema and tea house, **La Pagode** ⑫ in Rue de Babylone, about a 10-minute walk along Rue d'Estrées. The tea is strong, the gardens tropical and the films up-to-date.

When Parisian nobility moved out of the Marais in the 18th century, and Versailles tumbled, the rich and famous built new town houses across the river from the Tuileries. Beautifully preserved, they are now mostly behind heavily secured gates, since only French ministries and foreign governments can afford the rent. About 15 minutes further

on, across Boulevard Raspail (No. 45), stands **Hôtel Lutétia** ⑬, its extravagant statued facade fronting a deluxe, four-star hotel where Charles de Gaulle enjoyed his first night of married life. When the hotel was requisitioned by the Gestapo in 1940, the owner bricked up the vintage wine cellar and, even though the hotel staff were interrogated to reveal the whereabouts of the *cave*, no one talked.

Continue walking along Boulevard Raspail in the direction of the Seine until you come to Rue de Grenelle on the left, a narrow street stacked with beautiful buildings, including the Swiss and Dutch embassies, the Ministry of Education and the National Geographic Institute. Just into the street on the left is the Hôtel Bouchardon where the poet Alfred de Musset lived between 1824 and 1839, before going on an oriental voyage of discovery with George Sand. It is now the **Musée Maillol – Fondation Dina Vierny** ⑭ (6 rue de Grenelle, tel: 01 42 22 59 58; www.museemaillol.com; open Wed–Mon 11am–6pm, from 10am in sum-

The Musée d'Orsay has new permanent galleries on the ground floor (the side of the Rue de Lille) in order to exhibit, on a rotating basis, the 50,000 images in its photographic collection.

BELOW: the main hall, Musée d'Orsay.

Map
on page
160

mer; entrance fee), where the works of Aristide Maillol are on show, along with art by contemporaries Cézanne and Degas. Dina Vierny, owner of the private collection, was an art dealer and model for Maillol, whose sculptures adorn the Jardin des Tuileries. Next door, the grandiose **Fontaine des Quatre Saisons** was a monumental response to a local complaint about lack of water.

Rue de Varenne, one street over, has a collection of fine old houses, the most famous being the Paris residence of the French Prime Minister, **Hôtel Matignon ⑮**, which has the biggest private garden in the city.

Musée d'Orsay

No visit to Paris is complete without making the pilgrimage to the **Musée d'Orsay ⑯** (tel: 01 40 49 48 14; www.musee-orsay.fr; open mid-Jun–Sept Tues, Wed, Fri–Sun 9am–6pm, Thur until 9.15pm; from 10am in winter; entrance fee). The former railway station is crammed full of the finest art works (95 percent of which are French) spanning the period from 1848 until World War I broke out in 1914. The building, finished in two years in 1900, was almost torn down to make way for a hotel in 1970. Prompted by public outcry, government ministers fulfilled the prophesy of painter Edouard Detaille, who said at the opening ceremony in 1900 that the station would make a better museum. Its glass and iron construction was a triumph of modernity, rivalling Eiffel's tower, while the façade reflected the Palais du Louvre across the river. The museum was designed in 1977 by Italian architect, Gae Aulenti, and opened in 1986 *(see page 60)*.

The works are arranged on five levels around a vast central aisle, which makes a grand setting for sculpture by artists such as Rude, Pradier, Cavelier and Guillaume. But the best pieces are by Carpeaux, the major figure of Second Empire sculpture, including his controversial *La Danse*, for the Opéra Garnier.

Other artworks are shown chronologically starting on the ground floor which has works by Ingres

BELOW: *Crispin and Scapin (c. 1850)* by painter, sculptor and caricaturist Honoré Daumier, in the Musée d'Orsay.

Map on page 160

(notably *La Source*), Romantic painting by Delacroix, including the boldly colourful *Lion Hunt*, and Manet's nude *Olympia* (1863), which was pronounced pornographic at the 1865 Paris salon and is considered to be the first "modern" painting.

The museum's biggest draw, the Impressionist paintings, hang on the crowded top floor, bathed in soft light from the station's glass-vaulted roof. The galleries are full of paintings by Monet, Manet, Renoir, Pissarro, Degas, Cézanne and Van Gogh. At the end is a small café under a large clock with a terrace high above the Seine, offering sweeping views over Paris.

On the mezzanine are works by the Nabis painters, Vuillard, Bonnard and Denis. There is also a fine collection of Art Nouveau decorative arts including furniture by Majorelle, Guimard, Henri Van der Velde and a wood-panelled salon by Alexandre Charpentier.

If you are interested in medals and military decorations you should visit the next door museum, the **Musée National de la Légion d'Honneur et des Ordres de Chevalerie** ⓲ (tel: 01 40 62 84 25; open Tues–Sun 11am–5pm; entrance fee) tracing the history of France's most celebrated award, created by Napoleon I. The interior colonnaded courtyard is also a pleasant place to rest.

City sewers

For a surprisingly entertaining experience, descend into the bowels of the capital at Place de la Résistance, next to Pont de l'Alma. The **Musée des Egouts de Paris** ⓳ (tel: 01 53 68 27 81; open May–Sept Sat–Wed, 11am–5pm; Oct–Apr till 4pm; closed last three weeks of Jan; entrance fee) offers an excursion into the city's sewer system and an underground museum full of surprising facts about waste and water. Described by Victor Hugo in *Les Misérables* as the "other Paris", this network of tunnels follows the well-known streets above ground. Accompanied by a film and, unsurprisingly, a strong odour, it is the alternative tour of Paris. ❏

BELOW: details from two of the Musée d'Orsay's finest works: *L'Absinthe* by Edgar Degas and *L'Arlésienne* by Vincent Van Gogh.

RESTAURANTS & CAFÉS

Restaurants

L'Affriolé
17 rue Malar, 7th. Tel: 01 44 18 31 33. Open: L & D Tues–Sat. €€ (set menu) €€€ (à la carte).
One of the most appealing bistros in the neighborhood, with colourful mosaic tables and decorated with traditional objets de cuisine. The menu is seasonal and changes daily, and dishes are artfully presented with little *amuse-bouches* (appetisers). Reservations recommended.

Arpège
84 rue de Varenne, 7th. Tel: 01 45 51 47 33. Open: L & D Mon–Fri. €€€€.
Alain Passard is one of the heavyweights of French cuisine. His small restaurant is always crowded. The wine list is encylopedic and expensive (no wines by the glass).

L'Atelier Joël Robuchon
Hotel Pont-Royal, 7 rue de Montalembert, 7th. Tel: 01 42 22 56 56. Open: L & D daily. €€€ Superchef Robuchon came out of retirement to open this deluxe "snack bar". It's out with long sophisticated menus, and in with the tapas principal, involving small portions of outstandingly creative dishes (order as many as your appetite or budget will allow). Reservations or first seatings only (11.30am and 6.30pm). No smoking.

Au Bon Accueil
14 rue Montessuy, 7th. Tel: 01 47 05 46 11. Open: L & D Mon–Fri. €€ (set menu) €€€ (à la carte).
The Eiffel Tower can be seen looming from the pavement tables of this neighbourhood favourite. Inside is a cosy dining room. The daily menu is based on market-fresh produce and the prix-fixe menu is great value.

Bellota-Bellota
18 rue Jean-Nicot, 7th. Tel: 01 53 59 96 96. Open: L & D Tues–Fri, Br, L & D Sat non-stop 11am–11pm.€€-€€€
A gem of a tapas bar specialising in the fine Iberian ham after which it is named, as well as Spanish cheeses, wine, and seafood. Great for grazing or a light, romantic dinner. You can stop in and dine at the bar if you're early; otherwise reserve one of the handful of tables.

Le Café du Marché
38 rue Cler, 7th. Tel: 01 47 05 51 27. Open: Mon–Sat 7am–midnight, Sun 7am–5pm. £ € The best café on rue Cler, one of the most atmospheric and convivial pedestrian market streets in the city. Come here in the morning and enjoy a *café au lait* and a croissant on the spacious terrace. The kitchen whips up good salads and daily specials at lunchtime.

Le Café de l'Esplanade
52 rue Fabert, 7th. Tel: 01 47 05 38 80. Open: L & D daily (until 2am). €€€. This café-restaurant has it all: breathtaking views of Les Invalides, opulent decor by Jacques Garcia, a fashionable crowd and good, if expensive contemporary food.

Café Lenôtre
Pavillon Elysées, Carre Marigny, 10 avenue des Champs-Elysées, 8th. Tel: 01 42 65 85 10. Open: B, L & D daily. €€-€€€
This pretty, wedding-cake style pavilion in the gardens of the Champs-Elysées serves cosmopolitan food and is famous for its pastries.

La Fontaine de Mars
129 rue St-Dominique, 7th. Tel: 01 47 05 46 44. Open: L & D daily (until midnight). €€ (set menu) €€€ (à la carte). In a dinky arcaded square next to a handsome 19th-century fountain, this restaurant serves French classics. The house speciality, *cassoulet au canard confit*, is the real thing and so is the *île flottante*.

RIGHT: before the mid-day rush.

MUSÉE D'ORSAY

The national museum of 19th-century art is best known for its French Impressionist paintings but its collection also contains key pieces from other contemporary movements

Middle Level

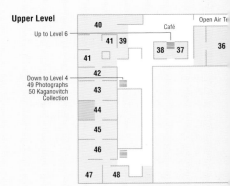

Upper Level

Most visitors to the museum come to see the Impressionist and Post-Impressionist paintings, contained in the Galerie des Hauteurs. Below is a brief tour. The first room (29) is dominated by Manet's controversial masterpiece *Déjeuner sur l'Herbe* while his pastels are exhibited further on (rooms 37, 38). Monet and Renoir (rooms 32, 34, 39) were the two artists who, in the 1870s, stuck closest to the Impressionist ideal of pure colour and modelling through light while Van Gogh (room 35) sought expression through both colour and the brushstrokes themselves, as in the uneasy, blue *Self-Portrait*. Cézanne (room 36) originally exhibited with the Impressionists, but differed from them in his search for fundamental underlying structure. Don't miss the two large panels by Toulouse-Lautrec depicting his favourite models, dancers and personalities. In room 44, are examples of Gauguin's later works painted in the Pacific. The paintings point to his rejection of modern Western civilisation and his championing of primitivism, both in his lifestyle and and in his use of colour, stylised forms and pattern.

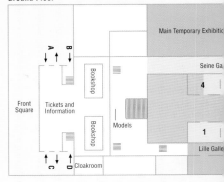

Ground Floor

ABOVE: the skylit sculpture aisle runs the length of the museum along the old railway tracks.
FAR RIGHT: Manet's *Olympia* caused a scandal in 1865.

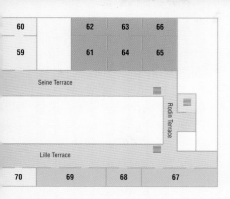

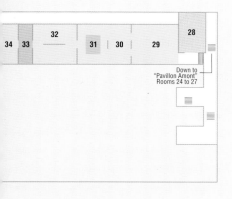

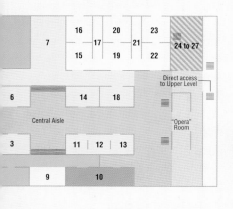

THE HIGHLIGHTS

The sculpture aisle

François Rude's monument *Napoleon Waking up to Immortality* expresses Romantic grandeur. Late neoclassical exercises by Pradier, Cavelier and Guillaume draw on antique sculpture while Mercié's *Young David* looks to the Renaissance. At the rear of the aisle is an interesting model of the opera district.

Ground floor paintings

Cabanel's sentimental *Birth of Venus* (1863); the shocking (at the time) *Olympia* by Manet; the expressive *Crispin et Scapin* and the 24 painted clay heads, *Célébritiés du Juste Milieu,* both by Daumier and *La Source* by Ingres are worth looking out for on this floor.

Upper level paintings

The Galerie des Hauteurs contains the wealth of the Impressionist and post-Impressionist paintings. Here are a few highlights: Manet's *Déjeuner sur l'Herbe*; Monet's *Poppyfield*; Degas' *L'Absinthe*; Van Gogh's blue *Self-Portrait;* the *Card Players* by Cézanne and *Tahitian Women on a Beach* by Gauguin.

Middle level works

The opulent Salle des Fêtes houses academic marble sculpture and also Fantin-Latour's famous group portraits *Table Corner* and *A Studio in the Batignolles Quarter* and Vuillard's work, *In Bed.*

Decorative arts works

The Decorative arts galleries on the ground floor and mezzanine parallel developments in fine art. The highlight on the ground floor is the wardrobe by Diehl and Brandoly. On the mezzanine there is a fine collection of Art Nouveau decorative arts.

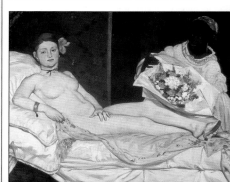

PARIS PARKS

On both sides of the city's busy ring road lie green havens, from the ancient woods and gardens of Boulogne and Vincennes to the new-age Parc André-Citroën and the futuristic Parc de la Villette

Map on page 177

BELOW: boating lake in the Bois de Boulogne.

In 1759 Voltaire declared "We must cultivate our garden", but it was not until the 19th century that Paris began to make parks and gardens a touchstone for the health of the capital. While the 1980s may be remembered as the decade of the *grands projets* and monumental building, the 1990s and the new millennium have seen the city's parks and gardens flourish. Politicians have realised that improving the urban environment is a vote-winner. Derelict industrial sites are flower-ing and blossoming into suburban parks with a fervour not seen since Haussmann's day. Now, more than ever, Parisians are looking to their green spaces as an escape from the increasing congestion and stress of urban living.

Bois de Boulogne

Past the necklace of the *périphérique* ring road to the west of Paris, the **Bois de Boulogne ❶** (Métro: Porte Maillot, Porte Dauphine, Porte d'Auteuil, Sablons; www.boisde-

boulogne.com) is one of the reasons that the 16th *arrondissement* alongside it is preferred by the wealthy as a place to live – Avenue Foch, perhaps the most expensive residential street in the capital, leads straight to its park gates. Embraced by an elbow of the Seine, this 860-hectare (2,125-acre) expanse of woods and gardens has been the Sunday afternoon playground for generations of Parisian families. Historically, it has also had a reputation for love, as successive kings used to house their mistresses here and, after Louis XIV opened the woods to the public in the 17th century, it was noted that "marriages from the Bois de Boulogne do not get brought before the Right Reverend".

In 1852, Napoleon III had the surrounding wall of the royal hunting ground, built by Henri II, demolished and the park was remodelled on Hyde Park in London. It now offers gardens, wild woods, horse racing at France's two famous racecourses, Longchamps and Auteuil, a sports stadium, boating, museums, restaurants and theatre.

A good place to start exploring the Bois de Boulogne is from the beautiful Art Nouveau Métro stop at Porte Dauphine and the best way is by bicycle, which can be rented (May–Sept daily; Oct–Apr Sat–Sun) near the Pavillon Royal, off the Route de Suresnes. A network of cycle paths and nature trails intersect the woods, enabling easy access to the vast park and its scenic lakes and waterfall. Be advised that walking around the park at night is not recommended.

To the north is the **Jardin d'Acclimatation** (tel: 01 40 67 90 82; www.jardindacclimatation.fr; open Oct–May 10am–6pm, Jun–Sept until 7pm; closed some public holidays; entrance fee), an amusement park for children, with a hall of mirrors, zoo, go-kart racing, a wooden fort,

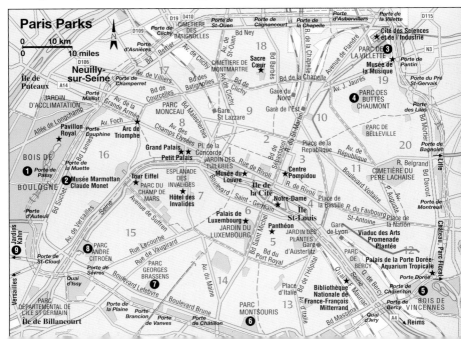

The great novelist Honoré de Balzac (1799–1850) lived at 47 rue Raynouard, east of the Bois de Boulogne (above), from 1840–47 under a false name, and wrote 16 hours a day to pay his creditors. Now Maison de Balzac is a museum (open daily except Mon and public holidays; entrance fee).

BELOW: Parc de la Villette, Cité des Sciences et de l'Industrie.

theatre and puppet show (Wed, Sat–Sun at 3pm and 4pm). Here, the **Musée en Herbe** (tel: 01 40 67 97 66; Sun–Fri 10am–6pm, Sat 2–6pm) organises art exhibits and workshops for future Picassos. Also here is the **Musée National des Arts et Traditions Populaires** (tel: 01 44 17 60 00; Wed–Mon 9.30am–5.15pm; closed some public holidays; entrance fee) which portrays life in France before industrialisation, incorporating local customs, crafts and folklore.

Westwards, the **Parc de Bagatelle** (open daily dawn until dusk; entrance fee) surrounds a small château built by the Count of Artois, later Charles X, who bet Marie-Antoinette he could construct a house in three months. The bet was won at great cost, hence the ironic name "bagatelle" (meaning "paltry sum"). The gardens are magnificent, with 8,000 roses blooming from June to October, a walled iris garden flowering in May and a display of waterlilies in August. Art exhibitions are held in the Trianon and Orangery during the summer season.

In the centre of the Bois, the Pré Catalan is the most romantic spot in western Paris. In spring, narcissi, tulips and daffodils carpet the manicured lawns, bathing the foot of the colossal copper beech, well over 200 years old, whose branches span over 500 metres/550 yds. Le Pré Catalan restaurant is a big attraction, offering sumptuous fare in elegant Belle-Epoque surroundings.

Nearby, the **Jardin Shakespeare** (open daily for guided tours 3–3.30pm, 4–4.30pm; entrance fee) is planted with flowers, trees and shrubs that feature in Shakespeare's plays, such as Macbeth's heather, Mediterranean herbs from *The Tempest* and Ophelia's stream. In summer, open-air productions are presented in the leafy theatre.

On the eastern border of the park, between the Place de la Porte de Passy and Porte de la Muette, is the **Musée Marmottan** ❷ (2 rue Louis Boilly, tel: 01 44 96 50 33; open Tues–Sun 10am–6pm; entrance fee). The museum contains 65 paintings by Monet, which were donated by his son, Michel, in 1971 and

include his celebrated *Impression du Soleil Levant* (1872), which gave its name to the Impressionist movement. Once home to avid art collector, Paul Marmottan, this beautiful 19th-century mansion also exhibits works by Pissarro, Renoir, Gauguin and Berthe Morisot.

Parc de la Villette

To the northeast of Paris, nestling against the *périphérique*, the **Parc de la Villette ❸** (Métro: Porte de Pantin, Porte de la Villette; open daily; entrance fee) is the third most visited site in France, after Disneyland Paris and the Centre Georges-Pompidou. Built on the site of a huge abattoir, which was rendered obsolete by improved refrigeration techniques and poor design (the cows could not even get up the steps), 55 hectares (136 acres) of futuristic gardens surround a colossal science museum, the **Cité des Sciences et de l'Industrie** (tel: 08 92 69 70 72; www.cite-sciences.fr; open Tues–Sat 10am–6pm, Sun until 7pm, entrance fee). It is not a museum for academics: the exhibits are interactive, with buttons, levers, keyboards and screens to keep mind and body alert. Begin at L'Univers with a spectacular planetarium and explanation of the inexplicable Big Bang. La Vie is an eclectic mix of medicine, agriculture and economics. La Matière reproduces a nuclear explosion and permits you to land an Airbus 320, and La Communication has displays of artificial intelligence, three-dimensional graphics and virtual reality.

La Géode (tel: 08 92 68 45 40; www.lageode.fr; open Mon–Fri 10.30am–6.30pm, Sat until 9.30pm, Sun until 8.30pm; entrance fee) is a giant silver ball housing a wrap-around cinema; there is also **L'Argonaute**, a retired naval submarine and **Cinaxe** (entrance fee), a flight-simulator-cum-cinema, which is definitely not for the queasy.

The former cattle market now houses a cultural and conference centre in the immense 19th-century Grande Halle. Next door, the Cité de la Musique is an edifice of angles in the complex designed by Christian de Portzamparc, housing the music

BELOW: the dragon slide, Parc de la Villette.

Enjoying the playground at Parc de la Villette.

and dance conservatory, concert hall and the **Musée de la Musique** (tel: 01 44 84 45 45; www.cite-musique.fr; open Tues–Sat noon–6pm, Sun 10am–6pm; entrance fee). The museum charts the development of classical, jazz and folk music and houses an impressive collection of over 4,500 musical instruments.

The gardens of the park are the biggest to be built in Paris since Haussmann's time. Designed by Bernard Tschumi and opened in 1993, they comprise several thematic areas such as the **Jardin des Frayeurs Enfantines** (Garden of Childhood Fears), with a huge dragon slide, and the **Jardin des Vents** (Garden of Winds), home to multicoloured bamboo plants. Abstraction continues in the form of Tschumi's folies: red, angular tree houses minus the trees, each with a special function such as play area, workshop, daycare centre or café.

Parc des Buttes-Chaumont

To the south of La Villette and on the city side of the *périphérique*, **Parc des Buttes-Chaumont** ❹

(Métro: Botzaris, Buttes-Chaumont; open daily 7.30am–11pm in summer, until 9pm in winter) was built by Haussmann in the 1860s on the site of a rubbish dump and gypsum quarry. The uneven ground provided a perfect setting for a wooded, rocky terrain, and a lake has been created around an artificial 50-metre (165-ft) "mountain", capped by a Roman-style temple, with a waterfall and a cave containing artificial stalactites. Ice-skating, boating and donkey rides are also on offer, and the puppet show or "Guignol" in the open-air theatre has been a popular attraction for over 150 years.

Bois de Vincennes

On the southeast edge of Paris lies the **Bois de Vincennes** ❺ (Métro: Château de Vincennes, Porte de Charenton, Porte Dorée; RER Fontenay-sous-Bois, Joinville), which is renowned for its château, racecourse and zoo. Philippe-Auguste enclosed the forest in the 12th century with a 12-km (7-mile) wall to protect the royal hunting ground. In 1370, Charles V completed the **château**

(tel: 01 48 08 31 20; www.monum.fr; open Sept–Apr daily 10am–noon and 1–5pm; May–Aug until 6pm; entrance fee), which, over the centuries, has had many uses. It has served as a prison – incarcerating among others the philosopher Diderot and Revolutionary Mirabeau – a porcelain factory and, under Napoleon I, an arsenal. Napoleon III started a restoration programme but the château was severely damaged by the Germans in 1944. Restoration is now complete and there is a museum in the 14th-century keep.

Just south of the château, **Le Parc Floral de Paris** (open daily; entrance fee) is a favourite with families who wander the Vallée des Fleurs, in bloom all year round, the pine wood and the water garden and take advantage of the adventure playground.

Close by is **La Cartoucherie**, once an ancient arsenal, now a complex of theatres where plays are staged by some of France's most avant-garde companies, including the Théâtre du Soleil.

On the western side of the Bois is the **Parc Zoologique** (open daily; entrance fee). This zoo was all the rage when it opened in 1934, because the animals roamed free. Each enclosure is different, inspired by the animal's natural environment, and a giant artificial mound is home to 60 species of animals including monkeys, gazelles and goats.

At Porte Dorée, a few minutes walk away from the zoo, is the **Palais de la Porte Dorée – Aquarium Tropical** (open daily; closed noon–1.30pm Mon–Fri, Sat–Sun am and public holidays; entrance fee) which houses a crocodile pit in the basement.

The building is a masterpiece of Art Deco design, built during the height of the French colonial era; its sculpted facade celebrates the "Glorie" of the French Empire in Africa, Asia and the South Pacific. It houses the collection of the Musée des Arts d'Afrique et d'Océanie, including Nigerian death masks, Algerian jewels and South Pacific fertility symbols, until the Musée du Quai Branly *(see page 57)* is finished.

Map on page 177

BELOW: blooms in Le Parc Floral de Paris.

Map
on page
177

To the west of Vincennes lies **Parc Montsouris** ❻ (Métro: Porte d'Orléans; RER: Cité Universitaire; tel: 08 20 00 75 75; open daily), a 19th-century park comprising 16 hectares (40 acres) of gently undulating grass and trees, much loved by Cubist Georges Braque and the exiled Lenin, who both used to live close by. On the day the park opened in 1878, the lake suddenly and inexplicably drained dry, and its engineer committed suicide.

New-age and horticulture

The far-flung southwest of Paris is the capital's most populated district and home to two of its newest parks. **Parc Georges-Brassens** ❼ on Rue des Morillons (Métro: Convention) was opened in 1982 on the site of another old abbatoir and is now a child's playgroud paradise, with play houses, rock piles, rivers and mini-lakes.

It includes a garden designed for the blind: close your eyes, follow the trickling of fountains and smell the fragrant foliage. Braille signs give relevant information on herbs

and shrubs. Along Rue des Morillons grow 700 vines, producing the annual Clos des Morillons wine (full-bodied, fine bouquet). At weekends, the ancient slaughter-houses host a giant book market.

Further west on the banks of the Seine, the once derelict site of the Citroën car factory on Rue Balard has been turned into the **Parc André-Citroën** ❽ (Métro: Balard, Javel/André Citroën; tel: 08 20 00 75 75; open daily). The industrial buildings have been transformed into floral palaces – two huge glasshouses glisten next to the esplanade where children leap in and out of spurting fountains.

Beyond the glass greenhouses lie two gardens – one "black" and one "white". On the northeast side of the park a series of six more colourful gardens have been planted to a different colour scheme – gold, silver, red, orange, green and blue. Each garden is linked to a metal, a planet, a day of the week, and a sense: thus gold is linked to the sun, Sunday and the intangible sixth sense. There's also a panoramic Paris in miniature.

More traditional horticulture is found beyond the southeast of the Bois de Boulogne at the **Jardins Albert Kahn** ❾ (14 rue du Port, Métro: Boulogne-Porte de St-Cloud), where the legacy of financier Albert Kahn (1860–1940) takes the form of an extraordinary park, created between 1895 and 1910. Japanese, English and French gardens lie alongside an Alpine forest and North American prairie. The grass is cut at different levels, from "beatnik" style to "sailorboy". Kahn called the gardens "the vegetal expression of my thoughts concerning a reconciled world", an idea complemented by 72,000 photographs of world landscapes taken between 1910 and 1931 and exhibited on permanent rotation. ❏

DISNEYLAND PARIS

America's fantasy world promises fun for all,
from the charm of a fairytale castle to the
thrills and spills of the Rock 'n' Roller Coaster

Map
on page
193

With twice as many annual visitors as the Eiffel Tower or the Louvre, **Disneyland Paris ❶** is the most popular tourist attraction in Europe. Located at Marne-la-Vallée, 32 km (20 miles) east of Paris on a 2,000-hectare (5,000-acre) site one-fifth the size of the city itself, this is, as Disney put it, the land "where dreams come true".

The park is easy to reach from Paris, at the end of RER line A (a regular TGV train service takes 15 minutes from Roissy-Charles de Gaulle

BELOW: the Mad
Hatter's Tea Cups ride.

airport and there's a shuttle bus service from Orly airport).

According to the Disney marketing machine, Disneyland Paris was something of a homecoming – Walt's family originally came from Isigny-sur-Mer in Normandy and their name d'Isigny (from Isigny) became Disney in America. But generous financial incentives from the French government rather than family history were behind the final decision to bring Disneyland to Europe.

The most recent addition to the site is Walt Disney Studios, a major new attraction which offers a behind-the-scenes look at the history of animation, film and television. But it doesn't end there. If present plans are maintained, the whole site will not be fully developed until 2017, by which time there will be another new golf course and 13,000 more hotel rooms.

Getting your bearings

Disneyland Paris theme park is divided into five main areas, or "lands", each with attractions, restaurants and shops following a particular theme – a floor plan cloned from the other Disneylands in California, Florida and Tokyo. Designed by "Imagineers", the artistic and mechanical wizards who

spend their lives thinking up weird and wonderful attractions, this is Disney's most technologically advanced park, benefiting from state-of-the-art robotics: the organisation's unique audio-animatronics, where life-size, lifelike figures speak, sing and dance with gusto.

Decide what you want to do in order of priority and get there early, as, by midday, queues at the most popular rides can be quite long – up to 45 minutes. Heading round the park in an anti-clockwise direction avoids the bigger crowds, since the circular train chugs clockwise.

Once through the Victorian turnstiles, already humming along to ubiquitous Disney music, you enter **Main Street USA**, the first of the five areas representing 19th-century, small-town America. City Hall, on the left, is the central information centre, a contact point for lost children and property. Here, too, is the Main Street Station, from where the Disneyland train circles the park. The station is often quite crowded, so it is a good idea to get on the train at one of the other stations en route,

such as Frontierland. The bandstand in Main Street square is the best place from which to view the parades (weekends, and daily in summer) which traverse the park, passing around the bandstand and out through the large green gates to the right, between Discovery Arcade and Ribbons and Bows Hat Shop. Mickey's Showtime Parade is at 11.30am, the Princess Parade is at 4pm and then there's the night-time Fantillusion Parade, with illuminated floats lit up by a million light bulbs. On weekends, and each summer night, the bandstand is also the best spot from which to view the five-minute Simba's FiROARworks display.

Frontierland

To the left of Main Street is **Frontierland**, evoking dreams of the Wild West (at least that's the idea). Its centrepiece, **Big Thunder Mountain**, is a towering triumph of red rock reminiscent of every Western movie you have seen. The small town of Thunder Mesa surrounding the mountain represents a pioneer

BELOW: the Walt Disney Studios.

Disneyland Made Easy

Different types of Disneyland passes are available and prices are reduced in low season during school term times. Probably the best ticket option is a two- or three-day passport, so your family can spread out their visit. The pass does not have to be used on consecutive days, has no date limit and is more economical. You could combine a two-day passport with a night in one of the resort hotels.

During peak season, resort hotel guests are granted access to the park an hour before it opens. This can be a real advantage in reducing queuing time and goes someway to balance out the high cost of the accommodation. The Star Nights pass allows entrance after 5pm at a reduced rate in summer when it closes at 11pm. Passports can be bought from the Disney Store and Virgin Megastore on the Champs-Elysées, from FNAC, and at the gate. A Combi-ticket, combining a return RER ticket and passport, is available from main stations on RER line A. For details, including accommodation, tel: 01 60 30 60 30 in France and 0990 030303 in the UK, or visit www.disneylandparis.com.

Big Thunder Mountain is a screaming good ride.

settlement of the late 1800s, including Cavalry Fort and Lucky Nugget Saloon, where Miss Lil entertains on a vaudeville stage. **Phantom Manor**, home to some spectacular audio-animatronics, provides a high-tech rollicking ride through a haunted house. If the house itself seems vaguely familiar, it may be because it is copied from Norman Bates's abode in Hitchcock's *Psycho*. Inside are singing cowboy skeletons and holographic ghosts.

The Rivers of the Far West, an artificial lake in the middle of Frontierland, can be enjoyed by Mississippi paddle steamer, keelboat or Indian canoe. The Indian canoe station, verdant and full of birdsong (taped, but it fools the real birds) is a tranquil contrast to the roller-coaster ride. Also in Frontierland is the Pocahontas Indian Village, inspired by the Disney film of the same name.

Adventureland

BELOW: the Orbitron ride in Discoveryland.

From Frontierland, paths lead almost imperceptibly to **Adventureland**. Sparse scrub gives way to lush bamboo and flowers, and the twang of Wild West guitar fades into the beat of African drums. Here is another top attraction, the unforgettable **Pirates of the Caribbean** (queues move quickly as a rule). As you descend into the castle, the air cools, water drips and the darkness is punctuated only by flickering firelight. The water ride, through tropical swamp to the open sea, is orchestrated by jovially barbaric Disney workers. For the six-minute journey you remain spellbound by animated pirates invading a treasure-rich port – here, a singing donkey, there, an inebriated pig that taps its trotters in time to the music.

Rival to Big Thunder Mountain, the first-ever 360° looping roller-coaster created by Disney is **Le Temple du Péril**, near Explorers' Club Restaurant. Hold on to your stomach as the ore-carts plunge through rainforest and turn upside down above a mock archaeological dig inspired by the Indiana Jones saga. As with other top rides, get here early. Elsewhere, Adventureland offers the ultimate treehouse,

La Cabane des Robinson, home of the Swiss Family Robinson; an **Adventure Isle** based on Robert Louis Stevenson's *Treasure Island*, complete with rope bridge and Ben Gunn's cave; and **Captain Hook's Pirate Ship** which, along with Skull Rock, acts as a playground.

Fantasyland

The most popular land for younger children is Fantasyland, containing Disney's emblem **Le Château de la Belle au Bois Dormant** (Sleeping Beauty's Castle), the centrepiece of the park. You can enter into the French-style château, where Sleeping Beauty's tale is told through rich tapestries and stained-glass windows. Underneath, through Merlin's Workshop, lies La Tanière du Dragon (The Lair of the Dragon), hiding a 27-metre (88-ft) long creature that roars, curls its claws and hisses smoke. Next door, Blanche-Neige et les Sept Nains (Snow White and the Seven Dwarfs) leads children through the classic fairytale in the cars from the dwarfs' mine and terrifies them with a holographic floating witch's head.

Peter Pan's Flight is another site to visit early in the day before the tour buses arrive; here you can take a pirate galleon into the skies above London, as far as Never-Never Land. More sedate amusement is found in It's a Small World, where national stereotypes live in a cheerful puppet kingdom of singing children, first designed by Walt Disney for Pepsi's stand at the 1964 World Fair and sponsored by France Télécom.

Discoveryland

The assortment of futuristic high-tech experiences in Discoveryland are great for older kids. **Space Mountain** is a roller-coaster ride into outer space inspired by Jules Verne's novel *From the Earth to the Moon*, and **Star Tours** offers a trip into space with George Lucas's *Star Wars* characters. To get there, you walk past hard-working robots complaining about the trials of life. Once at the ride itself, the five minutes spent in the Air Force-designed flight simulator are riveting as the spaceship crashes through meteors and engages in a laser battle with the enemy. For a voyage through time in 10 minutes join the robotic time-keeper at the **Visionarium**, where a 360° screen provides a panoramic view of Europe, from the Swiss Alps to Gérard Depardieu's nose. The view of Paris circa 2200 is the most interesting feature of the show.

Walt Disney Studios

Walt Disney Studios, built alongside the established Disneyland Paris park, is a new zone of rides and attractions inspired by European and American cinema. Guests learn about the movie-making process and can step into the action themselves. The Walt Disney Studios park is made up of four distinct zones: the Front Lot, Animation Courtyard, Production Courtyard and Back Lot.

Map on page 193

Disney Village

Open daily, the complex between the park and the hotels buzzes with shops, restaurants, nightclubs and a huge cinema complex. Dramatic family entertainment takes the form of Buffalo Bill's Legend, a 90-minute Wild West show with Indian chiefs, buffalo and carousing cowboys.

For places to eat, the LA Bar and Grill offers a pizza terrace and Beach Boys' music as a mood setter. Key West serves seafood dishes at the sign of the life-size shark, a source of endless fun for children. Upstairs, you can sip a Cyclone Special under an alligator at the Hurricane Disco.

Slightly more low-key, Annette's Diner is well priced and entertaining, and fills up early with young families. Taking the theme of an American 1950s diner, it serves burgers, fries and beer, brought by roller-skating waiters. The mood continues in Rock 'n' Roll America, a 1950s dance hall. Across the strip, Billy Bob's presents simple chicken dishes set to bluegrass tunes. The area surrounding the lake is more sedate and more expensive and appeals to couples on a romantic night out.

Front Lot

As you walk through the majestic Studio Gates, the first thing you see are palm trees, a Mickey Mouse "Sorcerer's Apprentice" water fountain and a 33-metre (110-ft) water tower, the traditional symbol of a Hollywood film studio. Strolling down the 1940s Hollywood Boulevard and watching Disney starlets in veiled hats pose for the cameras, you will soon realise that it is all an elaborate film set, complete with hundreds of movie props. Don't be surprised when "producers" try to recruit you as an actor.

Animation Courtyard

This zone is Disney's homage to the art of film animation – from its origins in Europe to the greatest animated pictures of the 20th century. A movie highlighting the very moments from Disney's animated classics is followed by a cartooning demonstration given by a Disney artist. Guests can then try out their own animation skills at special interactive play stations. **Animagique** is a colourful show in the great

tradition of Czech "black light" theatre, bringing to life famous scenes from pictures like *The Lion King* and *Pinocchio*. The Genie from *Aladdin* invites children of all ages onto a film set called the **Flying Carpets over Agrabah**. The mayhem begins when the actor turned director tries to organise a film-shoot with guest-actors who are whizzing round a giant lamp on magic carpets.

Production Courtyard

The heartbeat of the studio production facilities, this area has productions and shows taking place almost every day. The **Walt Disney Television Studios** is the home of the Disney Channel. You get a rare glimpse of a busy production facility via a glass corridor, and there's even a chance that guests might be selected to appear on TV during one of the shows. Combining live performers and special effects, **CinéMagique** offers a magical journey through the very best of 100 years of the moving image. The **Studio Tram Tour** takes you on a tour of the studio premises, offering a peek behind the

BELOW: riding on the Flying Carpets over Agrabah.

scenes at location sites, movie props, special effects, studio decor and costume. When the tram visits **Catastrophe Canyon**, a dam bursts, releasing a deluge of recycled water.

Back Lot

This is where most of the thrills are – the special effects facility, the music recording stages and the stunt workshops. The **Rock 'n' Roller Coaster**, starring Aerosmith, offers you the chance to "ride the music" in this sight-and-sound spectacular, featuring hairpin turns, loops and heart-stopping drops. However, it is too scary for small children. **Armageddon** is an introduction to special effects: it takes guests on a voyage through the history of special effects and into a full-sized set of a Mir Russian space station (from the Bruce Willis sci-fi hit, *Armageddon*). Wind tunnels howl, meteors crash through the walls and guests dodge fireballs until an explosion in the heart of the ship brings the action to a climax. The highlight of the back lot is the **Stunt Show Spectacular**. Staged up to five times a day in front of 3,000 people, the live action trashes cars, motorcycles and jet skis in a crescendo of movie stunts performed in a Mediterranean village seaside set. The final edit is broadcast on a giant screen, showing spectators how live action scenes from movies are put together.

Where to stay

The wider resort – **Disney Village** and the hotels – make up a celebration of "Americana", which is a direct response to Disney's vision of how Europeans view America. **Hotel Cheyenne** is the most imaginative: a film-set Western town, complete with saloon, sheriff's jail and wooden-planked stores. At the other "moderately priced" hotel, **Santa Fe**, Clint Eastwood grimaces down from a mock drive-in movie screen above the reception area. The hotel

is a series of blocks recalling Mexican villages.

The more expensive hotels, **Sequoia Lodge** and **Newport Bay Club**, overlook Lake Disney. One of them recalls Hitchcock's *North by North-West* in its pine surroundings, and the other is a New England mansion straight from F. Scott Fitzgerald's novel, *The Great Gatsby*. Across the lake, **Hotel New York** offers luxury rooms in a Manhattan-style skyscape designed by Michael Graves.

But the jewel of the resort's hotels is, naturally, the four-star **Disneyland Hotel** sprawling across the main entrance. Its Victorian style whispers late 19th-century elegance and it is here that Michael Jackson comes to stay when he jets in to enjoy the park after hours. Five kilometres (3 miles) from the theme park (you will need your own car) in natural forest is **Davy Crockett Ranch**, with 97 camping places for tents and caravans and 498 fully equipped cabins in rustic logged style. Set in a "pioneer" village, it provides sports facilities and bike hire. ❑

Map on page 193

BELOW: the dam bursts in Catastrophe Canyon.

TRIPS OUT OF TOWN

FRANCE

Paris

Within easy reach of Paris, you can visit Joséphine's Malmaison or the royal Château de Fontainebleau, go cycling in an ancient forest, or see the actual waterlily pond that inspired Claude Monet

Map on page 193

PRECEDING PAGES: Monet's lily pond at Giverny.
BELOW: Gare du Nord station is the starting point for many day trips.

Many of the interesting places beyond the city limits are just a train ride away. Alternatively, you can hire a car *(see page 205)* to venture off the beaten track – your meanderings may lead to quaint old auberges serving hearty evening meals by the fire or lunch on a riverside terrace. If time is limited, then a trip to Versailles or **Disneyland Paris ❶** *(see page 184)* is an obvious choice, but you could take a day or two to visit towns such as Rouen or Chartres further away,

stopping at sights along the way. The forests of the Ile de France and surrounding regions are dotted with châteaux and monuments. SNCF trains are generally efficient and, on arrival at your destination, you will find the needs of visitors well catered for, with maps and information on tourist sights, hotels, restaurants and taxis. Some places can be reached by the speedy RER train *(see page 204)*. In Compiègne and Fontainebleau, tour buses will take you into town or the countryside.

The shortest hops

Château de Versailles ❷ (tel: 01 30 83 78 00; www.chateauversailles.fr; open Oct–Apr Tues–Sun 9am–5.30pm, May–Sept until 6.30pm; closed some public holidays; entrance fee), 23 km (14 miles) southwest of Paris, can be reached via RER line C5, which will drop you a short distance from the Sun King's magnificent château and gardens *(see pages 200–1).* You will have to pick and choose what you most want to see as you will need much more than a day to take in everything.

Apart from the main palace there is the Grand Trianon in the north of the park, the Petit Trianon and the nearby Hameau de la Reine. In the formal gardens (open daily dawn until dusk), the fountains dance to music at 3.30pm on every Sunday from May to October.

Just half a day will suffice for a visit to **Sèvres ❸** (Métro: Pont de Sèvres), southwest of Paris. Situated on the left bank of the Seine, the suburb has been famous for its porcelain for more than 200 years and the ceramics workshops, set in a sloping, wooded park, include the **Musée National de la Céramique** (tel: 01 41 14 04 20; open Wed–Mon; entrance fee).

Further westwards, en route to **St-Germain-en-Laye ❹**, is the **Château de Malmaison** (tel: 01 41 29 05 55; www.chateau-malmaison.fr; open Wed–Mon, closed 12–1.30pm; entrance fee) in Rueil-Malmaison (RER line A to La Défense-Grande Arche then bus 258), which was the favourite home of Napoleon Bonaparte's first wife, Joséphine, and where she lived after their divorce. Napoleon used to come here between battles. Along with the neighbouring Château de Bois-Préau, it now forms an important museum of the First Empire with period interiors. The rose garden looks much as it did in Joséphine's day.

"I have just been to Versailles, where everything is grand and everything is magnificent.".

— MADAME DE SÉVIGNÉ

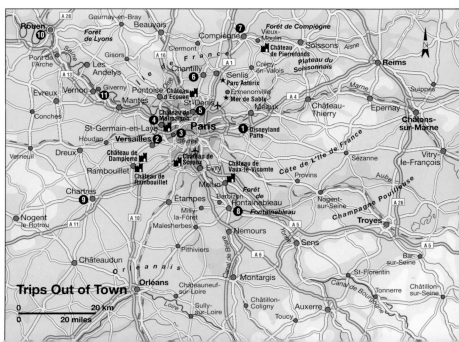

Trips Out of Town

0 ————— 20 km
0 ————— 20 miles

During the Revolution, the tombs in St-Denis (above) were vandalised and the royal bodies thrown into a pit. However, they were secretly rescued and finally returned to their original resting places in restored tombs by Louis XVIII in 1816.

BELOW: formal Versailles in bloom.

The wealthy Paris suburb of St-Germain-en-Laye, just 5 km (3 miles) away (at the end of RER line 1), has perched above Paris since the 12th century and was once a royal retreat. The château (tel: 01 34 51 53 65; open Wed–Mon; entrance fee), which still has a lovely Gothic chapel, was reconstructed under François I (his royal salamander and "F" can be seen in the courtyard) and again in the 19th century. Inside, you won't find any period furnishings or portraits, but rather a museum devoted to prehistoric and medieval times. The Gallo-Roman collection and the life-sized replica of the Lascaux cave drawings are favourite exhibits. The terrace gardens overlooking the Seine were designed by André Le Nôtre and later gave inspiration to the Impressionist painter Alfred Sisley (1839–99).

North of Paris, less than 4 km (3 miles) away, stands the **Basilica of St-Denis** ❺ (Métro: St-Denis–Basilique; tel: 01 48 09 83 54; www.monum.fr; open Mon–Sat 10am–5.15pm, Sun noon–5.15pm, until 6.15pm in summer; entrance fee), the final resting place of France's kings and queens. Revered as an early masterpiece of Gothic architecture, the basilica was mainly built by the charismatic Abbot Suger, close friend of Louis VII, in the 12th century on the site of an abbey church. According to legend, this is the spot reached by St Denis, first Bishop of Lutetia, when he walked out of Paris carrying his head, after being beheaded in Montmartre. Monarchs from as far back as Dagobert I (628–37) are buried here, and the medieval and Renaissance sculptures marking their tombs are some of the finest in France.

North to Chantilly and Compiègne

Chantilly ❻, about 50 km (30 miles) away from Paris (SNCF from Gare du Nord), is famous for horse racing, but also offers a sumptuous palace, a magnificent park created by Le Nôtre and the splendid, 18th-century, palatial Grandes Ecuries, stables built by Prince Louis-Henri de Bourbon, who believed that he

would be reincarnated as a horse. The **Château** (park open Mar–Oct daily 10am–7pm, closed Tues from 12.45–2pm; Nov–Feb Wed–Mon 10.30am–5pm) is a real fairytale castle – nestled in a forest grove, white walls topped by a blue-slate roof, and wild ducks bustling around the moat. Inside is the **Musée Condé** (tel: 03 44 62 62 62; www.chateauchantilly.com; open Wed–Mon 10am–6pm, until 5pm in winter; closed for lunch Nov–Feb, entrance fee) with works by Botticelli, Raphael, Giotto and Holbein.

You don't have to be a horse racing enthusiast to enjoy the **Musée Vivant du Cheval** (tel: 03 44 57 40 40; www.musee-vivant-du-cheval.fr; open Wed–Fri 10.30am–5.30pm, Sat–Sun until 6pm, shorter hours in winter; entrance fee), under the impressive dome of the Grandes Ecuries, with 30 horses of varying breeds on show and 31 exhibition rooms – these stables could once house 240 horses and 500 dogs. Riding displays are held on the first Sunday of each month. The Chantilly racecourse is the most

fashionable in France, and high society gathers here in June for the prestigious flat-racing trophies.

The town of **Compiègne** ❼, 30 km (20 miles) northeast of Chantilly and 80 km (50 miles) northeast of Paris (SNCF from Gare du Nord), sits between the Oise River and one of the largest forests in France. The town's Hôtel de Ville has the oldest bell in the country hanging in its clock tower, and *picantins* (little figures) strike every hour. The **Château de Compiègne** (tel: 03 44 38 47 02; www.musee-chateau-compiegne.fr; open Wed–Mon 10am–6pm; entrance fee) was once the favourite residence of Napoléon III and the Empress Eugénie, and contains three museums including one for vintage cars.

If you enjoy walking, make your way on foot to Les Beaux Monts, just outside the town, for a spectacular view of the château and the Oise. From here, a circular walk, lasting between one and two hours, has been marked out, guiding you through the beautiful Forêt de Compiègne, an ancient royal hunting forest full of old oaks and beech trees. By car or SNCF

Map on page 193

BELOW: solemnity in the Gothic Chartres cathedral.

There are no eating facilities at Château de Vaux-le-Vicomte; however, it's a 5-minute walk into town, where there are numerous cafés, brasseries and restaurants.

bus from Compiègne station, you can visit the **Musée-Wagon de l'Armistice** (tel: 03 44 85 14 18; open mid-Oct–Mar Wed–Mon 9am–noon and 2–5.30pm; Apr–mid-Oct until 6.15pm; entrance fee) in the Clairière de l'Armistice (Armistice Clearing), where the signing of the 1918 Armistice between France and Germany took place, and where Hitler humiliated the French by making them surrender there on 22 June 1940. On the eastern edge of the forest is Napoleon III's unusual hunting palace, the **Château de Pierrefonds** (tel: 03 44 42 72 72; open daily mid-May–mid-Sept 9.30am–6pm; mid-Sept–mid-May closed 12.30–2pm; entrance fee). Entirely reconstructed in the 19th century, in medieval military style by Viollet-le-Duc, with drawbridge, moat and towers, it is a remarkable architectural oddity, as inside the fanciful architect allowed his Romantic imagination a free rein.

Southeast to Fontainebleau

En route to **Fontainebleau ❽**, 40 km (25 miles) from Paris, is the luxurious 17th-century **Château de**

Vaux-le-Vicomte (SNCF from Gare de Lyon to Melun; tel: 01 64 14 41 90; www.vaux-le-vicomte.com; open Apr–mid-Nov daily 10am–6pm; entrance fee).

Built by Louis XIV's powerful royal treasurer, Nicolas Fouquet, a devoted patron of the arts, the impeccable house along with a beautiful garden *à la française* – the first created by Le Nôtre – was his undoing. Jealous advisers whispered to the King that Fouquet had paid for it with treasury funds. After a grand housewarming party for the young monarch, Fouquet was imprisoned at Vincennes and the upstaged Louis set out to build something even more splendid – Versailles – using the very same architect and designers.

The château, grounds and furnishings provide an intriguing visit. One room traces the history of its various owners, others are decorated in sumptuous period style, with coffered, painted ceilings and Gobelins tapestries, and the kitchen equipment is fascinating. The candlelit tour on Saturday evening (May to

BELOW: Château de Fontainebleau.

mid-Oct 8pm–midnight) gives an added atmospheric dimension.

Melun sits on the edge of the **Forêt de Fontainebleau**, which was once a royal hunting ground and is now the haunt of cyclists, mushroom hunters, birdwatchers, picnickers and rock climbers, attracted by the giant rock formations. The town of Fontainebleau (SNCF from Gare de Lyon) lies just 15 km (9 miles) away and is dominated by the first purpose-built royal **château** (tel: 01 60 71 50 70; www.musee-chateau-fontainebleau.fr; open Oct–May Wed–Mon 9.30am–5pm, Jun–Sept until 6pm; entrance fee), residence of French sovereigns from François I to Napoléon III.

Each one has added something to the palace, creating a mixture of styles, but Napoleon I outdid them all by building an ornate throne room – his grands *appartements* are definitely worth seeing.

If you are driving, **Barbizon**, 7 km (4 miles) away on the eastern edge of the forest, is a village that has attracted landscape painters since the 1840s, when Théodore

Rousseau (1812–67) and Jean-François Millet (1814–75) fled to the woods to escape the Industrial Revolution and rediscover nature. The Office du Tourisme is in Rousseau's former house and his workshop is now a museum to the **Ecole de Barbizon** (tel: 01 60 66 22 38; open Wed–Mon 10am–12.30pm and 2–5pm; entrance fee).

Southwest to Chartres

A trip to **Chartres** ❾ – 89 km (55 miles) from Paris – can be taken slowly, stopping off at the **Châteaux de Dampierre** and **Rambouillet** *(see below)* on the way, or you can go straight there by train (SNCF from Gare Montparnasse). The two spires of the magnificent Gothic cathedral (tel: 02 37 21 75 02; www.chartres.com; open daily; free) soar above the surrounding fields. Originally Romanesque, the cathedral dedicated to the Virgin Mary (Notre-Dame) was destroyed by fire in 1194, but everyone from peasant to lord contributed straight away to the rebuilding, either with labour or finances. The famous rose windows fill the cathedral with

Map on page 193

LEFT: classic image of France.

Châteaux around Paris

Ile de France is an area rich in châteaux, many built in the wake of the Sun King's extravagant palace at Versailles. The **Château de Sceaux** (tel: 01 46 61 06 71), 7 km (4 miles) south of Paris, was built in 1670 for Fouquet's successor, Colbert, with a beautiful park and gardens designed by Le Nôtre. Rebuilt in Louis XIII-style in 1856, the château contains the Musée de l'île de France. The museum serves as an introduction to the royal and rural history of Ile de France. More Le Nôtre gardens can be found at the **Château de Dampierre** (tel: 01 30 52 53 24), 35 km (22 miles) southwest of Paris, which has a touch of Versailles about it. The president's summer residence, **Château de Rambouillet** (tel: 01 34 83 00 25),15 km (9 miles) further on, was once a feudal castle and is open when the president is away. The **Château d'Ecouen** (tel: 01 34 38 38 50), 19 km (11 miles) north of Paris, is a masterpiece of Renaissance architecture. It is home to the Musée National de la Renaissance, with the finest tapestries preserved in France and some early mathematical instruments on display.

Map
on page
193

changing colours, along with 170 more of Europe's finest original stained-glass windows. Behind the cathedral is the **Musée des Beaux-Arts** (tel: 02 37 36 41 39; open Nov–Apr Mon, Wed–Sat 10am–noon and 2–5.30pm, Sun 2–5pm, May–Oct until 6pm; closed some public holidays; entrance fee) with Renaissance paintings and fine tapestries. The **Maison de l'Archéologie** (14 rue St-Pierre, tel: 02 37 30 99 38; open Jul–Sept Wed–Mon 2–6pm, Oct–May Wed and Sun 2–6pm), designed by the British architect Richard Rogers, tells the story of the recently excavated Gallo-Roman city. Along the banks of the Eure, a path passes typical medieval *lavoirs* (wash houses) and takes you past the medieval Benedictine abbey church of **St-Pierre** to the remains of the old city wall.

West to Monet's Giverny

For a longer break from Paris, head for the industrial city of **Rouen** ❿ (SNCF from Gare St-Lazare) on the Seine, about 110 km (70 miles) along the N13 from Paris. This road passes through Saint-Germain-en-Laye and close to Giverny, home of the Impressionist painter Claude Monet. Once the capital of Normandy, Rouen has a wealth of picturesque houses and narrow streets (despite the damage it suffered during World War II), mostly centred around the impressive Gothic cathedral, which was much loved and much painted by Monet. Joan of Arc was burned at the stake here in 1431, after a trial conducted by the bishop of Beauvais who was in cahoots with the English.

Giverny ⓫ (SNCF from Gare St-Lazare to Vernon 6 km/3 miles away) is set on a hillside above the Seine, and Monet lived and worked in the small village house for 43 years until his death in 1926, at the age of 86. Now known as the **Fondation Claude Monet** (tel: 02 32 51 28 21; www.fondation-monet.com; open Apr–Oct Tues–Sun 9.30am–6pm; entrance fee), the house is a museum decorated in the colours the painter loved. The gardens that the father of Impressionism designed and drew inspiration from are a living work of art – at their colourful best during May, June and July – with the Japanese bridge and the famous waterlilies on the pond. Arrive at 10am to avoid the crowds.

Only copies of Monet's works are on display at Giverny but, nearby, the modern **Musée d'Art Américain** (tel: 02 32 51 94 65; www.maag.org; open Apr–Oct Tues–Sun 10am–6pm; entrance fee) celebrates the original work of half a dozen American Impressionists who worked in France during Monet's time, and provides a restaurant. You can also head for the **Forêt de Lyons** (SNCF from Rouen or Gare St-Lazare to Pont de l'Arche). The centennial beech trees make a walk or cycle ride a particular pleasure, with fine views of Norman villages and their half-timbered houses. ❏

BELOW: the apse in Chartres cathedral.

La Défense

Heading west, crossing the city boundary at Porte Maillot, the historic avenues of Paris suddenly vanish. There, on the horizon, rises a city of gigantic glass blocks marching to the gates of the capital. This is La Défense, set around a vast concrete podium, with an enormous shopping complex, high-tech entertainment centres and, as its focus, the Grande Arche. The complex was intended to be the crowning glory of President Mitterrand's "progressive vision for the 1980s" but many of the buildings now seem dated rather than futuristic. However, the area is lively, busy with business people during the week and visitors at the weekend.

Over the Esplanade de la Défense at the entrance of the district, towers a white seemingly two-dimensional Grande Arche. When viewed from the sides, the third dimension mysteriously appears, an illusion created by the arch's alignment six degrees off the axis of the Triumphal Way, or Royal Axis (a design quirk shared by I.M. Peï's pyramid at the Louvre).

The Grande Arche (tel: 01 49 07 27 57; open daily 10am– 7pm, last lift to the top at 6.30pm; entrance fee) completes the Triumphal Way – the east-west axis that runs from the Louvre through the Carrousel arch to the Arc de Triomphe. In the words of its architect, Otto von Spreckelsen (he died two years before the arch was completed), it is "a window on the world. The arch will see far, in all directions".

The size of the arch is symbolic: measuring roughly 100 metres by 100 metres (330 ft by 330 ft), it has the same dimensions as the Cour Carrée at the Louvre. At 106 metres (348 ft) wide, the entire cathedral of Notre-Dame could fit within the archway. The architect Otto von Spreckelsen's monumental vision also respects the historic pattern of Parisian arches. The Arc de Triomphe du Carrousel is 25 metres (82 ft) high, the Arc de Triomphe 50 metres (164

ft) high, so La Grande Arche is 100 metres (330 ft) high.

The view from the top is vast. Two glass bubbles whisk lines of visitors up to the roof at vertiginous speeds, through the symbolic "cloud", a canvas net suspended between the twin towers designed to cut down wind resistance. On the roof terrace, Raynaud's *Carte du Ciel* (Map of the Sky) resembles an enormous sundial.

Next to the arch looms the immense silver globe of the Dôme IMAX. Designed by the IMAX Corporation of Canada, the screen is 1,000 sq metres (10,700 sq ft), and shows pictures 10 times the size of a normal cinema image at a viewing angle of 180 degrees, with seats tilted at 30 degrees. The giant forecourt of La Défense is something of an open-air art museum, with artworks by Miró, Calder, Utshori, and an imposing bronze thumb by César.

To get to La Défense, take the Métro Line 1 which cuts straight through the centre of Paris and ends up beneath the Grande Arche, the RER A line winds all the way from Disneyland Paris (a journey of only 40 minutes) before branching out to the suburbs. In addition, 20 bus routes converge here, making this small district one of the most accessible in France. ❑

RIGHT: La Défense is part business park, part modern sculpture park.

THE SPLENDOURS OF VERSAILLES

Paris was not always the capital of France. For a while, the country was run from a sumptuous palace at Versailles to the southwest of the city

ABOVE: There is an extra charge to enter the gardens on Sundays, when the fountains come to life and 17th-century music blasts over the parterres. While it's fabulous to see Louis's gardens in watery splendour, Sunday is the worst day to visit the château's interior, as it can become unbearably overcrowded.

The Château of Versailles is the ultimate expression of the French monarchy's power and ostentation prior to the Revolution. Built in 1624 as Louis XIII's hunting lodge, the building and surrounding land were developed by Louis XIV, who employed the celebrated creative trio of definite articles – Le Vau, Le Nôtre and Le Brun – and the architect Mansart. Versailles became the capital of France and, by 1774, after alterations by Louis XV and XVI, the palace had 2,143 windows, 67 staircases and was home to 10,000 courtiers and servants. The gardens were designed by Le Nôtre on the same grand scale as the château itself, and adorned with statues and fountains. The name Versailles evokes not just a building but also the world of Louis XIV's court.

ABOVE: the Hall of Mirrors (Galerie des Glaces) was built between 1678–82 under architect Jules Hardouin-Mansart. The corridor features 17 arched windows opposite 17 corresponding mirrored arcades; the decorated vaulted ceiling is embellished with captions by the playwright Jean Racine and 30 paintings by Lebrun, framed by stucco work. The best time to visit is in the afternoon when the sun streams in.

BELOW: The château's gardens and park are the work of André Le Nôtre who created the ultimate formal-style French playground for Louis XIV. A principal feature is the Grand Canal, an artificial stretch of water that covers 44 hectares (105 acres). Around the canal pathways, statues and fountains radiate symmetrically.

LEFT: The Royal Chapel is a Baroque masterpiece, the magnificent two-storey chapel is adorned with carved white marble, gilding and murals. The royal family worshipped from the gallery.

RIGHT: Other sites to visit at Versailles include the Jeu de Paume indoor real tennis courts, just outside the Versailles estate, on the Rue de Jeu de Paume, and Hardouin-Mansart's Great and Small stables, which are now home to Versailles' Carriage Museum.

THE HIGHLIGHTS

Versailles is the third most-visited monument in France. The château's main tour plus the gardens can be covered in a day but to assimilate fully the wealth of historical, political and architectural information visitors should allow two days.

The Main Tour

The main part of the château, which can be accessed without a guide, includes the lavish State Apartments of the King and Queen (Grands Appartements), notably the King's State Bedroom. Also included is the Queen's bedchamber and the vast Hall of Mirrors. Other highlights of the main tour include, in the Hercules Room, the ceiling painting *The Apotheosis of Hercules* (1733–36), by François Lemoyne, and, in the Battle Gallery towards the end of the tour, a copy of the imposing behemoth *The Crowning of the Empress Joséphine at Notre-Dame* (1804) by Jacques-Louis David. For a supplement access is granted to Louis XIV's private bedroom and the apartments of the Dauphin and Dauphine.

The Trianons and Hameau

The single-storey, Italianate Grand Trianon was erected by Louis XIV as a miniature palace in which he could escape the formality of the main château. The Petit Trianon was built for Louis XV from 1762–68 as a retreat for the king and his mistresses. A cluster of thatched cottages, the Hameau (the Hamlet), is linked to Marie-Antoinette; they were used as a dairy where food for the royal estate was produced.

TRANSPORT

GETTING THERE AND GETTING AROUND

GETTING THERE

By Air

Most of the major airlines fly regularly to Paris. Air France is the main agent for flights to France from the US and within Europe and also handles bookings for some of the smaller operators, such as Brit Air. For British travellers, operators such as the low-cost airlines Ryanair, easyJet and British Midland offer flights to Paris from London and other British cities.

Travellers from the USA and Canada can fly direct to Paris and to the larger provincial cities such as Nice and Lyon on Air France and most US airlines. For long-haul passengers, a charter flight to London then onward to Paris may prove cheaper.

For flights originating in the UK, check out Cheap Flights (www.cheapflights.com). In France, Nouvelles Frontières (www.nouvelles-frontieres.fr) and Lastminute (www.lastminute.fr) offer competitive fares on scheduled and charter flights. Opodo (www.opodo.com) is a Pan-European travel company that will offer you the best scheduled flight options available.

Students and those under 26 can get discount charter flights through specialist travel agencies. In the UK, try CTS Travel, 30 Rathbone Place, London W1T 1GQ, tel: 020-7290 0630. In the US, contact USIT, New York Student Centre, 891 Amsterdam Avenue, New York, NY 10025, tel: 212-663 5435, www.usitnow.com and www.usitworld.com.

AIRLINES

Air France: tel: 0845 0845 111 (UK), 800 237 2747 (USA), 08 20 32 08 20 (France), www.airfrance.com
American Airlines: tel: 08457 789 789 (UK), 800 433 7300 (USA), www.aa.com
British Airways: tel: 0870 850 9850 (UK), 800 247 9297 (USA), 08 25 82 54 00 (France), www.ba.com
British Midland: tel: 0870 6070 555 (UK), 800 788 0555 (USA), 08 00 05 01 42 (France), flybmi.com (discount applied when reservations are made on-line)
Continental Airlines: tel: 0800 776 464 (UK), 800 525 0280 (USA), www.continental.com
Delta: tel: 0800 414 767 (UK), 800 241 4141 (USA), 08 00 35 40 80 (France), www.delta.com

United Airlines: tel: 0845 844 777 (UK), 800 241 6522 (USA), www.united.com
Qantas Airways: tel: 0345 747 767 (UK), 13 13 13 (Australia), www.qantas.com

Budget Airlines
bmibaby.com: tel: 0870 264 2229 (UK), 800 788 0555 (USA), www.bmibaby.com
Brit Air: reservations through Air France, tel. 08 20 82 08 20, www.airfrance.fr
easyJet: tel: 0870 6000 000 (UK), 04 93 21 48 33 (France), www.easyjet.com
Ryanair: tel: 0871 246 0000 (UK), 0818 30 30 30 (Ireland), www.ryanair.com
Virgin Express: tel: 0870 7301 134 (UK), 08 00 52 85 28 (France), www.virgin-express.com

By Sea

Ferries from the UK, Ireland and the Channel Islands to the northern ports of France have reduced their prices since the Channel Tunnel opened. All ferries carry cars and foot passengers. Hovercraft were phased out in 2000 and replaced by Seacat catamarans. These offer the fastest

TRANSPORT

service but are subject to cancellation if the sea is really rough. Boulogne, Calais and Le Havre all have motorway links to Paris. Trains meet connecting ferries at Dover, Newhaven, Portsmouth, Weymouth and Folkestone.

The following companies operate from the UK:

Condor Ferries, tel: 01305 761 551, www.condorferries.co.uk, sail from Weymouth to St Malo and Portsmouth to Cherbourg.
Hoverspeed, tel: 08705 240 241, www.hoverspeed.co.uk, runs a two-hour Superseacat service from Newhaven to Dieppe and a one-hour Seacat service from Dover to Calais.
P&O Ferries, tel: 0870 242 4999, www.poferries.com, sails from Dover to Calais and Portsmouth to Le Havre and Cherbourg.
Irish Ferries, tel: 08705 171 1717, www.irishferries.ie, runs services from Rosslaire and Cork to both Le Havre and Cherbourg.

By Rail

The **Eurostar** has fast, frequent rail services from London (Waterloo International) or Ashford station to Paris (Gare du Nord). The service runs about 12 times a day and takes just under three hours (two hours from Ashford). For reservations, contact Eurostar at tel: 0990 134 909 (UK) or tel: 08 92 35 35 39 (France) or visit www.eurostar.com. There are reduced fares if you book in advance, and for children aged 4–11; those under 3 travel free but are not guaranteed a seat.

For those coming from the UK by car, **Eurotunnel** takes cars and passengers from Folkestone to Calais on a drive-on, drive-off service, known in French as *Le Shuttle*, taking 35 minutes platform to platform and about one hour from motorway to motorway. Payment is made at toll booths, which accept cash, cheques or credit cards, and the price applies to the car, regardless of the number of passengers or car

size. You can book in advance with Eurotunnel at tel: 0990 353 535 (UK), tel: 03 21 00 61 00 (France), www.eurotunnel.com (and may get a better deal by doing so) or simply turn up and take the next available service. *Le Shuttle* runs 24 hours a day, all year, and there are between two and five an hour, depending on the season and time of day.

Paris has six railway stations with lines radiating across France and Europe. Each connects with at least two Métro or RER lines and all have left-luggage facilities *(consignes)* and coin-operated lockers *(consignes automatiques).*The SNCF's much-publicised Train à Grande Vitesse (TGV) offers a rapid and comfortable service from Paris to Bordeaux, Brest, La Rochelle, Lille, Calais, Lyon and Marseille. It is not cheap, so it pays to travel off-peak. You must reserve in advance to travel on a TGV, and booking 30 days in advance could get you a reduction of up to 50 percent. Information and reservations are available from **Rail Europe**, tel: 08705 848 848 (UK), www.raileurope.co.uk, or **French Railways (SNCF)**, tel: 08 36 35 35 35 (France), www.sncf.com.

Note that before boarding an SNCF train you must have your ticket date-stamped *(composté)* for it to be valid. Simply insert your ticket in the orange *composteur* machine at the platform entrance.

By Bus

National Express Eurolines is a consortium of almost 30 European coach companies. Its services run from London (Victoria Coach Station) to Paris daily and it is one of the cheaper ways to get to the French capital. Discounts are available for young people and senior citizens and the ticket includes the ferry crossing (via Dover). For more information contact **National Express Eurolines** at 4 Cardiff Road, Luton, Bedfordshire, LU1

1PP, tel: 08705 143 219, www.nationalexpress.com, or **Eurolines France** at Gare Routière-Coach Station Galliéni, 28 avenue du Général de Gaulle, 93170 Bagnolet (Métro Galliéni), tel: 08 36 69 52 52 or visit www.eurolines.fr.

GETTING AROUND

From the Airports

From Roissy/Charles-de-Gaulle

Train

Trains are the quickest and most reliable way to get to central Paris. RER trains go direct from terminal 2 (Air France flights), or you can take the connecting shuttle bus *(navette)* from terminal 1. Trains run every 15 minutes between 5am and 11.45pm to Métros at Gare du Nord or Châtelet. The average journey time is about 45 minutes.

Bus

The Roissy bus runs between the airport and Rue Scribe, near the Place de l'Opéra from terminals 1 gate 30, 2A gate 10 and 2D gate 12. It runs every 15 minutes from 6am to 11pm and takes between 45 and 60 minutes. Alternatively, the Air France bus (to Métro Porte de Maillot or Charles-de-Gaulle Etoile) leaves from terminals 2A and 2B or terminal 1, arrival level gate 34. The bus runs every 12 minutes from 5.40am to 11pm.

Taxi

This is by far the most expensive but unquestionably the easiest way to get to Paris from the air-

BETWEEN AIRPORTS

An Air France bus links Roissy/Charles-de-Gaulle and Orly every 15 minutes from 5.45am to 11pm.

ACCOMMODATION

ACTIVITIES

A – Z

LANGUAGE

port. The journey can take from 30 minutes to over an hour, depending on the volume of traffic. The cost appears on the meter, but remember to account for the supplement that is charged for each large piece of luggage and bulky items like pushchairs.

From Orly

Train

Take the shuttle from gate H at Orly Sud or arrivals gate F at Orly Ouest to the Orly railway station. The RER stops at Austerlitz, Pont St-Michel and the Quai d'Orsay. It runs every 15 minutes from 5.50am to 10.50pm and takes approximately 30 minutes to Austerlitz.

The Orlybus (to Place Denfert-Rochereau) leaves from Orly Sud gate F or Orly Ouest arrivals gate D. It runs every 10–12 minutes from 6am to 11.30pm.

The Orlyval automatic train is a shuttle to Antony (the nearest RER to Orly). It runs every 5–8 minutes from 6.30am to 9.15pm Monday to Saturday and 7am–10.55pm on Sunday, and takes 30 minutes.

Bus

Air France buses (to Invalides and Gare Montparnasse) leave from Orly Sud, gate J or Orly Ouest arrivals gate E. They run every 20 minutes from 6am to 11pm and take 30 minutes. Tickets are available from the Air France terminus. For more information, visit www.airfrance.fr.

Taxi

Taxis are available outside the terminal buildings any time. The journey from Orly to the city centre takes 20–40 minutes, depending on the traffic.

Public Transport

Métro and RER

Run by the Régie Autonome des Transports Parisiens (RATP), the Paris Métro is one of the world's oldest subway systems. Used by around 9 million people every day, it is quick and efficient.

The Métro operates from 5.30am, with the last train leaving end stations at 12.30am. You can pick up a comprehensive map free at any Métro station. The lines are identified by numbers, colours and the names of their terminals, so Line 4 running north is shown as Porte de Clignancourt, while going south it is Porte d'Orléans. Follow the orange correspondance signs to change Métro lines.

TAXIS

Taxis are readily available at the airports and railway stations. In the city itself there are almost 500 taxi ranks, but be careful to hail only a genuine taxi – one with a light on the roof – as other operators may charge exorbitant fares. The white light will be on if a cab is free, while a glowing orange light means that the taxi is engaged.

Taxi drivers in Paris operate on three rates:

● **Tariff A** 7am–7pm Monday to Saturday
● **Tariff B** 7pm–7am Monday to Saturday and all day Sunday
● **Tariff C** at night in the suburbs and during the day in the outlying districts of Hauts-de-Seine, Seine St-Denis and Val-de-Marne, when the taxi has no client for the return journey.

The following taxi companies take phone bookings 24 hours a day:
Alpha: 01 45 85 85 85
Artaxi: 08 91 70 25 50
G7: 01 47 39 47 39
Taxis Bleus: 08 25 16 10 10.

If you have a complaint about Paris taxis, it should be addressed to: Services des Taxis, Préfecture de Police, 36 rue des Morillons, 75015, tel: 01 55 76 20 02.

The Métro runs in conjunction with the RER (suburban regional express trains), which operates five main lines, identified as A, B, C, D and E. RER trains run daily every 12 minutes from 5.30am to midnight (and till 1am Friday–Saturday).

The Métro and the bus system use the same tickets (€1.30 for a single fare at 2004 rates). A book or carnet of 10 tickets, which is available from bus or Métro stations and some tabacs (tobacconists), offers a considerable saving at just €10.

Another option is the Paris Visite card, valid for one, two, three or five consecutive days on the Métro, bus and railway in the Paris/Ile de France region, in zones one to three (approximate prices €9, €14, €19 and €27 and for children aged 4–11 it costs approximately €5, €7, €10 and €14). The card also entitles you to a discount at several tourist sites and can be bought from main Métro, RER and SNCF stations. It is only available to tourists. Check www.citefutee.com/informer/tarif.php for further information on the most up-to-date prices.

For shorter stays, you can buy the Mobilis card, which allows an unlimited number of trips for a day on the Métro, bus, suburban SNCF, RER and the night buses, extending as far as Disneyland Paris. It can be bought in all Métro stations.

A Carte Orange allows unlimited travel on the number of zones of your choice on any public transport system for a week or a month (approximately €15 or €49). A Carte Jaune gives you unlimited travel from Monday to Monday. To buy either of these you need to take along a passport photograph to any Métro or SNCF station. Sign your card and copy its number onto your ticket – you will be fined by ticket inspectors if you fail to do this.

For further information on the Paris Métro and RER network, contact RATP; www.ratp.fr.

Buses

Taking the bus is a pleasant way to see the city but is much slower than the Métro because of often heavy traffic. Tickets can be bought from the driver or from Métro stations, as buses accept the same tickets as the Métro. Remember to punch your ticket, and not your travel card, in the *composteur*.

Buses don't automatically stop, so when you want to get off push one of the request buttons and the *arrêt demandé* (bus stopping) sign will light up. Each bus has a map of its route posted at the front and back and at every bus stop. Most buses run from 6.30am to 8.30pm, although some routes continue until 12.30am.

A night service — the *Noctambus* – leaves Place du Châtelet (Avenue Victoria or Rue St-Martin) at 1.30am, 2.30am, 3.30am, 4.30am and 5.30am on 10 routes. Travel passes are valid on the night bus and stops are marked by a special black-and-yellow owl logo.

Look out for the *Balabus* service at certain stops. It visits the main tourist sites every Sunday and on public holidays between 11 April and 26 September, 12.30–8pm. The tour lasts about 50 minutes.

Private Transport

Driving in Paris requires confidence and concentration. In fact the best thing to do with a car in the city is to leave it in a car park and take public transport.

If you do intend to drive, here are a few guidelines. Seat belts are obligatory in both the front and back of the car, and the speed limit in town is 50kph (30mph). Do not drive in bus lanes at any time, and give priority to vehicles approaching from the right. This applies to some roundabouts, where cars on the roundabout stop for those coming on to it. Helmets are compulsory for motorbike riders and passengers.

Street parking is very difficult to find; it is usually metered Monday–Saturday 9am–7pm (paid for with a *Paris Carte*, currently €10 or €30, purchased from a local *tabac*) and the maximum stay is two hours; most car parks are underground (see www.parkingsdeparis.fr). Illegally parked cars may be towed away. Be sure not to leave any possessions visible to would-be thieves, as theft from cars is very common.

Petrol can be difficult to find in the city centre, so if your tank is almost empty you should head for a *porte* (exit) on the *Périphérique* (the multi-lane ring road), where there are petrol stations that are open 24 hours a day all year round.

Drivers are liable to heavy on-the-spot fines for speeding and drunk driving. The drink limit in France is 50mg/litre of alcohol in the blood (equivalent to about two glasses of wine) and is strictly enforced.

Car Hire

Hiring a car is expensive, partly because it incurs the highest rate of TVA tax, at 33 percent. Some fly/drive packages are good value, if you are on a short visit. The SNCF offers a good deal on its combined train/car hire bookings *(train + auto)*. Weekly rates often work out better than a daily rate, and it may be cheaper to hire a vehicle from the UK or the US before leaving. The minimum age for hiring a car is 23, or 21 if paying by credit card. The hirer must have held a full licence for at least a year.

Central reservation offices of the major car hire firms are:
Auto Europe, www.autoeurope.com (on-line bookings only; reservations are best made before your trip).
Avis, tel: 08 20 05 05 05, www.avis.com.
Europcar/National/InterRent, tel: 08 25 35 83 58, www.europcar.com.
Hertz, tel: 01 39 38 38 38, www.hertz.com.

Bicycles

If you know Paris well and have nerves of steel, a bicycle is an excellent way to explore. You can hire bicycles from:
Paris-Vélo, 2 rue du Fer à Moulin, 75005, tel: 01 43 37 59 22, fax: 01 47 07 67 45, www.paris-velo-rent-a-bike.fr.
Paris à Vélo C'est Sympa, 37 bvd Bourdon, tel: 01 48 87 60 01, fax: 01 48 87 61 01, www.parisvelosympa.com.

Hitchhiking

It can be difficult to get a lift out of the channel ports, so take a bus or train for the first leg of your journey. Hitching is forbidden on the *autoroutes* (motorways), but waiting on slip roads or at toll booths is allowed.

Allostop aims to connect hitchhikers with drivers. You simply pay a registration fee and a contribution towards the total petrol cost. Tel: 08 25 80 36 66, or visit www.allostop.net.

ACCOMMODATION

SOME THINGS TO CONSIDER
BEFORE YOU BOOK THE ROOM

Choosing a Hotel

Paris is renowned for the diversity of its hotels, from small, family-run guesthouses to four-star de-luxe hotels. It is advisable to reserve accommodation in advance, either with the hotel or via the Paris Tourist Office (*see Recommended Websites on page 226 and Tourist Offices on page 229*). They will book your first night's accommodation if you apply in person. The tourist offices supply a free booklet listing all hotels, pensions and similar establishments in Paris and the neighbouring suburbs that have been awarded a classification by the Direction de l'Industrie Touristique.

The following organisations also offer reservation services:
Paris Séjour Réservations, 90 ave des Champs-Elysées, tel: 01 53 89 10 50, fax: 01 53 89 10 59, www.psrparis.com.
Prestotel, 1 rue Condorcet, 75009, tel: 01 45 26 22 55, fax: 01 45 26 05 14.

Holiday Flats

The following companies let apartments to tourists. These range from bedsits to five-bedroom flats.
France-Ermitage, 5 rue Berryer, 75008, tel: 01 42 56 23 42, fax: 01 42 56 08 99, www.france-ermitage.com.
Flatotel Expo, 52 rue d'Oradour-

sur-Glane, 75015, tel: 01 45 54 93 45, fax: 01 45 54 93 07.
ABM Rent-a-flat, 12 rue Valentin Haüy, 75015, tel: 01 45 67 04 04, fax: 01 45 67 90 15, www.abmrentaflat.com.
At Home in Paris, 16 rue Médéric, 75017, tel: 01 42 12 40 40, fax: 01 42 12 40 48, www.at-home-in-paris.com.

Prices & Booking

Hotel prices in Paris are not subject to restrictions and can be changed without notice, so check before booking. The majority of hotels vary prices by season. State your arrival time if you book by phone or your room will not be held after 7pm.

ACCOMMODATION LISTINGS

ILE DE LA CITÉ, ILE ST-LOUIS AND THE MARAIS

HOTELS

Hôtel Britannique
20 ave Victoria
75001
Tel: 01 42 33 74 59
Fax: 01 42 33 82 65
www.hotel-britannique.fr

A comfortable hotel near the Ile de la Cité, furnished with some inviting leather sofas in the sitting room. Courteous service. 40 rooms. €€€
Hotel des Deux-Iles
59 rue St-Louis-en-l'Ile
75004

Tel: 01 43 26 13 35
Fax: 01 43 29 60 25
A peaceful and attractive hotel in a 17th-century mansion house in the heart of the Ile-St-Louis. There are 17 rooms, some with views over a pretty courtyard. €€€

Map, page 70

Hôtel Pavillon de la Reine
28 place des Vosges
75003
Tel: 01 40 29 19 19
Fax: 01 40 29 19 20
www.pavillon-de-la-reine.com
Arguably the smartest hotel in the Marais, housed in an imposing mansion. It has 55 rooms furnished with Louis XIII-style antiques, some of which overlook the lovely Pavillon de la Reine courtyards. €€€€

Les Argonautes
12 rue de la Huchette
75005
Tel: 01 43 26 79 86
Fax: 01 44 07 18 84
A comfortable hotel in a bustling part of town by the Théâtre de la Huchette. €€

Hôtel de la Place des Vosges
12 rue Birague
75004
Tel: 01 42 72 60 46
Fax: 01 42 72 02 64
An attractive former stables that has been carefully renovated. There are only 16 rooms, all with bath or shower, making the hotel intimate but comfortable. It's popular, so book ahead. Note that the lift only goes as far as the fourth floor. €€€

Castex Hôtel
5 rue Castex
75004
Tel: 01 42 72 31 52

Fax: 01 42 72 57 91
www.castex-paris-hotel.com
A small pristine hotel with 29 rooms, close to the Bastille and the Place des Vosges. It is very popular, so book well in advance. €€

Hôtel Saint-Louis Marais
1 rue Charles V
75004
Tel: 01 48 87 87 04
Fax: 01 48 87 33 26
A small, comfortable hotel with an impressive reception area. Offers 16 rooms, all with 17th-century beams. TV in rooms. €€

Hôtel Saint-Merry
78 rue de la Verrerie
75004

Tel: 01 42 78 14 15
Fax: 01 40 29 06 82
This is probably the most original hotel in Paris. The Saint-Merry was once a 17th-century presbytery, and the 11 rooms are decorated accordingly, with mahogany church pews and iron candelabra and, in one, a carved-stone flying buttress. The phone booth is in a confessional. The windows are, of course, stained glass. Affable Mr Crabbe, the owner, has devoted 35 years to renovating this Gothic masterpiece. No credit cards. €€

BEAUBOURG, LES HALLES, LOUVRE AND TUILERIES

HOTELS

Hôtel Tiquetonne
6 rue Tiquetonne
75002
Tel: 01 42 36 94 58
Fax: 01 42 36 02 94
Nicely situated in an old part of Paris close to Les Halles, the Tiquetonne is popular and well maintained, with 47 sizeable en-suite double rooms. Closed: August. €

Hôtel Victoria Chatelet
17 av. Victoria
75001
Tel: 01 40 26 90 17
Fax: 01 40 26 35 61
A small hotel in a bustling part of town with 24 rooms. €€€

Hôtel Vivienne
40 rue Vivienne
75002
Tel: 01 42 33 13 26
Fax: 01 40 41 98 19
Close to the Bourse, with 44 rooms. €€

Hôtel de Rouen
42 rue Croix-des-Petits-Champs
75001
Tel/fax: 01 42 61 38 21
Small, cosy hotel with 22 rooms; an excellent spot by the Louvre. €

Hôtel Andrea
3 rue St Bon
75004
Tel: 01 42 78 43 93
Fax: 01 44 61 28 36
This modest hotel with 26 rooms is handily situated just off the Rue de Rivoli. €€

Edouard VII
39 av. de l'Opéra
75002
Tel: 01 42 61 56 90
www.edouard7hotel.com
Historic hotel on one of the most beautiful avenues in Paris, L'Avenue de l'Opéra, close to the Garnier Opera house and the Louvre. The hotel features the newly-opened Angl'Opera

restaurant. €€€€/€€€€€

Hôtel Normandy
7 rue de l'Echelle
75001
Tel: 01 42 60 61 08
Fax: 01 42 60 45 81
Between the Louvre and the Opera, the Normandy offers traditional comfort; 115 well-appointed rooms, bar and restaurant. €€€€

Hôtel Costes
239 rue St-Honoré
75001
Tel: 01 42 44 50 00
Fax: 01 4 44 50 01
A fashionable hotel near the Tuileries in the chic Rue St-Honoré. A gorgeous terrace, where guests can dine in the summer, a fitness centre and a pool. €€€€

Hôtel Meurice
228 rue de Rivoli
75001
Tel: 01 44 58 10 10
Fax: 01 44 58 10 15
www.meuricehotel.com

Maps, pages 70, 94

Elegant, 18th-century-style salons and a Michelin-starred restaurant. The 152 sound-proofed, air-conditioned rooms, and 28 suites are located under the Rue de Rivoli arcades, with views over the beautiful Tuileries. €€€€

PRICE CATEGORIES

Price ranges, per double room, are as follows:
€30–€55 = €
€55–€100 = €€
€100–€200 = €€€
€200–€300 = €€€€
over €300 = €€€€€

TRANSPORT
ACCOMMODATION
ACTIVITIES
A – Z
LANGUAGE

GRANDS BOULEVARDS & CHAMPS-ELYSÉES

HOTELS

Hôtel Berne Opéra
37 rue de Berne
75008
Tel: 01 43 87 08 92
Fax: 01 43 87 08 93
Set in a quiet street, this is a comfortable and pleasant hotel with 36 rooms, that is welcoming to young families. €€€

Hôtel Le Bristol
112 rue du Faubourg St-Honoré
75008
Tel: 01 53 43 43 00
Fax: 01 53 43 43 01
www.lebristolparis.com
This is a discreetly upmarket 1920s' hotel with period furniture in all 195 rooms. Lovely gardens complete an extremely pleasant experience. Expensive, but worth it. €€€€

Hôtel Ritz
15 place Vendôme
75001
Tel: 01 43 16 30 70/71/72
Fax: 01 43 16 36 68/69
www.ritzparis.com
The Ritz offers pure, unashamed luxury in one of the finest squares in the capital. Sadly, it is now often remembered as the setting for the last supper eaten by Princess Diana and Dodi

Map, page 94

al-Fayed (son of the owner). Beyond most budgets, but for a taste of luxury, have a cocktail in the elegant Hemingway Bar. €€€€€

MONTMARTRE, BASTILLE AND EAST PARIS

HOTELS

Hôtel Beaumarchais
3 rue Oberkampf
75011
Tel: 01 53 36 86 86,
01 43 38 32 86
www.hotelbeaumarchais.com
A fun, designer hotel located in the trendy Oberkampf district. There's a terrace and private parking (for a separate charge); 31 rooms. €€/€€€

Hôtel Regyn's Montmartre
18 place des Abbesses
Tel: 01 42 54 45 21
75018
www.regynsmontmartre.com
In the heart of Montmartre, opposite Abbesses Métro station. Some of the rooms have great views. Breakfast available. €€

La Pavillon Bastille
65 rue de Lyon
Tel: 01 43 43 96 52
75012
www.pavillon-bastille.com
Classy, contemporary hotel situated behind an

attractive courtyard opposite the Opéra Bastille. Decor is modern and clean. Popular with business people. €€€/€€€€

Hôtel Gilden Magenta
35 rue Yves Toudic
75010
Tel: 01 42 02 59 66
Situated near to the Canal St-Martin, a little of the beaten track, this is a value-for-money hotel with a small garden terrace and even smaller lift. All the rooms are clean and compact. €€

Timhôtel Paris
11 rue Ravignan, 75018
Central reservations, tel: 01 53 38 40 00, fax: 01 53 38 37 38
www.timhotel.com
A reliable chain with several hotels around the capital, including ones at the Place d'Italie, St Lazare, the Louvre and on the Boulevard Clichy. All hotels are fairly modern, well equipped and individually decorated. This one in Montmartre is in an attractive, tree-lined square with a fountain. €€/€€€

Hôtel Apollo
11 rue de Dunkerque
75010
Tel: 01 48 78 04 98
A traditional railway hotel opposite the Gare du Nord is a pleasant surprise for this location. Rooms are comfortable in an old-fashioned way and the windows are double glazed. €

Libertel Terminus Est
5 rue du 8 mai
75011
Tel: 01 55 26 05 05
www.libertel-hotels.com
Reminiscent of the grand age of steam, this great railway hotel has an old-style charm and class mixed with modern luxury and sleek design. €€€/€€€

Maps, pages 122, 133

Terrass Hôtel
12–14 rue Joseph-Maistre
75018
Tel: 01 46 06 72 85
www.terrrass-hotel.com
The main attraction of this Montmartre hotel is the view from the rooftop restaurant – it is superb and takes in the whole of Paris. A favourite with some celebrities who favour the hotel's plush suites. The rest of the rooms are comfortable if unremarkable. €€€

LATIN QUARTER AND ST-GERMAIN-DES-PRÉS

HOTELS

Hôtel des Alliés
20 rue Berthollet
75005
Tel: 01 43 31 47 52
Fax: 01 45 35 13 92
Few rooms in this simple yet well-maintained hotel in the middle of the Latin Quarter have their own bath or shower, but it's a good bargain if you are on a tight budget. €

Hôtel Familia
11 rue des Ecoles
75005
Tel: 01 43 54 55 27
Fax: 01 43 29 61 77
www.familiahotel.com
An excellent location, within a few minutes' walk of the islands and St-Germain-des-Prés. Fifth- and sixth-floor rooms have a view of Notre-Dame cathedral. The many return guests appreciate the hospitable Gaucheron family who live on the hotel premises and take great pride in its every detail. €

Hôtel Marignan
13 rue du Sommerard
75005
Tel: 01 43 25 31 03
www.hotel-marignan.com
An elegant-fronted hotel in the lively Latin Quarter. It offers 30 rooms as well as free kitchen laundry facilities. No credit cards. €

Hôtel La Louisiane
60 rue de Seine
75006
Tel: 01 43 29 59 30
Fax: 01 46 34 23 87
www.hotel-lalouisiane.com
The Louisiane has 80 well-furnished rooms and overlooks the bustling Buci market in St-Germain. €€

Hôtel de Saint-Germain
50 rue du Four
75006
Tel: 01 45 48 91 64
Fax: 01 45 48 46 22
www.hotel-de-saint-germain.fr
In an excellent location on the Left Bank, with 30 comfortable rooms. €€

Hôtel Lutetia
45 bvd Raspail
75006
Tel: 01 49 54 46 46
Fax: 01 49 54 46 00
www.lutetia-paris.com
An early Art Deco palace conveniently situated in the heart of the bustling St-Germain-des-Prés and once frequented by such literary luminaries as Dorothy Parker, Ernest Hemingway and F. Scott Fitzgerald. It still attracts a few famous faces: Catherine Deneuve is a regular visitor nowadays. €€€€

Hôtel Ibis Gare Montparnasse
71 bvd de Vaugirard
75015
Tel: 01 43 20 89 12
Fax: 01 43 22 77 71
A pleasant hotel, conveniently situated for browsing in the antique shops in the area; 31 rooms. €€

Aramis Saint-Germain
124 rue de Rennes
75006
Tel: 01 45 48 03 75
Fax: 01 45 44 99 29
One of the Best Western Group, a well-known American chain, the Aramis offers 42 attractive and comfortable rooms, with well-equipped bathrooms and TV. Some rooms have air-conditioning. Not far from the Jardin du Luxembourg. €€€

Des Grandes Ecoles
75 rue du Cardinal-Lemoine
75005
Tel: 01 43 26 79 23
Fax: 01 43 25 28 15
www.hotel-grandes-ecoles.com
At first glance, you might think you were in the French countryside here. There are 50 large rooms set around a cobbled courtyard and a garden of old trees and trellised roses. Although it is a short uphill walk from the Métro, you are still close enough to everything you may want to visit, including the Place de la Contrescarpe and Rue Mouffetard, for it to be convenient. €€

Hôtel Keppler
12 rue Keppler
75016
Tel: 01 47 20 65 05
Fax: 01 47 23 02 29
www.hotelkeppler.com
The rooms are furnished in Scandinavian style and four of them have balconies overlooking this smart neighbourhood. There is a spiral staircase, a welcoming fireplace and a bar which also offers room service, all impeccably managed by the family that owns it, making this excellent value for the money; 49 rooms. €

Hôtel Lenox
9 rue de l'Université
75007
Tel: 01 42 96 10 95
Fax: 01 42 61 52 63
www.lenoxsaintgermain.com
This trendy hotel is decorated in Art Deco style and is very popular among creative types such as photographers, artists and dress designers. There's a bar, and the rooms are spotless. It's very popular, so you should reserve well in advance if you can. €€€

Hôtel Montalembert
3 rue de Montalembert
75007
Tel: 01 45 49 68 68
Fax: 01 45 49 69 49
www.montalembert.com
The Montalembert has an ornate Beaux-Arts-style exterior and stylish rooms furnished with antiques. The attic suite is Sir Terence Conran's pied à terre. €€€€

Hôtel Bac Saint-Germain
66 rue du Bac
75007
Tel: 01 42 22 20 03
Fax: 01 45 48 52 30
A very pleasant hotel in a popular location, with 21 comfortable rooms and a glassed-in terrace on the seventh floor. €€€

Map, page 142

PRICE CATEGORIES

Price ranges, per double room, are as follows:
€30–€55 = €
€55–€100 = €€
€100–€200 = €€€
€200–€300 = €€€€
over €300 = €€€€€

TRANSPORT

ACCOMMODATION

ACTIVITIES

A – Z

LANGUAGE

MONTPARNASSE, THE EIFFEL TOWER AND INVALIDES

Hôtel du Palais Bourbon
49 rue Bourgogne
75007
Tel: 01 44 11 30 70
This is a modern hotel with 33 rooms in a quiet area. It's popular, so book well in advance, especially for the cheaper rooms. €€

Hôtel d'Angleterre
44 rue Jacob
75006
Tel: 01 42 60 34 72
Fax: 01 42 60 16 93
This was once the home of the British Ambassador and was the site on which the US Treaty of Independence was drawn up in 1783. Elegant yet relaxed and very comfortable, it is located in a smart corner of the Left Bank. There are 27 good-sized rooms, all en suite. €€€

Bradford Elysées Hôtel
10 rue St-Philippe-du-Roule
75008
Tel: 01 45 63 20 20
Fax: 01 45 63 20 07
www.astotel.com
Large, light and airy rooms by the Champs-Elysées make it a pleasure to stay in this elegantly furnished, intimate 1900s' hotel. There are 50 rooms, some of them on the hotel's two non-smoking floors, plus air conditioning and a bar. Good facilities for children, too. €€€€

Hôtel Royal Monceau
37 ave Hoche
75008
Tel: 01 42 99 88 00
Fax: 01 42 99 89 90
www.royalmonceau.com
The Royal Monceau offers grand, marble-floored public areas,

lavish antique furnishings and a central location close to the Champs-Elysées and the Arc de Triomphe. Caters mainly for a business clientele. There are 220 rooms and 40 suites. €€€

Banville
166 bvd Berthier
75017
Tel: 01 42 67 70 16
Fax: 01 44 40 42 77
Located close to L'Etoile and the Porte Maillot, this family-run hotel is clean and cosy. There are 38 well-appointed rooms, with chic marble bathrooms. Some rooms have terraces looking out towards the Eiffel Tower. €€€

Saint-Thomas-d'Aquin
3 rue du Pré-aux-Clercs
75007
Tel: 01 42 61 01 22
Fax: 01 42 61 41 43
www.hotel-st-thomas-daquin.com
Close to the Eiffel Tower and the Musée d'Orsay, this hotel offers 21 rooms, each with TV and telephone. Good for those holidaying with pets, as animals are allowed. €€

Hôtel De Crillon
10 place de la Concorde
75008
Tel: 01 44 71 15 00
Fax: 01 44 71 15 02
www.crillon.com
The Crillon is perhaps the grandest hotel in the capital, and may be the best known, as well. It is set in a stunning location on the Place de la Concorde, and frequented by film stars, heads of state and the very, very rich. The grand building – Marie-Antoinette used

to have singing lessons here – is also home to the Michelin-starred Ambassadeurs restaurant. €€€€€

Four Seasons George V
31 ave George V
75008
Tel: 01 49 52 70 00
Fax: 01 49 52 70 10
www.fourseasons.com
The well-furnished rooms have lavish marble bathrooms, and the hotel can count a restaurant, a top-class wine cellar and a health club among its many facilities. The George V is supremely elegant, stylish and extremely exclusive. €€€€€

Hilton International
18 ave de Suffren
75015
Tel: 01 44 38 56 25
Fax: 01 44 38 56 10
In a good, quiet location on the Left Bank, the Hilton offers impressive views of the Eiffel Tower, along with all the usual modern conveniences and efficient service. €€€€

Plaza-Athénée
25 ave Montaigne
75008
Tel: 01 53 67 66 65
Fax: 01 53 67 66 66
www.plaza-athenee-paris.com
This palatial hotel, featuring lavish Versace decor, offers 190 soundproofed rooms, a disco, a restaurant and suites furnished in Louis XVI or Regency style. Super-chef Alain Ducasse is in charge of the fabulous restaurant (see page 119). If you can't stretch to the price of a room, treat yourself to a cocktail in the fashionable bar. €€€€

Map, page 160

BED & BREAKFAST

Alcôve & Agapes, Le Bed & Breakfast à Paris
8 bis rue Coysevox
75018
Tel: 01 44 85 06 05
Fax: 01 44 85 06 14.
A service with more than 100 homes on its register. Hosts range from artists to grandmothers. €50– 110.

Good Morning Paris
43 rue Lacépède
75505
Tel: 01 47 07 28 29
Fax: 01 47 07 44 45
This company offers about 40 rooms throughout the city (prices ranging from €38 for one person to about €75 for three).

HOSTELS

Youth Hostels
Holders of accredited Youth Hostel Association cards may stay in Paris hostels for approximately €20 per night. The hostels are run by two organisations:
Fédération Unie des Auberges de Jeunesse (FUAJ)
27 rue Pajol
75018
Tel: 01 44 89 87 27
Fax: 01 44 89 87 49
www.fuaj.fr

Affiliated to the International Youth Hostel Federation.

Ligue Française pour les Auberges de Jeunesse (LFAJ)
67 rue Vergniaud
750013
Tel: 01 44 16 78 78
Fax: 01 44 16 78 80
www.auberges-de-jeunesse.com

The British YHA publishes the International Youth Hostel Handbook Vol I (revised at the end of each year), which includes all the hostels in the Paris region. It is available by post from the Youth Hostel Association, Trevelyan House, Dimple Road, Matlock, Derbyshire DE4 3YH, tel: 01629 592600, fax: 01629 592702, www.yha.org.uk.

In the US, apply to Hosteling International-USA, National Administrative Office, 8401 Colesville Road, Suite 600, Silver Spring, MD 20910, tel: 301 495 1240, fax: 301 495 6697, www.hiayh.org.

Tourist information offices offer a booklet *Jeunes à Paris* (Young People in Paris) with addresses and telephone numbers of hostels (some of which cannot be reserved in advance, you just have to turn up and take a chance).

UCRIF (*Union des Centres de Rencontres Internationaux*), 27 rue de Turbigo, 75002, tel: 01 40 26 57 64, fax: 01 40 26 58 20, www.ucrif.asso.fr, is also a helpful resource for young visitors to France.

Some of the main youth hostels are:
Auberge Jules Ferry
8 bvd Jules-Ferry
75011
Tel: 01 43 57 55 60
Fax: 01 43 14 82 09
In a convenient location near the Bastille.

Auberge Internationale des Jeunes
10 rue Trousseau
75011
Tel: 01 47 00 62 00
Fax: 01 47 00 33 16
www.aijparis.com
Also close to the Bastille.

Centre International de Paris/Louvre (BVJ)
20 rue Jean-Jacques Rousseau
75001
Tel: 01 53 00 90 90
A large hostel that is well situated for visiting the Louvre.

Le Fauconnier
11 rue du Fauconnier
75004
Tel: 01 42 74 23 45
www.mije.com
A renovated 17th-century building located in the Marais (Métro St-Paul/Pont-Marie), this is one of three hostels in Paris operated by Les Maisons Internationales de la Jeunesse et des Etudiants.

Le Fourcy
6 rue de Fourcy
75004
Tel: 01 42 74 23 45
Fax: 01 40 27 81 64
In the heart of the Marais.

Maubuisson
12 rue des Barres
75004
Tel: 01 42 74 23 45
Impressive medieval building near the Hôtel de Ville.

PRICE CATEGORIES

Price ranges, per double room, are as follows:
€30–€55 = €
€55–€100 = €€
€100–€200 = €€€
€200–€300 = €€€€
over €300 = €€€€€

TRANSPORT

ACCOMMODATION

ACTIVITIES

A – Z

LANGUAGE

ACTIVITIES

THE ARTS, NIGHTLIFE, FESTIVALS, SHOPPING AND SPECTATOR SPORTS

THE ARTS

Theatre, Opera, Ballet and Concerts

There is a wonderful choice of theatre, concerts, ballet and opera in Paris. Some of the main venues are listed below:

Cité de la Musique
223 av. Jean-Jaurès, 75019, tel: 01 44 84 45 00, fax: 01 44 84 44 84, www.cite-musique.fr. Opened in 1995, this complex at La Villette includes a concert hall, information service, museum and bookshop dedicated to music.

Comédie Française
2 rue Richelieu, 75001, tel: 08 25 10 16 80, fax: 08 26 80 16 80, www.comedie-francaise.fr. This is the principal national theatre where work by such greats as Molière and Racine are performed. More recent plays, including those by Genet and Anouilh, are also shown here.

Opéra Bastille
130 rue de Lyon, 75012, tel: 08 92 89 90 90. www.opera-de-paris.fr. The late 20th-century addition to Paris's operatic/ballet scene, where both opera and ballet are performed. Booking tickets can be a lengthy process, so allow plenty of time.

Opéra National du Palais Garnier
Place de l'Opéra, 75009, tel: 08 92 89 90 90. www.opera-de-paris.fr. The sumptuous 19th-century Paris opera house. Opera and ballet are staged in grandiose surroundings.

Théâtre du Châtelet
2 rue Edouard Colonne, 75001, tel: 01 40 28 28 40, fax: 01 40 28 29 01, www.chatelet-theatre.com. Opera and some modern dance performances; also puts on lunchtime concerts.

Théâtre du Vieux Colombier
21 rue du Vieux-Colombier, 75006, tel: 01 44 39 87 00, fax: 01 44 39 87 01,

WHAT'S ON AND WHERE TO GET TICKETS

The listings magazines *L'Officiel des Spectacles* and *Pariscope* (www.pariscope.com), which includes a very useful section in English prepared by *Time Out*, both appear every Wednesday with full details of cultural events and venues in and around the city.

The tourist office publishes a monthly listing, *Paris Selection*, and its information service is updated weekly, tel: 08 92 68 31 12 (approximately €0.50 per minute). Details are also available on their website: www.paris-touristoffice.com.

Main ticket agencies
Agence Spectaplus, Salle Pleyel, 252 rue du Faubourg St-Honoré, 75008, tel: 01 53 53 58 60; and other branches.
FNAC Billeterie, at the FNAC stores, 136 rue de Rennes, 75006, and 26 av. des Ternes, 75017. Bookings can also be made online at: www.fnac.fr.
Virgin Megastore, 52 av. des Champs-Elysées, 75008, tel: 01 49 53 50 00. Ticket bookings can be made by phone, tel: 01 44 68 44 08, and in person, Monday to Saturday 10am–midnight, and 12pm–midnight on Sunday.
Kiosque, 15 place de la Madeleine, 75008, sells tickets on the day at half price. Open Tuesday to Friday 12.30–8pm; on Saturday from 12.30pm for matinées and from 2pm for evening shows; on Sunday 12.30–4pm.
CROUS (Centre Régional des Oeuvres Universitaires et Scolaires), 39 av. Georges-Bernanos, 75005, tel: 01 40 51 36 00, www.crous-paris.fr. Offers reduced-price seats for students (with valid student cards).

www.theatreduvieuxcolombier.com.
Small-scale productions of classical and modern drama from the Comédie Française troupe.

Museums

Most national museums charge an entrance fee, but municipal museums are all free. Entrance is often cheaper on Sunday, and reductions are usually given for children, senior citizens and students with a valid student card. If you plan to visit several museums during your stay, buying a *Carte Musées* means you queue only once to visit 70 museums or monuments in Paris and the Ile de France region and you also save money on entrance prices. Tickets are available for one, three or five days and can be purchased from tourist offices, Métro stations or from museum ticket offices.

Many museums are open daily, although times vary on public holidays. As a general rule, national museums are closed on Tuesday and municipal museums close on Monday. Major museums stay open throughout the day, especially in summer, but smaller ones usually close for a long lunch from noon or 12.30pm to about 2.30pm.

NIGHTLIFE

Paris nightlife offers something for everyone, from elitist bars and clubs where you can do a bit of celebrity-spotting to underground cafés run by squatters. You can find jazz, salsa, tango, Congolese storytelling, shiatsu massages and, of course, traditional French *chansons*.

Cabarets

Chez Michou
80 rue des Martyrs, 75018, tel: 01 46 06 16 04, fax: 01 42 64 50 50, www.michou.fr. Drag shows every night.

The Crazy Horse
12 av. George V, 75008, tel: 01 47 23 97 90, fax: 01 47 23 54 54, www.lecrazyhorseparis.com. Two or three shows every night.

Aux Folies-Bergère
32 rue Richer, 75009, tel: 01 44 79 98 98, fax: 01 47 70 98 28, www.foliesbergere.com. You can hardly get near for the tour buses and it's expensive. Dine at 7pm for a 9.30pm show. Closed Monday.

Au Lapin Agile
22 rue des Saules, 75018, tel: 01 46 06 85 87, fax: 01 42 54 63 04, www.au-lapin-agile.com. Old-fashioned mayhem in Picasso's old haunt. Arrive early for a seat. It helps if you understand French.

Le Lido
116 bis av. des Champs-Elysées, 75008, tel: 01 40 7656 10, fax: 01 45 61 19 41, www.lido.fr. Three shows daily. The slickest of Parisian cabarets and home to the Bluebell Girls.

Moulin Rouge
82 bvd de Clichy, 75018, tel: 01 53 09 82 82, fax: 01 46 40 06 00, www.moulinrouge.fr. Two shows a night. Tourist prices and a host of tour buses.

Paradis Latin
28 rue Cardinal-Lemoine, 75005, tel: 01 43 25 28 28, fax: 01 43 29 63 63, www.paradis-latin.com. One show on every week night.

Nightclubs

Alcazar (Mezzanine)
62 rue Mazarine, 75006, tel: 01 53 10 19 99. A cool bar and even cooler DJs pull in a mixed crowd of Parisians and tourists.

Le Balajo
9 rue de Lappe, 75011, tel: 01 47 00 07 87. Popular club with a chic crowd; Latin and rock-and-roll music. Open Thursday and Sunday afternoon, and Thursday to Sunday evening.

Les Bains Douches
7 rue du Bourg-l'Abbé, 75003, tel: 01 48 87 01 80, fax: 01 48 87 13 70. Former Turkish baths

frequented by the smart set; some are there more for rubber necking than dancing. Open daily 11.30pm–5am.

Batofar
11 quai François-Mauriac 75013, tel: 01 56 29 10 33, www.batofar.org. A top candidate for coolest club in Paris, on a barge moored across from the new Bibliothèque Nationale. Electronic and world music concerts are a prelude to all-nighters with leading DJs. Open Tuesday to Sunday 8pm–2am.

Le Divan du Monde
75 rue des Martyrs, 75018, tel: 01 44 92 77 66. Cheap and friendly, this former café (where Toulouse-Lautrec was a regular) is now a throbbing, eclectic nightclub (R&B, Brazilian, trance, etc.); no elitist door policy or dress code. Open daily 8.30pm–dawn.

Elysée Montmartre
72 bvd Rochechouart, 75018, tel: 08 92 68 36 22. Fun for all ages, with theme evenings from rock 'n' roll to salsa (check listings magazines for details on any specific evening). Open Friday and Saturday 11pm–5am.

Les Etoiles
61 rue du Château-d'Eau, 75010, tel: 01 47 60 60 56. This is a stylish Latino club in an old cinema. Attracts top-quality musicians and a hip crowd. Open Thursday 9pm–3.30am, Friday to Saturday 9pm–4.30am.

Folies Pigalle
11 place Pigalle, 75018, tel: 01 48 78 55 25. A very popular disco in an area that never sleeps. Open Thursday to Saturday midnight to dawn, Sunday 6pm–midnight.

La Java
105 rue du Faubourg-du-Temple, 75010, tel: 01 42 02 20 52. Latin American music in a Belleville dance hall. Open Thursday to Saturday 11pm–6am, Sunday 2–7pm.

La Locomotive
90 bvd de Clichy, 75018, tel: 01 53 41 88 88. Rough, ready, mainstream and enormous.

Situated right next door to the Moulin Rouge. Daily 11pm–dawn.

Le Moloko
26 rue Fontaine, 75009, tel: 01 48 74 50 26. Chic, sharp and bedraggled – they're all here for cocktails, wine or a boogie.

Pubs and Bars

Bar du Crillon
Hôtel de Crillon, 16 rue Boissy d'Anglas, 75008, tel: 01 44 71 15 39. This is where Hemingway drank when he had the money. The turn-of-the-20th-century decor has been given a designer facelift by Sonia Rykiel.

La Belle Hortense
31 rue Vieille-du-Temple, 75004, Tel: 01 48 04 71 60. This wine bar and bookshop is one of the few non-smoking bars in Paris.

Flann O'Brien's
6 rue Bailleul, 75001, tel: 01 42 60 13 58. One of the first Irish pubs in Paris and now a venue for watching televised Irish football and rugby internationals.

La Flèche d'Or
102 bis rue de Bagnolet, 75020, tel: 01 43 72 04 23, www.flechedor.com. A hip Mecca for eastern Paris, The Golden Arrow occupies the premises of a former railway station. Free concerts on weeknights at 6pm.

The Frog & Rosbif
116 rue St-Denis, 75002, tel: 01 42 36 34 73, www.frogpubs.com. An English pub serving home-brewed ales, as well as Guinness and lagers on tap.

Le Fumoir
6 rue de l'Admiral-de-Coligny, 75001, tel: 01 42 92 00 24. This "smoking room" is not particularly smoky but does feel more like a club than a bar. Regulars sit in plush leather chairs sipping *mojitos* (rum-based Cuban cocktails) while perusing something from the 3000-plus library or the rack of newspapers.

Harry's Bar
5 rue Daunou, 75002, tel: 01 42 61 71 14. A legendary Parisian landmark that is said to be the birthplace of the Bloody Mary.

F. Scott Fitzgerald was a regular in the 1920s.

The Honest Lawyer
176 rue de la Pompe, 75016, tel: 01 45 05 14 23. A short walk from Place Victor Hugo, this yuppie pub has three televisions and reasonably-priced pub grub. There is a jazz brunch on Sunday.

The Lizard Lounge
18 rue du Bourg-Tibourg, 75004, tel: 01 42 72 81 34. Lots of students, Anglophone au pairs, and Anglophile French perch at the bar that undulates around the room, or retreat to the intimate basement.

Man Ray
34 rue Marbeuf, 75008, tel: 01 56 88 36 36, www.manray.fr. Jointly owned by actors Johnny Depp, Sean Penn and John Malkovich (and you don't get any cooler than that), this former cinema near the Champs-Elysées is now an opulent bar/restaurant, serving Californian-Asian cuisine.

Rosebud
11 bis rue Delambre, 75014, tel: 01 43 35 38 54. The decor is a throwback to the 1930s when the likes of Jean-Paul Sartre sometimes drank here. It draws an older crowd, including many arty and media types.

Xtremes Bar
10 rue Caumartin, 75009, www.xtremes.fr. Something for everyone, with a lounge and chill-out music on the top floor and sports broadcast live from the bar on the ground floor.

Music Venues

Jazz Bars

Caveau de la Huchette
5 rue de la Huchette, 75006, tel: 01 43 26 65 05. Frequented by GIs in WW II it now hosts a young clientele for cellar jazz. Open Monday to Thursday 9.30pm to 2.30am, Saturday to Sunday 9.30pm–3.30am.

La Chapelle des Lombards
19 rue de Lappe, 75011, tel: 01 43 57 24 24. Lively music in a

popular club. Open Thursday to Saturday 10.30pm–dawn.

La Cigale
120 bvd de Rochechouart, 75018, tel: 01 49 25 89 99. A popular club hosting up-and-coming bands. Telephone beforehand for concert details.

New Morning
7–9 rue des Petites-Ecuries, 75010, tel: 01 45 23 51 41. For aficionados. Concerts usually start at 9pm.

Le Sunset
60 rue des Lombards, 75001, tel: 01 40 26 46 60. There's a restaurant on the ground floor and jazz in the basement at 10pm (9pm on Sunday).

CINEMA

Paris has a high concentration of multi-screen cinemas showing the latest films, but if you'd rather see a French classic than the most recent Hollywood blockbuster, there are a number of good retro and art-house cinemas too. The majority of cinemas in the centre of Paris show films in their original language with subtitles in French (these are marked "VO" – *version originale*), though once you get out of the city centre, mainstream films are usually dubbed (and marked "VF" – *version française*). Ticket prices are reduced by up to 30 percent on Monday and/or Wednesday.

For an up-to-date programme, *Pariscope*, the city's weekly listings magazine, has a section in English giving programme details. The following cinemas frequently show films in English:

Action Ecoles
23 rue des Ecoles, 75005, tel: 01 43 29 79 89. Screens new copies of old classics, English and French.

Le Champo
51 rue des Ecoles, 75005, tel: 01 43 54 51 60. Ever-popular art-house cinema in the Latin Quarter.

Le Cinéma des Cinéastes
7 av. de Clichy 75017, tel: 01 53
42 40 20. A three-screen cinema
for film buffs, with a varied international programme of films.
Gaumont Marignan
27–33 av. des Champs-Elysées,
75008, tel: 08 92 69 66 96. One
of many multi-screen complexes
on the Champs-Elysées.
Gaumont Grand Ecran Italie
30 place d'Italie, 75013, tel: 08
36 68 75 55. With the biggest
screen in the city, this is the place
to see the latest blockbusters.
La Géode
Parc de la Villette, 75019, tel: 08
92 66 45 40. An OMNIMAX cinema
housed inside a huge glittering
dome. Mainly nature- or science-
themed films.
Le Grand Rex
1 bvd Poissonnière, 75002, tel:
08 92 68 05 96. Art Deco cinema with one huge screen.
Max Linder Panorama
24 bvd Poissonnière, 75009, tel:
08 92 68 50 52. A panoramic
screen and state-of-the-art acous-
tics in a 1930s setting – which
gives you the best of both worlds.
MK2 Quai de la Seine
14 quai de la Seine, 75019, tel:
08 92 68 14 07. The first of nine
cinemas in the MK2 chain, with
six screens and a restaurant.
La Pagode
57 bis rue de Babylone, 75007,
tel: 01 45 55 48 48. The latest
films are shown in a tranquil Japanese setting. Serves good tea.
UGC Ciné-Cité Les Halles
7 place de la Rotonde, Nouveau
Forum des Halles (level 3),
75001, tel: 08 92 70 00 00. A
huge, 16-screen cinema showing
mainstream and art-house films.
UGC Ciné-Cité Bercy
2 cour St-Emilion, 75012 tel: 08
92 70 00 00. The city's biggest
multiplex cinema with 18 screens.

FOR CHILDREN

Most children are not interested in
city sightseeing; Disneyland *(see
pages 184–9)* is what they are

after. Or an afternoon in one of
Paris's parks *(see pages 176–82)*.
For details of other activities
which should appeal to children,
such as plays, films, puppet
shows and circuses, refer to
L'Officiel des Spectacles and
Pariscope.
   In terms of accommodation,
most hotels have family rooms,
so children are not separated
from their parents. A cot *(lit
bébé)* can often be provided for a
small supplement, but ask first if
booking in advance.
   Taking your children out to a
restaurant should not be a problem (although check beforehand
with the more upmarket places).
French children are used to eating out from an early age and are
therefore generally well behaved.
Many restaurants offer a children's menu. If not, they may
split a *prix-fixe* menu between
two. With very young children,
just request an extra plate and
give them food from your own.
Alternatively, order a simple dish
from the *à la carte* menu, such
as an omelette or soup. With the
bread that comes automatically
to a French table, and ice-cream

or fruit to follow, most children
will be well fed.

Puppet Shows
**Théâtre de Marionettes du
Jardin du Luxembourg**
Tel: 01 43 26 46 47 or 01 43 29
50 97 for a recorded message (in
French) about current children's
puppet shows.

Babysitting
L'Officiel des Spectacles and
Pariscope list babysitting services. High-grade hotels should
be able to arrange babysitters for
you. Here are two services:
Kids' Service
75 bvd Péreire, 75005, tel: 01
47 66 00 52 (Métro Wagram).
Open Monday to Friday
8am–8pm, Saturday 10am–8pm.
Reduced hours during August.
One of the oldest babysitting
agencies in Paris with a young,
dependable team of qualified
nannies and play supervisors.
Home Service
2 rue Pierre-Semard, 75009, tel:
01 42 82 05 04, fax: 01 40 16
48 88, www.homeserviceidf.com.
For babysitting services at any
time of the day or night.

FESTIVALS AND EVENTS

A listing of the major events in
Paris is available from the Tourist
Office *(see page 229)*. Here are
some of the festivals and
events that occur every year:
● **January** fashion shows at
Paris-Expo, Métro: Porte de
Versailles
● **late March–early May** *Foire
du Trône.* France's biggest
funfair; Pelouse de Reuilly,
Métro: Porte Dorée
● **late March–early April** Paris
Film Festival; Champs-Elysées
● **late May–early June** French
Tennis Open, Grand Slam
event; Roland Garros stadium,
Métro: Porte d'Auteuil
● **June** *Fête de la Musique* (21
June). Huge street music festival, with free concerts and
dancing everywhere.

● **July** Bastille Day. Celebrations
to mark the storming of the
Bastille usually begin the
evening of 13 July. Military
parade on 14 July starts at
10am on the Champs-
Elysées.
● **September** *Journée du Patrimoine* (3rd weekend). Open
day at otherwise off-limits government and private buildings.
Festival d'Automne (until
Dec). Annual festival of theatre, music and dance.
● **November** The Beaujolais
Nouveau is celebrated in bars
and cafés (3rd Thur of month).
● **December** Notre Dame is
packed for the 11pm Christmas Eve service. New Year's
Eve crowds fill the Champs-
Elysées; fireworks at Trocadéro.

SHOPPING

What to Buy

Paris is the designer city of the world. Alongside France's chains such as Naf Naf and Kookaï, all the top-name couturiers have boutiques. The top couture houses are in the Avenue Montaigne area and around the Faubourg St-Honoré, with more individual boutiques clustering around the Marais and St-Germain-des-Prés.

Other main shopping areas include the Rue de Rivoli, which runs from the Marais to the Louvre, the streets around the Opéra and the Boulevard Haussmann. For smaller boutiques and more individual designs you're best advised to visit the appealing narrow alleys of the Marais.

Where to Buy

Department Stores

Le Bon Marché Rive Gauche
22 rue de Sèvres, 75007, tel: 01 44 39 80 00, www.lebonmarche.fr. One of Paris's most stylish *grands magasins*, housed in a building designed by the architect Gustave Eiffel. Once called *"une cathédrale du commerce"* it sells haute couture fashions and make-up. Highlights of the ground floor are the Theatre of Beauty, devoted to the hottest make-up artist brands, and the men's section, Balthazar, with polished wood floors and designer boutiques.
La Grande Epicerie de Paris
38 rue de Sèvres, 75007, tel: 01 44 39 81 00, www.lagrandeepicerie.fr. Le Bon Marché's gourmet grocery store sells every delicacy under the sun.
Galeries Lafayette
40 bvd Haussmann, 75009, tel: 01 42 82 34 56, www.galerieslafayette.com. An entire floor devoted to lingerie, and the largest perfume department in

TAX

the world, beneath a breathtakingly beautiful Art Nouveau steel and glass dome – just some of the delights of this massive department store that carries over 75,000 brand names.
Au Printemps
64 bvd Haussmann, 75009, tel: 01 42 82 50 00, www.printemps.com. The store is situated in three separate buildings – each devoted to a theme: L'Homme (men's fashion), La Maison (home) and La Mode (women's fashion). There is a good selection of new designer collections, plus large departments specialising in china, kitchenware and stationery.
La Samaritaine
19 rue de la Monnaie, 75001, tel: 01 40 41 20 20, www.lasamaritaine.com. Located at the north end of the Pont-Neuf and occupying a fine example of metal and stone Art Deco architecture, this store is a less flashy version of its Haussmann sisters, but with the addition of a DIY department. It also has large linen and toy departments. The rooftop café of store number 2 gives way to fantastic 360° views over Paris.

Designer Names

Agnès b
2, 3, and 6 rue du Jour (the street numbers refer to stores for children's, men's and women's fashions, respectively), 75001, tel: 01 45 08 56 56, www.agnesb.fr. The quintessential French designer clothes that are relatively affordable.
Emporio Armani
149 bvd St-Germain, tel: 01 53 63 33 50, www.emporioarmani.com. Classic, chic Italian design.
Azzedine Alaïa
7 rue de Moussy, 75004, tel: 01 42 72 19 19. Slinky couture.
Cerruti
15 place de la Madeleine, 75008, tel: 01 47 42 10 78. Fashions for men and women, fragrances and watches.
Chanel
31 rue Cambon, 75001, tel: 01 42 86 27 27, www.chanel.fr. You can still find that quilted black bag and tailored suit, or Chanel No. 5 perfume (first made in 1921) but the classics are displayed alongside Karl Lagerfeld's take on sportswear, as he plays games with the Chanel logo on ski pants or tracksuits.
Chloé
54–56 rue du Faubourg St-Honoré, 75008, tel: 01 44 94 33 00. Delicate, hip fashions, now created under designer Phoebe Philo.
Christian Lacroix
26 av. Montaigne, 75008, tel: 01 47 20 68 95. Christian Lacroix's exuberant colours evoke the vibrant palettes of Provençal artists.
Christian Dior
30 av. Montaigne, 75008, tel: 01 40 73 54 44. Join the well-heeled mothers, daughters and

granddaughters vacuuming up flimsy, bias-cut outfits, teetering talons, gilded cosmetics and household knick-knacks.

Colette
213 rue St-Honoré, 75008, tel: 01 55 35 33 90. The "lifestyle boutique" for the new millennium generation.

Comme des Garçons (RED)
54 rue du Faubourg St-Honoré, 75008, tel: 01 53 30 27 27. Trends from Rei Kawakubo displayed in chilli-pepper red interiors designed by Sir Richard Rogers' son, Abe, and partner Shona Kitchen.

Givenchy
3 av. George V, 75008, tel: 01 44 31 50 00, www.givenchy.com. French couture by British designer Julien MacDonald, who replaced Alexander McQueen.

Gucci
23 rue Royale, 75008, tel: 01 44 94 14 70, www.gucci.com. Italian-style house for die-hard fashionistas.

Hermès
24 rue du Faubourg St-Honoré, 75008, tel: 01 40 17 47 17, www.hermes.com. For that perfect silk scarf.

Jean-Paul Gaultier
6 rue Vivienne, 75002, tel: 01 42 86 05 05. Outlandish tailoring for men and women, plus accessories.

Jil Sander
52 av. Montaigne, 75008, tel: 01 44 95 06 70. Trend-setting German fashion.

Kenzo
3 place des Victoires, 75001, tel: 01 40 39 72 03, www.kenzo.com. Flamboyant colours from the celebrated Japanese designer.

Louis Vuitton
54 av. Montaigne, 75008, tel: 08 10 81 00 10, www.vuitton.com. Trademark leather goods.

Patrick Cox
62 rue Tiquetonne, 75002, tel: 01 40 26 66 55, www.patrickcox.fr. The shoes to be seen in, from the British designer.

Plein Sud
21 rue des Francs-Bourgeois,

75004, tel: 01 42 72 10 60. Sexy fashion for women by top Moroccan designer, Fayçal Amor.

Prada
10 av. Montaigne, 75008, tel: 01 53 23 99 40, www.prada.com. For a pair of the mules all Parisian women seem to favour in warm weather.

Sonia Rykiel
175 bvd St-Germain, 75006, tel: 01 49 54 60 60, www.sonia rykiel.fr. Witty, wearable and beautifully cut designs. Menswear is across the road. Also at 70 rue du Faubourg St-Honoré.

Lolita Lempicka
78 av. Marceau, tel: 01 40 70 96 96. Romantic and feminine clothing, accessories and perfumes.

Thierry Mugler
45 rue du Bac, 75007, tel: 01 45 44 44 44, www.thierrymugler.com. Innovative clothing from the Strasbourg-born designer.

Yohji Yamamoto
3 rue de Grenelle, 75007, tel: 01 42 84 28 87. New fashion that draws its inspiration from traditional Japanese and Tibetan costumes.

SALES

Traditionally the sales *(soldes)* are held in July, just after Christmas and throughout January. However, many shops have mid-season reductions so you may pick up bargains all year round.

Boutiques

Abou Dhabi
10 rue des Francs-Bourgeois, 75003, tel: 01 42 77 96 98. This stylish shop sells a range of pretty women's wear by up-and-coming young designers.

Barbara Bui
23 rue Etienne Marcel, 75001, tel: 01 40 26 43 65. Super-smart garments for the woman about town.

La Boutique de Floriane
17 rue Tronchet, 75008, tel: 01 42 65 25 95. Top-quality chil-

dren's clothes – plus Babar the elephant.

Cartier
13 rue la Paix, 75001, tel: 01 42 18 53 70. Cartier is the place for glittery diamond sparklers. Perhaps the most desirable item is the square tank watch, which has been produced with variants ever since the 1920s. There is also a selection of vintage pieces.

Corinne Sarrut
4 rue du Pré au Clercs, 75007, tel: 01 42 61 71 60. Very Parisian fashion label. Distinctly feminine silhouettes in an original mix of materials and colours.

Editions de Parfums Frédéric Malle
37 rue de Grenelle, 75007, tel: 01 42 22 77 22. The grandson of Parfums Christian Dior's founder, Frédéric Malle, gave seven of the world's leading "noses" carte blanche to create a fragrance under their own names. Judge the results for yourself in his elegant boutique.

L'Habilleur
44 rue de Poitou, 75003, tel: 01 48 87 77 12. End-of-line and ex-catwalk clothes from some of the top designers.

Loft Design By
12 rue du Faubourg St-Honoré, 75008, tel: 01 42 65 59 65. Gap, French-style.

Maria Luisa
2–4 rue Cambon, 75001, tel: 01 47 03 96 15. One of the hottest multi-label stores in Paris with an eye not only for the avant-garde but for what is wearable.

Paul et Joe
62 rue des Saints-Pères, 75007, tel: 01 42 22 47 01, www.paulandjoe.com. The fetish boutique of Parisian fashionistas filled with weathered-looking creations that emulate the continuing vintage craze.

Pronuptia
87 rue de Rivoli, 75001, tel: 01 42 60 16 92. Elegant wedding gowns and accessories.

Tara Jarmon
18 rue du Four, 75006, tel: 01 46 33 26 60. Elegant, pretty fashions from this Canadian designer.

Ursule Beaugeste
15 rue Oberkampf, 75011, tel:
01 49 23 02 48. Selling dinky,
hand-made bags, this cute shop is
one of a growing number of lovely
Bohemian boutiques around the
trendy Rue Oberkampf.

High-street Fashions

There is a growing number of
high-street chains in France,
many of which have branches
across the capital – only one
branch of each is listed for most
of the following. This selection
should start you off.

Cacharel
36 rue Tronchet, 75009, tel: 01
42 68 38 88. Delicate, feminine
designer lingerie and perfume.

Etam
73 rue de Rivoli, 75001, tel: 01
47 67 73 73, www.etam.com.
The megastore branch of a chain
selling pretty, affordable lingerie,
aimed at the younger market.

Gap
102 rue de Rivoli, 75001, tel: 01
44 88 28 28, www.gap.com. The
US chain has gone down a storm
in the French capital and there
seem to be branches of Gap
everywhere. Practical urban wear
for the family at good prices.

Kookaï
2 rue Gustave-Courbet, 75016,
tel: 01 47 55 18 00, www.kookai.fr.
Inexpensive fashion for the
young. Other branches can be
found throughout Paris.

Morgan
165 rue de Rennes, 75006, tel:
01 45 48 96 77. Familiar to the
young UK market, this French
chain offers groovy styles.

Promod
60 rue Caumartin, 75009, tel: 01
45 26 01 11, www.promod.com.
One of several branches in Paris.
French fashions at reasonable
prices. Good for jumpers,
jewellery and coats.

Zara
44 av. des Champs-Elysées,
75008, tel: 01 43 59 09 51.
Expanding Spanish chain offering
funky designs for men, women
and children at high-street prices.

Shoes

The main shoe chains (which
have branches across the
city) include the following, all
offering this-season's styles at
affordable prices:

André Chaussures
106 and 138 rue de Rivoli,
75001, tel: 01 53 40 96 84
and 01 55 34 94 88.

France Arno
98 rue de Rivoli, 75001, tel: 01
40 28 00 10.

Mephisto
78 rue des Saints-Pères,
75007, tel: 01 45 44 03 04,
www.mephisto.com. French
walking shoes for getting around
Paris on foot.

Rodolphe Ménudier
14 rue de Castiglione, 75001,
tel: 01 92 60 86 27. Chic shoes
for the well heeled.

Gifts

Androuet
49 rue St-Roch, 75001, tel: 01
42 97 57 39. This is an excellent
cheese shop connected to the
Androuet restaurant.
Other branches include:
83 rue St-Dominique, 75007,
tel: 01 45 50 45 75, and
19 rue Daguerre, 75014,
tel: 01 43 21 19 09.

Bains Plus
51 rue des Francs-Bourgeois,
75004, tel: 01 48 87 83 07.
Everything you could possibly
imagine for the bathroom.

Bon Ton
82 rue de Grenelle, 75007,
tel: 01 44 39 09 20. Fun kids'
clothes and accessories.

The Conran Shop
117 rue du Bac, 75007, tel: 01
42 84 10 01, www.conran.com.
Sir Terence Conran's emporium
in a former Bon Marché warehouse designed by Gustave
Eiffel. All manner of designer
gifts and household items.

Debauve et Gallais
30 rue des Saints-Pères,
75007, tel: 01 45 48 54 67,
www.debauveetgallais.com.
Chocolates fit for the kings
of France.

Diptyque Candles
34 bvd St-Germain, 75005, tel:
01 43 26 45 27. Heavenly
scented candles.

Fauchon
26 place de la Madeleine,
75008, tel: 01 47 42 60 11,
www.fauchon.fr. Luxury foodstore,
much-celebrated for its gourmet
buffets, an excellent in-house
brasserie and Italian trattoria.

FNAC
74 av. des Champs-Elysées,
75008, tel: 01 53 53 64 64,
www.fnac.fr. Books, music, hi-fi
and videos are all sold in this
giant, long-established French
chain. Concert tickets can
also be bought here. Branches
across the city. Late opening
most nights.

Guerlain
68 av. des Champs-Elysées,
75008, tel: 01 45 62 52 57,
www.guerlain.com. The French
perfumier in a breathtakingly
beautiful flagship store.

La Maison du Chocolat
8 bvd de la Madeleine, 75009,
tel: 01 47 42 86 52 (see
www.lamaisonduchocolat.com for
other branches). Mouth-watering
chocolate emporium.

Maître Parfumeur et Gantier
84 bis rue de Grenelle, 75007,
tel: 01 45 44 61 57, www.maitre-
parfumeur-et-gantier.com. Natural, hand-crafted perfumes not
found on the mass market, and
beautiful leather gloves.

Marie Papier
26 rue Vavin, 75006, tel: 01 43
26 46 44. Paper products,
including hand-made stationery,
albums and folders.

Pétrossian
18 bvd La Tour-Maubourg,
75007, tel: 01 44 11 32 22,
Caviar specialists who are also
renowned for their smoked
salmon and foie gras.

QuatreHomme Fromagerie
62 rue de Sèvres, 75006, tel: 01
47 34 33 45. Cheeses and more.

Sennelier
3 quai Voltaire, 75007, tel: 01
42 60 72 15, www.magazin
sennelier.com. One of Paris's
oldest art supplies shops.

COIFFURE

If you need a haircut while in Paris, you could head for the ubiquitous Toni and Guy (try 248 rue St-Honoré, 75001, tel: 01 40 20 98 20) or one of Jean-Claude Biguine's many salons (check www.biguine.com for the addresses).

Séphora
70 av. des Champs-Elysées, 75008, tel: 01 53 93 22 50 (see www.sephora.com for other branches). Part of a perfume chain with branches across the capital. This branch is huge.

Children

Apache
84 rue du Faubourg-St Antoine, 75012, tel: 01 53 46 60 10, www.apache.fr. Colourful toy store with an activities studio and cyber-café.

Chantelivre
13 rue de Sévres, 75006, tel: 01 45 48 87 90. Children's bookshop with a small English-language section, plus CDs, videos, paints, stationery.

Les Cousines d'Alice
36 rue Daguerre, 75014, tel: 01 43 20 24 86). Stuffed animals, books, construction games and much more.

Les Deux Tisserins
36 rue des Bernardins, 75005, tel: 01 46 33 88 68. A large collection of wooden toys, alongside clothing and accessories.

Du Pareil au Même
1 rue St-Denis, 75001, tel: 01 40 13 07 43 (www.dpam. com for other branches). Affordable French children's clothes.

FNAC Junior
19 rue Vavin, 75006, tel: 01 56 24 03 46, www.fnacjunior.fr. Educational and fun games, toys, videos and CDs for young kids.

Pain d'Epices
29 passage Jouffroy, 75009, tel: 01 47 70 08 68. A doll enthusiast's paradise.

Markets

Le Marché d'Aligre
Rue and Place d'Aligre, 75012. General. Tues–Sun 7.30am–12.30pm.

Le Marché Biologique
Place Brancusi, 75014. Organic produce. Sat 9am–2pm. Also at Boulevard Raspail, 75014, on Sun.

Ile de la Cité
Place Louis-Lépine, 75004. Flowers. Daily 8am–7.30pm. Birds. Sun 8am–7pm. The adjacent **Quai de la Mégisserie** sells birds, fish and small animals.

Le Marché Maubert
Place Maubert, 75005. Produce and flowers. Tues, Thur, Sat 7am–2.30pm.

Place de la Madeleine
East side of the church, 75008. Flowers. Tues–Sun 8am– 7.30pm.

Le Marché Place Monge
Place Monge, 75005. Produce, flowers, cheese and a variety of home-made comestibles. Wed, Fri and Sat 7am–2.30pm.

Le Marché St-Germain
Rue Lobineau, 75006. Produce, cheese, wine and flowers. Tues–Sat, 8am–1pm and 4–7.30pm, Sun 8.30am–1pm.

Le Marché Aux Puces de Clignancourt
Av. de la Clignancourt, 75018. Popular flea market. Sat–Mon, 7am–7pm.

Le Marché Aux Puces de Vanves
Av. Marc Sagnier, 75014. Flea market. Sat–Sun, 7am–7.30pm (5pm in winter).

BROCANTES

If you are interested in buying antiques and bric-a-brac, look out for the *brocantes* held in various parts of Paris, usually at weekends. They are publicised by posters and banners in the streets. They sell ceramics and jewellery, tools and small pieces of furniture and, because many of the traders come from outside Paris and are keen to sell their goods, they are often as cheap as the flea markets.

SPORTS

Participant

You probably wouldn't go to Paris primarily in search of sporting facilities or events (unless you were going for the Tennis Open in June), but nevertheless the city caters fairly well for the sports enthusiast. You can find information on sporting events in *Le Figaro* each Wednesday or by phoning *Allô-Sports*, tel: 08 20 00 75 75. The latter can give you information (in French) about sporting facilities in Paris.

Cycling

The Bois de Boulogne and Bois de Vincennes offer good cycling, as do the Quais de Seine and the Canal St-Martin (for more leisurely rides). Call the **Fédération Française de Cyclotourisme** for your nearest cycling club, tel: 01 44 16 88 88.

Fitness Centres

Club Quartier Latin
19 rue Pontoise, 75005, tel: 01 55 42 77 88, www.clubquartier latin.com. Health club with squash courts and pool. The gym has plenty of machines, and offers a variety of exercise classes.

Club Med Gym
17 rue du Débarcadère, 75017, tel: 01 45 74 14 04. One of a chain of health clubs that offer step classes, weights, martial arts and sauna. Not all clubs have a pool, so check first. Reductions for students and members of some organisations. Tel: 01 44 37 24 24, or check www.clubmedgym.fr for clubs.

Swimming

Aquaboulevard
4–6 rue Louis Armand, 75015, tel: 01 40 60 10 00. A massive water world offering an exciting choice of waves, flumes and both indoor and outdoor pools. Ideal fun for the kids, and makes a change from sightseeing.

TRANSPORT
ACCOMMODATION
ACTIVITIES
A – Z
LANGUAGE

Piscine Armand-Massard
66 bvd du Montparnasse,
75015, tel: 01 45 38 65 19. An
underground sports centre with
three pools.

Piscine Georges-Vallery
148 av. Gambetta, 75020, tel:
01 40 31 15 20. Built for the
1924 Olympic Games, where
Johnny Weissmuller (aka Tarzan in
films of old) won the gold medal.

Piscine des Halles
Centre Suzanne-Berlioux, 10
place de la Rotonde, 75001,
tel: 01 42 36 98 44. Part of
the Forum des Halles, with a
50-metre/yd pool.

Piscine Jean-Taris
66 rue Thouin, 75005, tel: 01
43 25 54 03. A very pleasant
25-metre/yd pool with a view
of the Panthéon.

Piscine du Marché St-Germain
12 rue Lobineau, 75006, tel:
01 43 29 08 15. Underground
25-metre/yd pool in St-Germain.

Tennis

Jardins du Luxembourg
75006, tel: 01 43 25 79 18.
Anyone can play tennis here
in the heart of the city, and it's
not expensive. Summer, daily
8am–9pm; rest of year,
8am–sunset.

Centre Sportif d'Orléans
7 av. Paul-Appell, 75014, tel: 01
45 40 55 88. A variety of sports
are on offer here (athletics, football, basketball) in addition to
nine tennis courts.

Courcelles
149 bis rue Blomet, 75015, tel:
01 45 30 07 00. A tennis club
offering all levels of lessons.

Spectator

Stade de France

Football fans should pay homage
at the massive new stadium,
designed by architects Zubléna,
Macary, Regembal and Constan-
tini and built in 1997 for the
1998 World Cup. The stadium is
also used for rock concerts, seating around 100,000 spectators.
Located at Rue Francis de

Pressensé, 93200 St-Denis, tel:
01 55 93 00 00, fax: 01 55 93
00 03, www.stadefrance.fr (Métro
Porte de Paris; take RER B to La
Plaine–Stade de France or RER D
to Stade de France–St-Denis).
Open 10am–6pm daily, except
when events are taking place.
Entrance fee. Guided tours are
available.

Palais Omnisports de Bercy
8 bvd de Bercy, 75012, tel: 01
44 68 44 68, fax: 01 40 02 61
15, www.bercy.fr. The huge Bercy
sports stadium, built in 1984,
offers a vast range of events
including football, ice sports,
motor sports and horse riding.

Major sporting events include
the Marathon in April, the French
Tennis Open in May/June at the
Stade Roland-Garros, and the
Paris Triathlon in September.
For those keen on racing, the
Grand Prix de l'Arc de Triomphe
takes place at **Hippodrome de
Longchamp**, Bois de Boulogne,
in October.

Other Activities

Courses

Paris hosts numerous schools
and courses for people of all ages,
ranging from language study
breaks and cookery courses to
far more in-depth education at
the celebrated Grandes Ecoles
created by Napoléon.

    **Le Centre d'Information et de
Documentation Jeunesse (CIDJ)**
has information sheets on
education in France that can be
bought for a nominal sum from
101 quai Branly, 75015 Paris,
tel: 01 44 49 12 00.

    Language and cookery
schools will be able to send you
detailed information about their
courses, plus general information
on Paris, and they may also be
able help you with your travel and
accommodation arrangements,
once you've signed up.

French Language
A good reference site for locating
a French language course centre
is www.fle.fr. Otherwise, you

could begin with the following
schools:

Alliance Française
101 bvd Raspail, 75006, tel: 01
42 84 90 00, www.alliancefr.org

Ecole Eiffel
3 rue Crocé-Spinelli, 75014,
tel: 01 43 20 37 41, www.ecole-
eiffel.fr. Has a variety of courses
on offer.

**Ecole de Langue Française pour
Etrangers (ELFE)**
8 villa Ballu, 75009, tel: 01 48
78 73 00, www.elfe-paris.com.
All levels of language courses in
small classes of between four
and six students.

Eurocentre
13 passage Dauphine, 75006,
tel: 01 40 46 72 00. Organises
courses on language and civilisation. They are held on sites in
Paris, Amboise and La Rochelle.

France Langues
2 rue de Sfax, 75116, tel: 01 45
00 40 15. Various levels of
French-language courses.

Cookery
Le Cordon Bleu
8 rue Léon-Delhomme, 75015,
tel: 01 53 68 22 50, fax: 01 48
56 03 77, www.lecordonbleu
paris.com. Courses are taught in
French, English and Japanese at
this renowned institution.

Ritz Escoffier
15 place Vendôme, 75001,
tel: 01 43 16 30 30, fax: 01 43
16 36 68, www.ritzparis.com.
A variety of culinary courses.

History and Culture
**Cours de Civilisation Française
à la Sorbonne**
47 rue des Ecoles, 75005, tel:
01 40 46 26 70, www.paris4.
sorbonne.fr. Courses are run at
several levels throughout the
year.

**Institut Parisien de Langue et
de Civilisation Française**
87 bvd de Grenelle, 75015,
tel: 01 40 56 09 53, fax: 01 43
06 46 30. Courses in language
and culture combined at the
Parisian Institute.

A - Z

A HANDY SUMMARY OF PRACTICAL INFORMATION, ARRANGED ALPHABETICALLY

Addresses

Paris is divided into numbered districts – *arrondissements* – and most people still refer to them by number, saying, for example, that they live "in the 5th", but this system is no longer used officially. Street names are now always followed by a five-digit post code, and the final digit corresponds to the old *arrondissement* number, so an address with a 75008 code, for example, will be in the 8th *arrondissement*.

Budgeting for your Trip

The price of accommodation ranges across the spectrum. You can get a double room in a small pension for under €50 a night, or you can pay €300 in a luxury hotel. An average price, however, for an en suite double room in a centrally located, comfortable hotel is around €100–150.

Meals also cover a wide price range but on average you can expect to pay around €30–40 for a three-course meal with a half-bottle of house wine.

The average entrance price to a national museum or gallery is €7–8 (municipal ones are free).

A taxi from the airport will cost around €45–60, depending on traffic, plus €1 per bag and a tip of about 5 percent. Single Métro and bus fares cost €1.30 (at 2004 rates). A *carnet* of 10 tickets costs €10. For various ticket deals, refer to Public Transport (see page 204).

Business Hours

Office workers normally start early (8.30am is not uncommon) and often stay at their desks until 6pm or later. This is partly to make up for the long lunch hours (two hours, from around noon) that are traditional in public offices. Many companies are changing to shorter lunch breaks as employees appreciate the advantages of getting home earlier in the evening. Most banks in Paris open from Monday to Friday 9am to 4.30pm, and are closed on Saturday and Sunday.

Food shops, especially bakers, tend to open early. Most boutiques and department stores open about 9am, although some do not open until 10am. Traditionally in France, most shops close from around noon to 2.30pm, but in Paris, many shops remain open until 7 or 7.30pm. The larger department stores do not close at lunchtime and are open until 9 or 10pm on Thursday. Most shops close on Sunday, although bakers and patisseries are usually open in the morning.

In the suburbs, hypermarkets usually stay open until 8 or 9pm. Most shops are closed on Monday morning, some all day Monday. If you want to buy a picnic lunch, remember to get everything you need before midday.

Business Visitors

Business travel accounts for approximately a third of French tourism revenue. This important market has led to the creation of a special Conference and Incentive Department at the French Government Tourist Offices in both London and New York. The department deals with business-travel enquiries, and will also help organise hotels, conference centres and incentive deals.

Conferences and Exhibitions

Paris is a world leader for conferences, exhibitions and trade fairs, and the building development at La Défense is the largest business district in Europe. For further information, call Info-

BUSINESS SPECIALISTS

There are several tour operators who specialise in conference organisation. Try: Le Palais des Congrès de Paris, 2 porte Maillot, 75017, tel: 01 40 68 22 50, fax: 01 40 68 27 40, www.palais-congres-paris.fr.

Défense, tel: 01 47 74 84 24. For a list of exhibitions and details about particpating, contact Promo Salons, The Colonnades, 82 Bishops Bridge Road, London W2 6BB, tel: 020-7221 3660, fax: 020-7792 3525 or visit www.promosalons.com.

Many châteaux offer luxurious accommodation for smaller gatherings, and it's even possible to organise a congress at Disneyland Paris.

Chambers of Commerce

An excellent source of business information about local companies, assistance with technicalities of export and import, interpretation and translation agencies and conference centres is the Chambre de Commerce et d'Industrie, 45 av. d'Iéna, 75016, tel: 01 40 69 37 00, fax: 01 47 20 61 28, www.acfci.cci.fr. Most countries' Chambers of Commerce have conference facilities of some kind. There are French Chambers of Commerce in key cities around the world promoting business with France. In London, the Chamber of Commerce is at 21 Dartmouth Street, London SW1H 9BP, tel: 020-7304 4040, fax: 020-7304 4034, www.ccfgb.co.uk

C limate

France is the only European country that is both north European and Mediterranean. In Paris, the climate is similar to that of southern England, although less changeable, and temperatures can be much higher in mid-summer. The average maximum temperature in July and August is 25°C (76°F), the average minimum 15°C (58°F), but a temperature of 27°C (80°F) is not unusual. In January, expect a maximum average of 6°C (43°F), a minimum of 1°C (43°F). To check the weather at the time you visit, go to www.weather.com.

When to Visit

Spring, when the temperature is ideal for sightseeing, is probably

the best time to visit Paris, although you should be prepared for showers. Autumn mornings can be sharp, but by midday the skies are usually clear and bright. Some believe that winter light shows Paris at its best.

What to Wear

Paris is a great city to explore on foot, so comfortable walking shoes are essential. Bring warm clothes if you're coming to Paris in winter, as the weather can be very chilly, and remember waterproofs (or at least an umbrella) in spring or autumn, as showers are typical. Most Parisians are very style-conscious and won't brave even the corner shop without displaying a fair amount of élan. Casual tourists might therefore consider taking a smart change of clothes, for a night out at one of the city's many upmarket restaurants, for example.

Complaints

To complain about a purchase, return it to the shop as soon as possible. In a serious dispute, contact the local Direction Départementale de la Concurrence, de la Consommation et de la Répression des Fraudes (consult the telephone directory for details).

Crime and Safety

Police

In the event of loss or theft, a report must be made in person at the nearest police station (commissariat) as soon as possible after the event. This will also be required if you wish to claim from your insurance company. Visit www.prefecture-police-paris.interieur.gouv.fr for locations, or for emergency help call tel: 17.

Security

If you take sensible precautions with your personal possessions, you should be safe in Paris.

There is a problem with pickpockets in some of the Métro stations. Obvious centres of prostitution (such as Les Halles and parts of the Bois de Boulogne) are best avoided at night. As anywhere else, use care when withdrawing money with debit or credit cards at a bank, currency exchange office, or ATM machine and make sure others cannot see your PIN. It's always a good idea to keep a photocopy of your passport in case of theft (see also Police).

Customs Regulations

There are no official restrictions on the movement of goods within the European Union, provided that the goods were purchased within the EU. Note that it is no longer necessary for EU nationals to exit Customs through a red or green channel. However, people of all nationalities must declare, upon arrival or departure, sums of cash exceeding €7,600.

Duty-paid goods If you buy goods in France on which you pay tax, there are no longer any restrictions on the amounts you may take home with you. However, EU law has set "guidance levels" on the following:
• **Tobacco** 3,200 cigarettes, or 400 cigarillos, or 200 cigars, or 1kg of tobacco
• **Spirits** 10 litres
• **Fortified wine/wine** 90 litres (not more than 60 litres may be sparkling wine)
• **Beer** 110 litres
If you exceed these amounts you must be able to prove that the goods are for personal use, for example a family wedding.
Duty-free goods If you are from outside the EU and buy goods duty-free in France, the following restrictions still apply (these quantities may be doubled if you live outside Europe):
• **Tobacco** 200 cigarettes, or 100 cigarillos, or 50 cigars, or 250g of tobacco
• **Alcohol** 1 litre of spirits or

liqueurs over 22 percent volume, or 2 litres of fortified, sparkling wine or other liqueurs.
• **Perfume** 50g of perfume, plus 250ml of toilet water.
There are no restrictions on the amount of currency you can take into France.
For more information contact Centre de Renseignements des Douanes, tel: 08 25 30 82 63.

D isabled Travellers

Travellers with mobility problems are advised to book accommodation in advance. Most official lists of hotels use a symbol to denote wheelchair access, but it is always a good idea to check with the hotel regarding the facilities available. Check the Paris Tourist Office website for further information at www.paris-touristoffice.com.
Budget rooms in the hotels in the Campanile chain have at least one room for guests with disabilities and all public areas are accessible.
Contact Hôtel Campanile, 18 rue du Pont-des-Halles, 94656 Rungis Cedex, tel: 01 49 78 01 45, fax: 01 46 86 50 18.
Balladins is a chain of newly built, budget hotels across France, which all have at least one room designed for guests with disabilities, plus restaurants and public areas that are easily accessible for wheelchair users. For a full list of these hotels, contact: Hôtel Balladins, 6 rue Turgot, Paris, 75009, www.balladins.com.
Maison des Clubs UNESCO, 43 rue de la Glacière, 75013, tel: 01 43 36 00 63, has accommodation for disabled young people.

Wheelchairs to rent

CRF Matériel Médical, 153 bvd Voltaire, 75011, tel: 01 43 73 98 98, fax: 01 43 73 17 37, www.crf-medical.com.

UK Organisations

RADAR, The Royal Association for Disability and Rehabilitation,

12 City Forum, 250 City Road, London EC1V 8AF, tel: 020-7250 3222, www.radar.org.uk. They will give helpful and friendly advice.
Disabled Drivers' Association (DDA) tel: 0870 770 3333, www.dda.org.uk.
Disabled Drivers' Motor Club (DDMC) tel: 01832 734724, www.ddmc.org.uk
Disabled Motorists' Route Map Service tel: 01743 761181.

French Organisations

Association des Paralysés de France, Service Information, 17 bvd Auguste Blanqui, 75013, tel: 01 40 78 69 00, www.apf.asso.fr. The association may be able to answer specific enquiries and can provide branch addresses.
The CIDJ (see Student Travellers) has information on services for less able young travellers. It publishes Vacances pour Personnes Handicapées and annual leaflets on activity and sports holidays for young disabled people.

USEFUL BOOKS

The following guides are useful for people with disabilities:
● **Access in Paris** A guide book that provides information for anyone with a mobility problem, including the elderly and for parents travelling with young children. It can be purchased from Access Project, 39 Bradley Gardens, West Ealing, London W13 3HE, tel: 020-7250 3222.
● **Door-to-Door** is a Department of Transport guide to all types of travel abroad for people with disabilities, from Stationery Office Bookshops or mail order, tel: 0870 600 5522, fax: 020-7873 8200 (orders), fax: 020-7873 8247 (enquiries).
● **Michelin Red Guides** Both France and Camping-Caravanning indicate hotels that welcome and have facilities to cater for people with disabilities.

Union Nationale des Associations de Parents d'Enfants Inadaptés (UNAPEI), 15 rue Coysevox, 75018, tel: 01 44 85 50 50, www.unapei.org. Parents may wish to contact this organisation for information about facilities for children with disabilities.

Comité de Liaison pour le Transport des Personnes Handicapées, Conseil National des Transports, 34 av. Marceau, 75009, tel: 01 53 23 85 85, www.coliac.cnt.fr. This gives brief information on the accessibility and arrangements for less able passengers on public transport, and contacts for special transport schemes in France.

US Organisations

Society for Accessible Travel and Hospitality (SATH), 347 Fifth Avenue, Suite 610, New York, tel: 212-447 7284, www.sath.org. A non-profit educational organisation that actively represents travellers with disabilities.

MossRehab Resource Net www.mossresourcenet.org. An information-only website.

E lectricity

The standard voltage is 220/230 volts, although in a few areas it is only 110 volts. Round-pin plugs are used everywhere, so pack an adapter (available at airports as well as any store selling travel-related items). Visitors from the US will also need a transformer for the higher voltage.

Entry Requirements

Visas and Passports

All visitors to France require a valid passport. No visa is required by visitors from European Union (EU) member states, the US, Australia, Canada or Japan. Nationals of other countries need a visa. If in doubt, check with the French Consulate in your home country. Anyone (including EU nationals) wishing to stay for longer than 90 con-

EMBASSIES & CONSULATES

● **Australia**
4 rue Jean-Rey
75015
Tel: 01 40 59 33 00
● **Canada**
35 av. Montaigne
75008
Tel: 01 44 43 29 00
● **New Zealand**
7 ter rue Léonard-de-Vinci
75116
Tel: 01 45 00 24 11
● **Republic of Ireland**
12 av. Foch
75116
Tel: 01 44 17 67 00
Consulate:
4 rue Rude, 75116

● **South Africa**
59 quai d'Orsay
75007
Tel: 01 53 59 23 23
● **United Kingdom**
35 rue du Faubourg St-Honoré
75008
Tel: 01 44 51 31 00
Consulate:
18-bis rue d'Anjou, 75008
Tel: 01 44 51 31 02
● **United States**
2 av. Gabriel
75001
Tel: 01 43 12 22 22
Consulate:
2 rue St-Florentin, 75001
Tel: 08 36 70 14 88

secutive days will need a *carte de séjour*, obtainable from their French Consulate or the Préfecture de Police, 9 bvd du Palais, 75004 Paris.

G ay Travellers

The Marais (the 4th *arrondissement*) is the most gay-friendly district in Paris, with gay-oriented restaurants, wine bars, boutiques, bookstores, beauty salons, hotels, bars and discos. For more information check out the websites www.legayparis.fr, www.paris-gay.com and www.gay-paris.net (all in French and English). There are various free magazines you can pick up in most gay bars in the 3rd and 4th *arrondissements*. The gay magazine *Têtu* is another useful source of information, and can be bought at most news kiosks in the city.

H ealth & Medical Care

If you are an EU national and you fall ill in France, you can receive emergency medical treatment from doctors, dentists and hospitals. You will have to pay the cost of this treatment, but are entitled to claim from the French *Sécurité Sociale*, which refunds up to 70

percent of your medical expenses. To receive a refund you must, prior to leaving the UK, complete form E111 (or E112 for those already undergoing treatment). This form can be obtained from main post offices and, once completed, must be given back to the post office where it will be stamped, signed and returned to you. Failure to do this will render the form E111 unusable. Once abroad, keep the form safe with your passport. It may be used on subsequent trips.

If you need to see a doctor, expect to pay at least €45 per consultation, with prescription charges on top of that. The doctor will provide a statement of treatment *(feuille de soins)*. With this, EU citizens can reclaim around 70 percent of the cost of the treatment. Check that the price stamp *(vignette)* from any prescribed medicine has been attached to the *feuille de soins* by the chemist so that you can also reclaim that cost. When complete, the *feuille de soins*, prescription and your form E111 should be sent to the local *Caisse Primaire d'Assurance Maladie* (the doctor or chemist will have the address, or consult the phone book under *Sécurité Sociale*) for your refund, which will be sent on to your home. This will probably take about a month. If you have any difficulties, contact the **Service Juridique des Relations Internationales**, 173–5 rue de Bercy, 75586 Cedex 12, tel: 01 53 38 70 00.

For more information, consult the leaflet **Health Advice for Travellers** (available from post offices, online at www.doh.gov.uk or by tel: 0800 555777) which outlines the health arrangement that the UK has with France. As this reciprocal arrangement does not cover all medical expenses, such as the cost of bringing a sick person back to the UK, the Department of Health advises travellers also to take out holiday insurance. If you plan to drive in France, you should check that your motor insurance covers you for accidents abroad.

In North America, contact the **International Association for Medical Assistance to Travellers (IAMAT)**, 40 Regal Road, Guelph, Ontario N1K 1B5, Canada, tel: 519 836 0102. This is a non-profit-making group that offers members fixed rates for medical treatment from participating physicians. Members receive a passport-sized medical record completed by their doctor and a directory of English-speaking IAMAT doctors in France, who are on call 24 hours a day. Membership is free, but a donation is requested.

In Paris, you can reach English-speaking health services at the **American Hospital** (Hôpital Américain de Paris, tel: 01 46 41 25 25) or the **British Hospital** (Hôpital Franco-Britannique, tel: 01 46 39 22 22). However, neither of these hospitals has a casualty department and both are private, which means the French *Sécurité Sociale* will refund only a small percentage of your medical expenses.

Pharmacies

Most pharmacies display flashing green neon crosses and are open from 9 or 10am to 7 or 8pm. At night, they all post the address of the nearest late-opening pharmacy in their window or doorway. Staff can provide basic medical advice and services. Some late night pharmacies are:
Dhéry, 84 av. des Champs-Elysées, 75008 (Métro Georges V), tel: 01 45 62 02 41, is open all hours.
Pharmacie Européenne de la Place de Clichy, 6 pl. de Clichy, 75009 (Métro Place de Clichy), tel: 01 48 74 65 18, is open all hours.
Pharmacie des Halles, 10 bvd de Sébastopol, 75004 (Métro Châtelet), tel: 01 42 72 03 23, fax: 01 42 72 52 10, is open 9am–midnight, Monday to Saturday, and 9am–10pm on Sunday.
Publicis Drugstore, 133 av. des Champs-Elysées, 75008 (Métro Etoile), tel: 01 47 20 78 00 is open daily 9am–2am. Recently reopened after a face lift of applied sculptural glass forms by architect Michele Saee.

HOSPITALS

All state hospitals in Paris have casualty departments. The following are some of the larger ones:
● **Hôpital Boucicaut**
78 rue Convention, 75015
Tel: 01 53 78 80 00
● **Hôpital Necker**
(Children's Hospital)
149 rue de Sèvres, 75015
Tel: 01 44 49 40 00
● **Hôpital Bichat**
46 rue Henri-Huchard, 75018
Tel: 01 40 25 80 80
● **Hôpital Hôtel-Dieu**
1 place du Parvis-Notre-Dame, 75004
Tel: 01 42 34 82 34
● **Hôpital Saint-Louis**
1 av. Claude-Vellefaux, 75010
Tel: 01 42 49 49 49
● **Hôpital Fernaud-Widal**
(Poisons)
200 rue du Faubourg St-Denis, 75010
Tel: 01 40 05 45 45

EMERGENCIES

Ambulance:	15
Police:	17
Fire:	18
SOS English Helpline: tel: 01 47 23 80 80	

Internet

There is no shortage of places to surf the net in Paris. You could try the following.

Internet Cafés

Enjoy a drink or light meal and surf the web at:
Bistrot Internet Galeries Lafayette
40 bvd Hausmann
75009
Tel: 01 42 82 30 33
Café Orbital
13 rue de Médicis
75006
Tel: 01 43 25 76 77
Cyber Cube Bastille
12 rue Daval
75011
Tel: 01 49 29 67 67
Cyberia
Centre Pompidou
75004
Tel: 01 44 54 53 49
easyEverything
Bvd Sébastopol
Tel: 01 40 41 09 10
www.easyeverything.com
Open daily, 24 hours
Le Shop
3 rue d'Argout
75002
No phone
Net Coffee
27 rue Lacépède
75005
Tel: 01 43 36 70 46
Virgin Café
Virgin Megastore
52 av. des Champs-Elysées
75008
Tel: 01 49 53 50 00
www.virginmega.fr
Web Bar
32 rue de Picardie
75003
Tel: 01 42 72 66 55

TRANSPORT

ACCOMMODATION

ACTIVITIES

A – Z

LANGUAGE

LOST PROPERTY

If your personal documents, cash, belongings or travellers cheques are lost or stolen, go to the *Commissariat de Police* closest to the scene of the crime as soon as possible – even before contacting the travellers cheque service or your embassy or consulate.

If you lose your passport, report it to your consulate as soon as possible (there is a full list in both *Pages Blanches* and *Pages Jaunes* phone books under *Ambassades et Consulats*; www.pagesjaunes.fr).

If your credit card is lost or stolen, the numbers to ring are:
American Express, tel: 01 47 77 72 00
Diner's Club, tel: 08 20 00 07 34
Visa or **Carte Bleue**, tel: 08 92 70 57 05
Mastercard-Eurocard, tel: 01 45 67 84 84

To reclaim anything else you have lost, you should go (with ID) to the Bureau des Objets Trouvés, 36 rue des Morillons, 75732 Cedex 15, tel: 08 21 00 25 25 (Métro Convention), open weekdays 8.30am–5pm, except Friday when it shuts at 4.30pm. You need to visit the office in person, as no information is given over the telephone.

Recommended Websites

There is an enormous wealth of tourist information available over the web, from pages telling you the best way to get to your destination, to how to speak the language when you get there. The following sites are only the tip of the iceberg.
www.paris-touristoffice.com (official site of the Paris Tourist Office, with information on hotels, sites, events, exhibitions, transport, weather and more)
www.france.com (official site

of the French Tourist Office, Maison de la France, for general information on France)
www.paris.org (general information on Paris)
www.magicparis.com (travel, shops, hotels, etc.)
www.pariscope.com (*Pariscope* on-line)
www.ratp.fr (the official Paris transport system site)
www.musexpo.com (guide to museums and exhibitions, in French)
www.rmn.fr (guide to national museum exhibitions)
www.centrepompidou.fr (Pompidou Centre)
www.louvre.fr (Musée du Louvre)
www.tour-eiffel.fr (Eiffel Tower)
www.musee-orsay.fr (Musée d'Orsay)
www.musee-rodin.fr (Musée Rodin)
www.invalides.org (Les Invalides)
www.chateauversailles.fr (Château de Versailles)
www.meteo.fr (the weather on-line)
www.pagesjaunes.fr (the French Yellow Pages)
www.monum.fr (guide to national monuments)
www.opera-de-paris.fr (Opéras Palais Garnier and Bastille)
www.mairie-paris.fr (site of the Mairie de Paris, the town hall/ mayor's office)
www.eurostar.com (fares and timetables for trains to/from London)
www.worldmedia.fr/fashion (on-line fashion guide)
www.disneylandparis.com (holiday plans; fun for kids)
www.lemonde.fr (France's most respected newspaper, in French)
www.mondediplo.com (Le Monde in English)
www.fashion.net (on-line fashion guide)
www.ttc.org (French news and analysis in English)
www.timeout.com/paris (*Time Out* city guide for Paris)
www.vogue.com (Paris fashion magazine)

Maps

Paris Pratique par Arrondissement is the most useful map for visitors. It can be bought for €5.50 at any of the ubiquitous newsstands and kiosks around the city. You may also be able to get by on the tourist office maps.

Media

Newspapers

The two main national dailies are *Le Monde*, which has a rather dry and leftish slant on politics and economic news, and the more conservative *Le Figaro*; both sell about 400,000 copies. The paper representing the Communist Party is *L'Humanité*, and not veering quite so heavily left is Jean-Paul Sartre's brainchild, *Libération*. The major weekly news publications are *Le Point* (right) and *L'Express* (left), which both sell approximately 300,000–500,000 copies. British, American and other European dailies are available at city-centre kiosks and shops showing *journaux* or *presse* signs.

The *International Herald Tribune*, published in Paris, has listings for the city. To find out what is going on in the capital try *L'Officiel des Spectacles* or *Pariscope* (both out on Wednesday), which give cultural listings (museums, galleries, theatres, concerts, cinema, nightlife, etc.).

Radio

France Inter (87.8 MHz) is the main national radio station, offering something to suit all tastes. Radio Classique (101.1 MHz) plays uninterrupted lightweight classical music. If you're looking for something a little less mainstream, try France Musique (91.7 and 92.1 MHz). RTL (104.3 MHz) is the most popular station throughout France, playing music from the charts, interspersed with chat shows, etc.

Television

TF1, France 2, France 3, France 5 and M6 are the five main television stations on offer. Most larger hotels receive cable as well. Canal+ is a subscription channel, which shows big-name new releases. CNN is sometimes also available in hotel rooms.

Money

Currency

The euro (€) is the official French currency and is available in 500, 200, 100, 50, 20, 10 and 5 euro notes, and 2 euro, 1 euro, 50 cent, 20 cent, 10 cent, 5 cent, 2 cent and 1 cent coins. There are 100 cents to one euro.

Credit Cards

The majority of large shops and restaurants, and almost all hotels, accept credit cards. The most common in France are Visa and *Carte Bleue* (often referred to as "CB"). American Express (Amex), Diner's Club (DC) and Mastercard are widely recognised and many places also now accept Maestro and Cirrus, but if you don't see your card's sticker in the hotel, shop or restaurant window, it's always advisable to double check beforehand.

Exchange

Most banks have an exchange counter, or *bureau de change*, which is open from Monday to Friday, usually from 9am to 4.30pm. Note that a few smaller branches close for lunch.

    Bureaux de change at railway stations vary their hours according to high or low season but most are open Monday to Friday 7am–7pm.

    Airport Orly Sud Exchange, on the departure level at gate H, is open daily until 11pm.

Airport Roissy Exchange at terminals 2A, 2B and 2D, is also open daily until 11pm.

Travelex at 194 rue de Rivoli, 75001, tel: 01 42 60 37 61,

or for other locations visit: www.travelex.com.

American Express Bureau de change at 11 rue Scribe, 75009, 01 47 777 928, www.american express.com. Open Monday to Friday, 9am–6.30pm, Saturday 9am–6.30pm. Take your passport if you want to cash travellers cheques.

Machines

You can draw cash from bank dispensing machines (ATMs) using a credit card or European bank cashpoint card, using your PIN. Visa is widely accepted in France but you can take out money from most cash machines if your card is one of the following: Visa, Mastercard, Maestro or Cirrus. Be sure to verify with your bank before leaving that both your card and PIN can be used abroad.

Tipping

Restaurants Most restaurant bills include a service charge. If in doubt ask, *"Le service est-il compris?"* Even when this charge is included, it is common to leave a small additional tip (not more than 5 percent) for the waiter if the service has been especially good. Remember to address waiters as *Monsieur* (never *Garçon*) and waitresses as *Mademoiselle,* if they are young, or *Madame,* if they are older.

Taxis A small tip – a couple of euros, depending on the fare, is common practice.

P ostal Services

The French post office is run by the PTT (*Poste et Télécommunications*). The main branches are open Monday to Friday 8am–7pm, Saturday 8am–noon. The central post office at 52 rue du Louvre, 75001, tel: 01 40 28 76 00, www.laposte.fr, operates a daily 24-hour service. Another large post office is at Place de la Bourse, 75001, tel: 01 44 88 23 00, fax: 01 42 33 38 49, Monday to Friday 8.15am–6.30pm,

New Year's Day, Easter Sunday, Easter Monday, 1 May (Labour Day), 8 May (end of World War II), Ascension Day – mid/late May, Whit Monday – late May, 14 July (Bastille Day), 15 August (Assumption), 1 November (All Saints' Day), 11 November (Armistice Day), 25 December (Christmas).

Saturday 8.15am–noon. Internet, fax and photocopying facilities are available here, as they are in all larger post offices.

    Stamps *(timbres)* are available at most *tabacs* (tobacconists) and other shops selling postcards or greetings cards. For postcards and letters weighing up to 20g, postage within France and to most of the EU currently costs €0.50 (2004 rates). Sending a letter airmail to Ireland, Australia, the US and Canada costs €0.90.

R eligious Services

France is predominantly Roman Catholic, and the many churches in Paris, including Notre-Dame, are open to the public. For a list of all denominational churches, temples and synagogues, look out for the guide Plan de Paris par Arrondissement from a kiosk or bookshop; or contact the Service d'Information Religieuse, tel: 01 49 24 10 21, www.catholique-paris.com. There are services in English around Paris, notably in the American church, which is situated at 65 quai d'Orsay, 75007, tel: 01 40 62 05 00 or visit www.acparis.org.

S tudent Travellers

Students and young people under the age of 26 can get cut-price travel to Paris (*see Transport*). For a prolonged stay, it may be worth finding out about an exchange visit or study holiday.

The following organisations provide information or arrange visits.

UK Services

The **British Council** provides opportunities for international youth experience, exchange and other projects. Contact the **Education and Training Group**, British Council, 10 Spring Gardens, London SW1A 2BN, tel: 020-7930 8466, www.british-council.org/education.

Those who can speak French could approach a UK-based camping holiday operator. Many of these, such as **Holidaybreak** (Hartford Manor, Greenbank Lane, Northwich, Cheshire CW8 1HW, tel: 01606 787474, www.holidaybreakjobs.com) employ students as site attendants in France and other European countries during the summer months.

US Services

American Council for International Studies (ACIS), Boston Regional Office, 343 Congress Street, Suite 3100, Boston, MA, 02210, tel: 800 888 ACIS or 617 236 2051, www.acis.com.
Council on International Educational Exchange (CIEE), 633 Third Avenue, 20th floor New York, NY 10017, tel: 800 40 STUDY, fax: 207 553 7699, www.ciee.org. Offers a wide range of services, including travel.
Youth for Understanding, 6400 Goldsboro Road, Suite 100, Bethesda, MD 20817, tel: 240 235 2100, fax: 240 235 2104, www.yfu.org. One of the world's oldest and largest international exchange organisations.

Study in France

Several French tour operators can organise study tours and language courses. The **Office National de Garantie des Séjours Linguistiques**, 8 rue César Franck, 75015, tel: 01 42 73 36 70, www.loffice.org, is a national association that quality-checks

the 30 members of the organisation offering language courses. Write for a list of schools, or try the following organisations:
Résidence OTU Bastille (Temporary housing), 151 av. Ledru Rollin, 75011, tel: 01 43 79 53 86, www.crous-paris.fr. Offers French study programmes, inexpensive accommodation and tours for individuals or groups.
Centre des Echanges Internationaux, 1 rue Gozlin, 75006, tel: 01 43 29 17 34, www.cei-frenchcentre.com. This is a non-profit-making group offering sporting and cultural holidays and educational tours for young people aged between 15 and 30. Students will find a student identity card useful for discounts, including admission to museums, galleries, cinema, theatre, etc. If you don't have your card, your passport may prove your status, but it depends on the discretion of the particular venue or organisation.
Centre d'Information et de Documentation Jeunesse (CIDJ), 101 quai Branly, 75015, tel: 08 25 09 06 30 (from Monday to Friday 1–6pm), www.cidj.com. A national organisation that disseminates information on youth and student activities.

T elephone

All telephone numbers in France have 10 digits. Paris and Ile de France numbers begin with 01, while the rest of France is divided into four zones: North West 02; North East 03; South East and Corsica 04; and South West 05. Toll-free phone numbers begin with 0800; all other numbers beginning with 08 are charged at variable rates; and 06 numbers are mobile phones. There are two kinds of phone boxes in Paris from which you can make local and international calls: coin-operated phones, and the more common, card-operated phones. Remember that you get 50 percent more call-time for your money if you ring between

10.30pm and 8am on weekdays, and from 2pm at weekends.

A *télécarte* can be bought from kiosks, *tabacs* and post offices for 50 or 120 units (currently €7.50 or €15). Insert the card and follow the instructions on the screen. Note that you can only receive telephone calls at telephone boxes displaying a blue bell sign.

You can also dial from all post offices, which have both coin- and card-operated phones. To call long distance, ask at one of the counters and you will be assigned a booth – you pay when your call is over. Cafés and *tabacs* often also have public phones, which usually take either coins or *jetons*, coin-like discs bought at the bar.

Direct Dialling to Paris from the UK: 00 (international code) + 33 (France) + 1 (Paris) + an eight-figure number. To call other countries from France, first dial the international access code (00), then the country code: Australia 61, UK 44, USA and Canada 1. If using a US credit phone card, call the company's access number: Sprint, tel: 08 00 99 00 87; AT&T, tel: 08 00 99 00 11; MCI, tel: 08 00 99 00 19.

Time zone

France is one hour ahead of Greenwich Mean Time (GMT) and six hours ahead of Eastern Seaboard Time. Most French people use the 24-hour clock, so 1pm appears as 13h00 on timetables and is referred to as *treize heures*.

Tour Operators

By Boat

Cruises on the Seine last an hour with commentaries in several languages. In the high season, boats leave every half hour between 10am and 10pm.
Batobus eight-stop service, Port de la Bourdonnais, tel: 01 44 11 33 99, www.batobus.com.
Bateaux Mouches depart from Pont de l'Alma, tel: 01 42 25 96 10, www.bateaux-mouches.fr.
Bateaux Parisiens depart from Quai Montebello, evening cruises from the Eiffel Tower, tel: 01 44 11 33 55, www.bateaux-parisiens.com.
Vedettes Paris-Ile-de-France depart from Port de Suffren, tel: 01 44 18 08 03, www.vedettes-deparis.com.
Vedettes du Pont-Neuf depart from Pont-Neuf, tel: 01 46 33 98 38, www.vedettesdupontneuf.com. There are several interesting boat trips along the Canal St-Martin, starting at Port de l'Arsenal (Bastille) and continuing almost to the *périphérique* at the northeast of the city. Lasting three hours they are well worth the money, but take warm clothes as you spend a lot of time in shaded locks and under bridges.
Canauxrama, 13 quai de la Loire, 75019, tel: 01 42 39 15 00, www.canauxrama.com.
Paris Canal, 19–21 quai de la Loire, 75019, tel: 01 42 40 96 97, www.pariscanal.com.

By Coach

Coach trips allow you to see Paris with minimum effort. Most companies provide a cassette commentary in several languages and will pass the major sights but do not stop along the way.

Cityrama leaves from 4 place des Pyramides, 75001, tel: 01 44 55 61 00 (www.cityrama.com).
Paris Vision leaves from 214 rue de Rivoli, 75001, tel: 01 42 60 30 01, www.parisvision.com.
Parisbus runs double-decker buses to the main tourist sites. You can hop off, sightsee, then catch a later bus. A commentary runs in both English and French. Tel: 01 43 65 55 55.
Paris L'Open Tour, operated by RATP, runs a similar service, also with open-topped double-decker buses, tel: 01 42 66 56 56, www.paris-opentour.com.

By Bicycle

Fat Tire Bike Tours – Paris, 24 rue Edgar Faure, 75015, tel/fax: 01 56 58 10 54, www.fattirebiketoursparis.com, has guided bike tours.

Tourist Offices

French Travel Centre 178 Piccadilly, London W1J 9AL, tel: 0906-824 4123 (calls cost 50p per minute), www.franceguide.com Open 10–6pm Mon–Fri, 10am–5pm Sat. Useful source of information before you travel.
Tourist Offices in Paris
The following centres can provide tourist information and make reservations. Note that most are closed 1st May and 25th Dec. Call beforehand to check, tel: 08 92 68 30 00 (€0.34 per minute).
• 11 rue Scribe, 75009, Métro: Opéra. Open Mon–Sat 9am–6.30pm.
• 20, bvd Diderot, 75012, Métro: Gare de Lyon. Open Mon–Sat 8am–6pm.
• Tour Eiffel, between east and north pillars, Métro: Bir-Hakeim. Open daily May–Sep 11am–6.40pm.
• 18 rue de Dunkerque, 75010. Métro: Gare du Nord. Open daily 8am–6pm.

TOURIST INFORMATION

● www.paris-touristoffice.com for full details of the tourist offices listed below.
● To call the Paris tourist office, tel: 08 92 68 30 00. Calls cost €0.34 per minute.
● For information on the area around Paris (Ile de France), tel: 01 44 50 19 98.

• 21 place du Tertre, 75018. Métro: Abbesses. Open daily 10am–7pm.
• Carrousel du Louvre, 99 rue de Rivoli, 75001. Métro: Palais Royal/Musée du Louvre. Open daily 10am–7pm.

Useful Addresses

Air France, 119 av. des Champs-Elysées, 75008, tel: 08 20 82 08 20, www.airfrance.fr.
Automobile Club de France, 6–8 place de la Concorde, 75008, tel: 01 43 12 43 12, tel: 01 43 12 43 43.
Information Service for general details about Paris, in English, tel: 08 92 68 41 14.
RATP information, Métro, RER, and bus details in English, tel: 08 36 68 77 14, www.ratp.fr.
SNCF, tel: 08 36 35 35 35, www.sncf.fr, for train information.
Weather Information in French, tel: 08 92 68 00 00, www.meteo.fr.

Weights & Measures

The metric system is used for all weights and measures. For a quick conversion: 2.5cm is approximately 1in, 1 metre is about a yard, 100g is just under 4oz, and 1kg is 2lb 2oz. Distance is quoted in kilometres. One kilometre equals five-eighths of a mile, so 80km is 50 miles.

LANGUAGE

UNDERSTANDING THE LANGUAGE

French pronunciation

French is the native language of more than 90 million people and the acquired language of 180 million. It is a Romance language descended from the Vulgar Latin spoken by the Roman conquerors of Gaul. It still carries the reputation of being the most cultured language in the world and the most beautiful. People often tell stories about the impatience of the French towards foreigners who do not attempt to speak their language. In general, however, if you attempt to communicate with them in French, they will appreciate it and may even overcome their reluctance to respond in English.

Since much of the English vocabulary is related to French, thanks to the Norman Conquest in 1066, travellers will often recognise many helpful cognates: words such as *hôtel, café* and *bagages* hardly need to be translated. You should be aware, however, of some misleading "false friends" *(faux amis)*, words that look like English words but mean something different.
le car coach, also railway carriage
le conducteur bus driver
personne can mean either person or nobody, depending on the context.

BASIC RULES

If you speak no French at all, it is worth trying to master a few simple phrases. The fact that you have made an effort is likely to break the ice. More and more French people like practising their English on visitors, especially waiters and the younger generation. Pronunciation is the key; they really will not understand if you get it very wrong. Remember to **emphasise each syllable**, but not to pronounce the last consonant of a word as a rule, unless it is followed by a vowel. Also bear in mind "er", "et" and "ez" endings are pronounced "ay" (this includes the plural "s") and "h"s are silent.

The Alphabet

Learning the pronunciation of the French alphabet is a good idea. In particular, learn how to spell out your name.
a = ah, **b** = bay, **c** = say, **d** = day, **e** = uh, **f** = ef, **g** = zhay, **h** = ash, **i** = ee, **j** = zhee, **k** = ka, **l** = el, **m** = em, **n** = en, **o** = oh, **p** = pay, **q** = kew, **r** = ehr, **s** = ess, **t** = tay, **u** = ew, **v** = vay, **w** = dooblah vay, **x** = eex, **y** = ee grek, **z** = zed.

Whether to use "**vous**" or "tu" is a vexed question; increasingly the familiar form of "tu" is used, but it is safer to be formal, and use "vous". It is very important to be courteous; always address people as **Mademoiselle, Madame** or **Monsieur**, and address them by their surnames until you are confident first names are acceptable. When entering a shop always say, *"Bonjour Monsieur/ Madame/Mademoiselle,"* and *"Merci, au revoir,"* when leaving.

Garçon is the word for waiter but is never used directly; say *Monsieur, Madame* or *Mademoiselle*, to attract a waiter's attention.

Useful Words & Phrases

How much is it? *C'est combien?*
What is your name? *Comment vous appelez-vous?*
My name is... *Je m'appelle...*
Do you speak English? *Parlez-vous anglais?*
I am English/American *Je suis anglais(e)/américain(e)*
I don't understand *Je ne comprends pas*
Please speak more slowly *Parlez plus lentement, s'il vous plaît*
Can you help me? *Pouvez-vous m'aider?*
I'm looking for... *Je cherche...*
Where is...? *Où est...?*
I'm sorry *Excusez-moi/Pardon*
I don't know *Je ne sais pas*
No problem *Pas de problème*
Have a good day! *Bonne journée!*
That's it *C'est ça*
Here it is *Voici*
There it is *Voilà*
Let's go *On y va/Allons-y*
See you tomorrow *A demain*
See you soon *A bientôt*
Show me the word in the book *Montrez-moi le mot dans le livre*
At what time? *A quelle heure?*
When? *Quand?*
What time is it? *Quelle heure est-il?*
yes *oui*
no *non*
please *s'il vous plaît*
thank you *merci*
(very much) *(beaucoup)*
you're welcome *de rien*
excuse me *excusez-moi*
hello *bonjour*
hi/bye *salut*
OK *d'accord*
goodbye *au revoir*
good evening *bonsoir*
here *ici*
there *là*
left *gauche*
right *droite*
straight on *tout droit*
far *loin*
near *près d'ici*
opposite *en face*
beside *à côté de*
over there *là-bas*

today *aujourd'hui*
yesterday *hier*
tomorrow *demain*
now *maintenant*
later *plus tard*
right away *tout de suite*
this morning *ce matin*
this afternoon *cet après-midi*
this evening *ce soir*

On Arrival

I want to get off at... *Je voudrais descendre à…*
Is there a bus to the Louvre? *Est-ce qu'il y a un bus pour le Louvre?*
What street is this? *A quelle rue sommes-nous?*
Which line do I take for...? *Quelle ligne dois-je prendre pour...?*
How far is...? *A quelle distance se trouve...?*
Validate your ticket *Compostez votre billet*
airport *l'aéroport*
railway station *la gare*
bus station *la gare routière*
Métro stop *la station de Métro*
bus *l'autobus, le car*
bus stop *l'arrêt*
platform *le quai*
ticket *le billet*
return ticket *aller-retour*
hitchhiking *l'autostop*
toilets *les toilettes*
This is the hotel address *C'est l'adresse de l'hôtel*
I'd like a (single/double) room... *Je voudrais une chambre (pour une/deux personnes)...*
...with shower *avec douche*
...with bath *avec salle de bain*
Is breakfast included? *Le prix comprend-il le petit-déjeuner?*
May I see the room? *Puis-je voir la chambre?*
washbasin *le lavabo*
bed *le lit*
key *la clé*
elevator *l'ascenseur*
air-conditioned *climatisé*

Emergencies

Help! *Au secours!*
Stop! *Arrêtez!*
Call a doctor *Appelez un médecin*

Call an ambulance *Appelez une ambulance*
Call the police *Appelez la police*
Call the fire brigade *Appelez les pompiers*
Where is the nearest telephone? *Où est le téléphone le plus proche?*
Where is the nearest hospital? *Où est l'hôpital le plus proche?*
I am sick *Je suis malade*
I have lost my passport/purse *J'ai perdu mon passeport/porte-monnaie*

Shopping

Where is the nearest bank (post office)? *Où se trouve la banque (Poste) la plus proche?*
I'd like to buy *Je voudrais acheter*
How much is it? *C'est combien?*
Do you take credit cards? *Est-ce que vous acceptez les cartes de crédit?*
I'm just looking *Je regarde seulement*
Have you got? *Avez-vous...?*
I'll take it *Je le prends*
I'll take this one/that one *Je prends celui-ci/celui-là*
What size is it? *C'est quelle taille?*
Anything else? *Avec ceci?*
size (clothes) *la taille*
size (shoes) *la pointure*
cheap *bon marché*
expensive *cher*
enough *assez*
too much *trop*
a piece of *un morceau de*
each *la pièce (eg ananas, €2 la pièce)*
receipt *le reçu*
chemist *la pharmacie*
bakery *la boulangerie*
bookshop *la librairie*
library *la bibliothèque*
department store *le grand magasin*
delicatessen *la charcuterie/le traiteur*
fishmonger's *la poissonnerie*
grocery *l'alimentation/l'épicerie*
tobacconist *tabac (also sells stamps and newspapers)*

TRANSPORT
ACCOMMODATION
ACTIVITIES
A – Z
LANGUAGE

markets *le marché*
supermarket *le supermarché*
junk shop *la brocante*

Sightseeing

town *la ville*
old town *la vieille ville*
street *la rue*
square *la place*
abbey *l'abbaye*
cathedral *la cathédrale*
church *l'église*
keep *le donjon*
mansion *l'hôtel*
hospital *l'hôpital*
town hall *l'hôtel de ville/la mairie*
nave *la nef*
stained glass *le vitrail*
staircase *l'escalier*
tower *la tour (La Tour Eiffel)*
walk *le tour*
country house/castle *le château*
Gothic *gothique*
Roman *romain*
Romanesque *roman*
museum *le musée*
art gallery *la galerie*
exhibition *l'exposition*
tourist information office *l'office du tourisme/le syndicat d'initiative*
free *gratuit*
open *ouvert*
closed *fermé*
every day *tous les jours*
all year *toute l'année*
all day *toute la journée*
swimming pool *la piscine*
to book *réserver*
town map *le plan*
road map *la carte*

Dining Out

Table d'hôte (the "host's table") is one set menu served at a set price. *Prix fixe* is a fixed-price menu. *A la carte* means differently priced dishes chosen from the menu.
breakfast *le petit-déjeuner*
lunch *le déjeuner*
dinner *le dîner*
meal *le repas*
first course *l'entrée/les hors d'œuvre*
main course *le plat principal*

made to order *sur commande*
drink included *boisson comprise*
wine list *la carte des vins*
the bill *l'addition*
fork *la fourchette*
knife *le couteau*
spoon *la cuillère*
plate *l'assiette*
glass *le verre*
napkin *la serviette*
ashtray *le cendrier*
I am a vegetarian *Je suis végétarien(ne)*
I am on a diet *Je suis au régime*
What do you recommend? *Que'est-ce que vous recommandez?*
Do you have local specialities? *Avez-vous des spécialités locales?*
I'd like to order *Je voudrais commander*
That is not what I ordered *Ce n'est pas ce que j'ai commandé*
Is service included? *Est-ce que le service est compris?*
May I have more wine? *Encore du vin, s'il vous plaît*
Enjoy your meal *Bon appétit!*

Breakfast and Snacks

baguette **long thin loaf**
pain **bread**
petits pains **rolls**
beurre **butter**
poivre **pepper**
sel **salt**
sucre **sugar**
confiture **jam**
miel **honey**
œufs **eggs**
...à la coque **boiled eggs**
...au bacon **bacon and eggs**
...au jambon **ham and eggs**
...sur le plat **fried eggs**
...brouillés **scrambled eggs**
tartine **bread with butter**
yaourt **yoghurt**
crêpe **pancake**
croque-monsieur **ham and cheese toasted sandwich**
croque-madame **...with a fried egg on top**
galette **type of cake**
pan bagna **bread roll stuffed with salad Niçoise**

quiche **tart of eggs and cream with various fillings**
quiche lorraine **quiche with bacon**

First Course

An *amuse-bouche, amuse-gueule* or appetiser is something to "amuse the mouth", before the first course
anchoïade **sauce of olive oil, anchovies and garlic, served with raw vegetables**
assiette anglaise **cold meats**
potage **soup**
rillettes **rich fatty paste of shredded duck rabbit or pork**
tapenade **spread of olives and anchovies**
pissaladière **Provençal pizza with onions, olives and anchovies**

Main Courses

La Viande **Meat**
bleu **rare**
à point **medium**
bien cuit **well done**
grillé **grilled**
agneau **lamb**
andouille/andouillette **tripe sausage**
bifteck **steak**
boudin **sausage**
boudin noir **black pudding**
boudin blanc **white pudding (chicken or veal)**
blanquette **stew of veal, lamb or chicken with creamy egg sauce**
bœuf à la mode **beef in red wine with carrots, onions, mushroom and onions**
à la bordelaise **beef with red wine and shallots**
Bourguignon **cooked in red wine, onions and mushrooms**
brochette **kebab**
caille **quail**
canard **duck**
carbonnade **casserole of beef, beer and onions**
carré d'agneau **rack of lamb**
cassoulet **stew of beans, sausages, pork and duck from southwest France**
cervelle **brains (food)**
châteaubriand **thick steak**
choucroute **Alsace dish of**

sauerkraut, bacon and sausages
confit duck or goose preserved in its own fat
contre-filet cut of sirloin steak
coq au vin chicken in red wine
côte d'agneau lamb chop
daube beef stew with red wine, onions and tomatoes
dinde turkey
entrecôte beef rib steak
escargot snail
faisan pheasant
farci stuffed
faux-filet sirloin
feuilleté puff pastry
foie liver
foie de veau calf's liver
foie gras goose or duck liver pâté
gardian rich beef stew with olives and garlic from the Camargue
cuisses de grenouille frog's legs
grillade grilled meat
hachis minced meat
jambon ham
langue tongue
lapin rabbit
lardons small pieces of bacon, often added to salads
magret de canard breast of duck
médaillon round piece of meat
moelle beef bone marrow
mouton navarin stew of lamb with onions, carrots and turnips
oie goose
perdrix partridge
petit-gris small snail
pieds de cochon pig's trotters
pintade guinea fowl
Pipérade Basque dish of eggs, ham, peppers and onion
porc pork
pot-au-feu casserole of beef and vegetables
poulet chicken
poussin young chicken
rognons kidneys
rôti roast
sanglier wild boar
saucisse fresh sausage
saucisson salami
veau veal

Poissons **Fish**
à l'Américaine made with white wine, tomatoes, butter and cognac

anchois anchovies
anguille eel
bar (or loup) sea bass
barbue brill
belon Brittany oyster
bigorneau sea snail
Bercy sauce of fish stock, butter, white wine and shallots
bouillabaisse fish soup, served with grated cheese, garlic croutons and spicy rouille sauce
brandade salt cod purée
cabillaud cod
calamars squid
colin hake
coquillage shellfish
coquilles Saint-Jacques scallops
crevette shrimp
daurade sea bream
flétan halibut
fruits de mer seafood
hareng herring
homard lobster
huître oyster
langoustine large prawn
limande lemon sole
lotte monkfish
morue salt cod
moule mussel
moules marinières mussels in white wine and onions
oursin sea urchin
raie skate
saumon salmon
thon tuna
truite trout

Légumes **Vegetables**
ail garlic
artichaut artichoke
asperge asparagus
aubergine eggplant, aubergine
avocat avocado
bolets boletus mushrooms
céleri rémoulade grated celery with mayonnaise
champignon mushroom
cèpes boletus mushrooms
chanterelle wild mushroom
cornichon gherkin
courgette zucchini, courgette
chips potato crisps
chou cabbage
chou-fleur cauliflower
concombre cucumber
cru raw
crudités raw vegetables
épinards spinach

frites chips, French fries
gratin dauphinois sliced potatoes baked with cream
haricot dried bean
haricots verts green beans
lentilles lentils
maïs corn
mange-tout snow pea
mesclun mixed-leaf salad
navet turnip
noix nut, walnut
noisette hazelnut
oignon onion
panais parsnip
persil parsley
pignon pine nut
poireau leek
pois pea
poivron bell pepper
pomme de terre potato
pommes frites chips, French fries
primeurs early fruit and vegetables
radis radis
roquette arugula, rocket
ratatouille Provençal vegetable stew of aubergines, courgettes, tomatoes, peppers and olive oil
riz rice
salade niçoise egg, tuna, olives, onions and tomato salad
salade verte green salad
truffe truffle

Fruit **Fruit**
ananas pineapple
cerise cherry
citron lemon
citron vert lime
figue fig
fraise strawberry
framboise raspberry
groseille redcurrant
mangue mango
mirabelle yellow plum
pamplemousse grapefruit
pêche peach
poire pear
pomme apple
raisin grape
prune plum
pruneau prune
reine claude greengage

Sauces **Sauces**
aïoli garlic mayonnaise
béarnaise sauce of egg, butter, wine and herbs

forestière **with mushrooms and bacon**
hollandaise **egg and butter**
lyonnaise **with onions**
meunière **fried fish with butter, lemon and parsley sauce**
meurette **red wine sauce**
Mornay **sauce of cream, egg and cheese**
Parmentier **served with potatoes**
paysan **rustic style, ingredients depend on the region**
pistou **Provençal sauce of basil, garlic and olive oil; vegetable soup with the sauce**
provençale **sauce of tomatoes, garlic and olive oil**
papillotte **cooked in paper**

Dessert **Pudding, dessert**
poire Belle-Hélène **pear with ice cream and chocolate sauce**
clafoutis **baked pudding of batter and cherries**
coulis **purée of fruit or vegetables**
gâteau **cake**
Ile flottante **whisked eggs whites floating in custard sauce**
crème anglaise **custard**
pêche melba **peaches with ice cream and raspberry sauce**
tarte tatin **upside-down tart of caramelised apples**
crème caramel **caramelised egg custard**
crème Chantilly **whipped cream**
fromage **cheese**
chèvre **goat's cheese**

In the Café

les boissons **drinks**
café **coffee**
...au lait or *crème* **...with milk or cream**
...déca/décaféiné **...decaffeinated**
...espresso/noir **...black espresso**
...filtre **...filtered coffee**
thé **tea**
tisane **herb infusion**
verveine **camomile**
chocolat chaud **hot chocolate**
lait **milk**
eau minérale **mineral water**
gazeux **fizzy**
non-gazeux **non-fizzy**

limonade **fizzy lemonade**
citron pressé **fresh lemon juice served with sugar**
orange pressée **fresh squeezed orange juice**
entier **full (eg full cream milk)**
frais, fraîche **fresh or cold**
bière **beer**
...en bouteille **...bottled**
...à la pression **...on tap**
apéritif **pre-dinner drink**
kir **white wine with cassis, blackcurrant liqueur**
kir royale **kir with champagne**
avec des glaçons **with ice**
sec **neat**
rouge **red**
blanc **white**
rosé **rosé**
brut **dry**
doux **sweet**
crémant **sparkling wine**
vin de maison **house wine**
vin de pays **local wine**
carafe/pichet **pitcher**
...d'eau/de vin **...of water/wine**
demi-carafe **half litre**
quart **quarter litre**
panaché **shandy**
digestif **after-dinner drink**
Armagnac **brandy from the Armagnac region of France**
calvados **Normandy apple brandy**

Where is this wine from?
De quelle région vient ce vin?
cheers! *santé!*
hangover *gueule de bois*

Days of the Week

Days of the week, seasons and months are not capitalised in French.

Monday	*lundi*
Tuesday	*mardi*
Wednesday	*mercredi*
Thursday	*jeudi*
Friday	*vendredi*
Saturday	*samedi*
Sunday	*dimanche*

Seasons

spring	*le printemps*
summer	*l'été*
autumn	*l'automne*
winter	*l'hiver*

Months

January	*janvier*
February	*février*
March	*mars*
April	*avril*
May	*mai*
June	*juin*
July	*juillet*
August	*août*
September	*septembre*
October	*octobre*
November	*novembre*
December	*décembre*

Saying the date
20th October 2004 *le vingt octobre, deux mille quatre*

Numbers

0	*zéro*
1	*un, une*
2	*deux*
3	*trois*
4	*quatre*
5	*cinq*
6	*six*
7	*sept*
8	*huit*
9	*neuf*
10	*dix*
11	*onze*
12	*douze*
13	*treize*
14	*quatorze*
15	*quinze*
16	*seize*
17	*dix-sept*
18	*dix-huit*
19	*dix-neuf*
20	*vingt*
21	*vingt-et-un*
30	*trente*
40	*quarante*
50	*cinquante*
60	*soixante*
70	*soixante-dix*
80	*quatre-vingt*
90	*quatre-vingt-dix*
100	*cent*
200	*deux cent*
500	*cinq cent*
1000	*mille*
1,000,000	*un million*

• Note that the number 1 is often written like an upside down V, and the number 7 is always crossed.

FURTHER READING

History

A Concise History of France, by Roger Price. Cambridge University Press, 1993. Excellent historical overview.
The Eiffel Tower: And Other Mythologies, by Roland Barthes. University of California Press, 1997. A collection of essays by this influential French critic.
Foreign Correspondents: Paris in the Sixties, by Peter Lennon. Picador/McClelland & Stewart) Irish journalist Lennon spent the decade in Paris where he witnessed the 1968 student riots.
The Illustrated History of Paris and the Parisians, by Robert Laffont. New York: Doubleday & Co., 1958.
A Woman's Life in the Court of the Sun King, by Duchesse d'Orléans. Trans. Elborg Forster. Baltimore: Johns Hopkins University Press, 1984. The Duchesse's letters reveal court-life in the 17th century.

Art & Architecture

Guide to Modern Architecture in Paris, by Hervé Martin. For descriptions and locations of buildings by *arrondissement*.
Paris: A City in the Making, by Le Pavillon de l'Arsenal. A catalogue of the architectural evolution of Paris.
A Propos de Paris, by Henri Cartier-Bresson. Bulfinch Press, 1998. Some 130 stunning black-and-white photographs of the capital, spanning 50 years.
Brassaï: The Eye of Paris, by Richard Howard. Abrams, 1999. Part biography, part catalogue of a photography exhibition of Brassaï's pictures of Paris.

The Cathedral Builders, by Jean Gimpel. New York: Harper & Row, 1984. The story of the hands and minds behind the cathedrals of France.
Paris: An Architectural History, by Anthony Sutcliffe. Yale University Press. A great book on the architecture of the capital across the ages.
Three Seconds of Eternity, by Robert Doisneau. Neues Publishing Company, 1997. Gorgeous photographs of 1940s and 1950s Paris, chosen by the champion of black-and-white photography himself.

Food

Paris Bistro Cooking, by Linda Dannenberg. Clarkson Potter, 1991. Tasty dishes from a wealth of Paris brasseries.
The Paris Café Cookbook, by Daniel Young. William Morrow & Co, 1998. Recipes and excerpts on recommended cafés in the capital.

Other Insight Guides

Insight Guide: France is the major book in the French series covering the whole country, with features on food and drink, culture and the arts. Other titles cover Alsace, Brittany, Burgundy, Corsica, The French Riviera, The Loire Valley, Normandy and Provence & the Côte d'Azur.
Insight Pocket Guides are particularly useful for people making short visits. Titles include Alsace, Brittany, Corsica, The French Riviera, The Loire Valley, Paris and Provence.
Compact Guides are inexpensive, mini-encyclopaedias with

a star-rated system of all the sites worth seeing. Titles include Brittany, Burgundy, The French Riviera, Normandy, Paris and Provence. **Insight Fleximaps** have a tough, laminated rainproof finish and feature a list of the top 10 sites in a city or area, and an in-depth index. Fleximaps in the French series include Paris and Corsica. Paris features in three new Insight Guide series: **Shopping in Paris**, **Eating in Paris** and **Museums in Paris**, all handy-sized, illustrated guides, packed with useful information.

FEEDBACK

We do our best to ensure the information in our books is as accurate and up-to-date as possible. The books are updated on a regular basis, using local contacts, who painstakingly add, amend and correct as required. However, some mistakes and omissions are inevitable and we are ultimately reliant on our readers to put us in the picture. We would welcome your feedback on any details related to your experiences using the book "on the road". We will acknowledge all contributions, and we'll offer an Insight Guide to the best letters received.

Please write to us at:
Insight Guides
PO Box 7910
London SE1 1WE
United Kingdom
Or send an e-mail to:
insight@apaguide.co.uk

ART & PHOTO CREDITS

PICTURE SPREADS

PARIS STREET ATLAS

The key map shows the area of Paris covered by the atlas section. An index of street names and places of interest shown on the maps can be found on the following pages. For each entry there is a page number and grid reference.

Map Legend

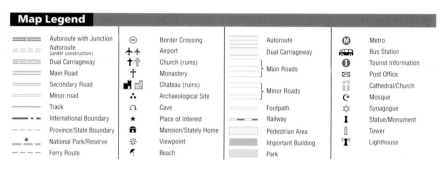

Autoroute with Junction		Border Crossing		Autoroute		Metro
Autoroute (under construction)		Airport		Dual Carriageway		Bus Station
Dual Carriageway		Church (ruins)				Tourist Information
Main Road		Monastery	Main Roads			Post Office
Secondary Road		Chateau (ruins)				Cathedral/Church
Minor road		Archaeological Site	Minor Roads			Mosque
Track		Cave		Footpath		Synagogue
International Boundary		Place of Interest		Railway		Statue/Monument
Province/State Boundary		Mansion/Stately Home		Pedestrian Area		Tower
National Park/Reserve		Viewpoint		Important Building		Lighthouse
Ferry Route		Beach		Park		

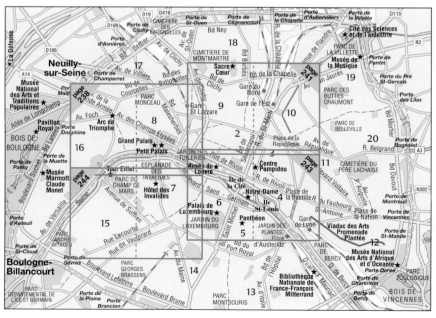

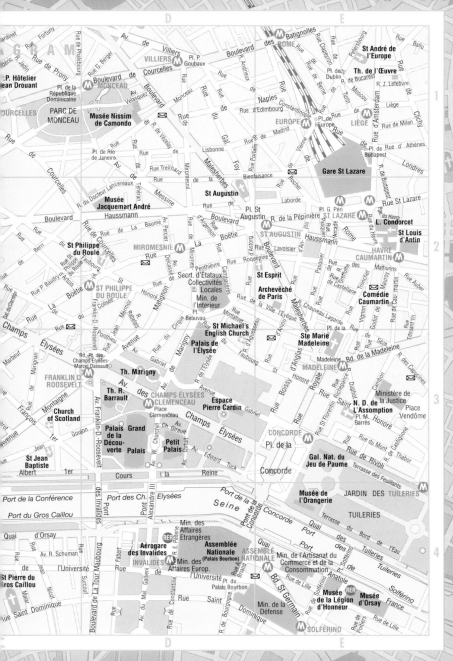

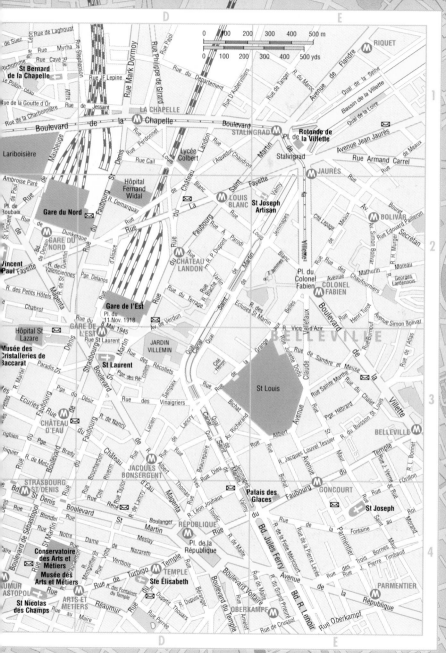

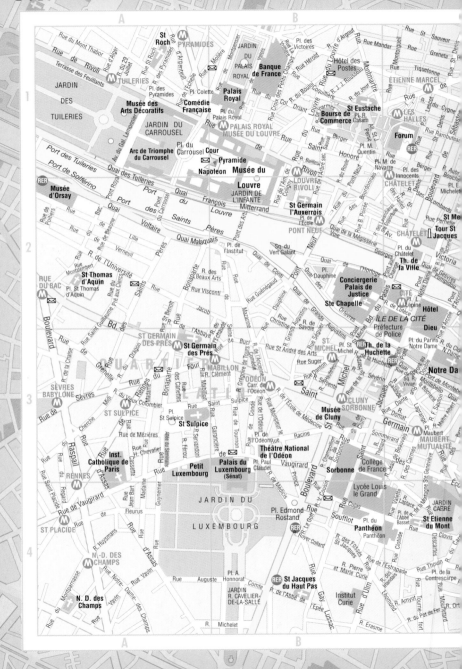

RÉAUMUR SÉBASTOPOL

Musée des Arts et Métiers

Ste Élisabeth

PARMENTIER

la République

St Nicolas des Champs

ARTS ET MÉTIERS

R. de Turbigo

R. Dupetit Thouars

R. Dupuis

Réaumur

OBERKAMPF

Richard

Oberkampf

Voltaire

Avenue Parmentier

Rue au Maire

Sq. du Temple

R. Perrée

Cirque d'Hiver

JARDIN ST AIGNAN

RAMBUTEAU

FILLES DU CALVAIRE

R. des Filles du Calvaire

St Ambroise

tre Nat. rt et de ure G. Pompidou

Musée de la Chasse et de la Nature

St Sébastien

ST SÉBASTIEN FROISSART

RICHARD LENOIR

Archives Nat.

Musée de l'Histoire de France

Hôtel de Rohan

Musée Picasso

St Denys du St Sacrement

Vert

Musée Bricard

Pl. de Thorigny

Musée Cognacq-Jay

Francs

CHEMIN VERT

Richard

Chemin

Musée Carnavalet

BRÉGUET SABIN

HÔTEL E VILLE

Rue

Biblio-thèque Hist.

Bourgeois

Rue des Minimes

Roquette

Hôtel de Ville

Pl. St Gervais

St Gervais-St Protais

ST PAUL

St Paul/ St Louis

Pl. des Vosges

Maison de Victor Hugo

Théâtre de la Bastille

ort de l'Hôtel de Ville

Mémorial de a Déportation

PONT MARIE

Hôtel de Sens

Centre des Monuments Nationaux

BASTILLE

Pl. de la Bastille

Rue de Faubourg St Antoine

LEDRU ROLLIN

ÎLE

ST LOUIS

St Louis-en-île

SULLY MORLAND

Opéra National de Paris Bastille

Institut du Monde Arabe

Bibliothèque de l'Arsenal

Avenue

GARE DE LYON

Universités Paris VI-Paris VII Pierre et Marie Curie

ARDINAL EMOINE

Jussieu

JUSSIEU

QUAI DE LA RAPÉE

Boulevard Diderot

GARE DE LYON

Arènes de Lutèce

Ménagerie

RER

Gare de Lyon

MONGE

JARDIN DES PLANTES

Place Valhubert

GARE D'AUSTERLITZ

Gare d'Austerlitz

Institut Musulman

Grande Galerie de l'Evolution

Rue Buffon

RER

0   100   200   300   400   500 m

0   100   200   300   400   500 yds

A B

Av. Paul Doumer Rue R.R. Franklin Av. de Camoens Pont d'Iéna Av. Franco Russe
Rue de Montessuy Rue du Gal. Camou Avenue Rapp

Pl. de Passy **Musée du Vin** Sq. Alboni PASSY Suffren **Tour Eiffel** PARC DU
Pl. du Général Gouraud

N. D. de Grace de Passy Stade Émile Anthoine Av. Gustave Eiffel Pl. Jacques Rueff CHAMP DE MARS
Maison de Balzac

Pl. des Martyrs Juifs du Vélodrome Rue d'Hiver BIR HAKEIM
Maison de Radio-France RER Grenelle Boulevard Bd St Léon LA MOTTE PICQUET GRENELLE

Port de Javel Pont de Grenelle Quai André Citroën Linois DUPLEIX GRENELLE CAMBRONNE

R. L. N. Orfila Place Martin Nadaud Gambetta GAMBETTA Belgran
Boulevard de Ménilmontant

Avenue de la République Pl. Auguste Métivier PÈRE LACHAISE
Basilique N. D. du Perpétuel Secours Columbarium CIMETIÈRE DU St Germain Charonne

Square de la Roquette PÈRE LACHAISE Mur des Fédérés
Place Léon Blum VOLTAIRE PHILIPPE AUGUSTE Boulevard de Charonne ALEXANDRE DUMAS
Bon Pasteur

A B

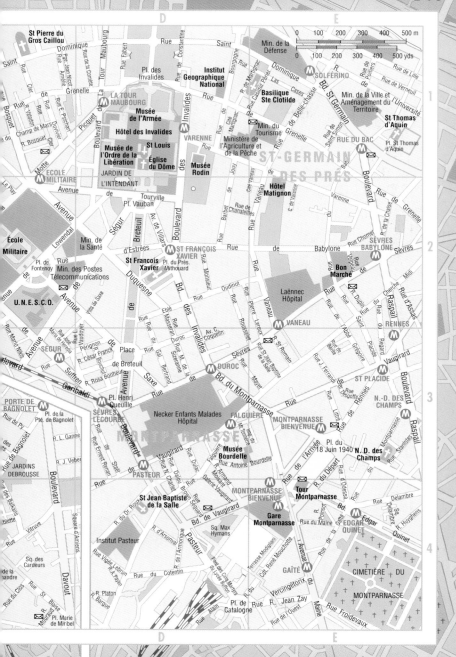

246 ◆ PARIS

STREET INDEX

STREET INDEX 247

GENERAL INDEX

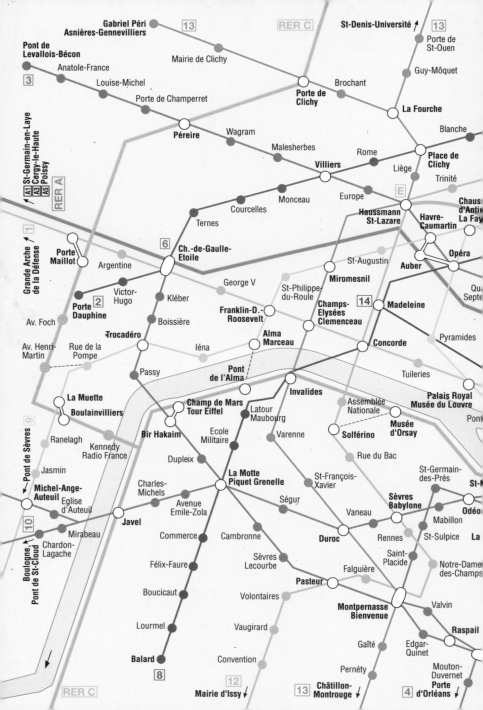